The School Psychologist and the Exceptional Child

geraldine t. scholl
editor

A product of the ERIC Clearinghouse on
Handicapped and Gifted Children
The Council for Exceptional Children

Library of Congress Cataloging Publication Data
Main entry under title:

The school psychologist and the exceptional child.

"A product of the ERIC Clearinghouse on Handicapped and Gifted Children"
Includes bibliographies.
    1. Exceptional children—Education—United States—Evaluation. 2. School
psychologists—United States. I. Scholl, Geraldine T. II. Council for Exceptional Children.
III. ERIC Clearinghouse on Handicapped and Gifted Children.

LC3981.S36 1985   371.9   84-23685
ISBN 0-86586-153-6

A product of the ERIC Clearinghouse on Handicapped and Gifted Children.

Published in 1985 by The Council for Exceptional Children, 1920 Association Drive,
Reston, Virginia 22091-1589.

NIE This publication was prepared with funding from the National Institute
of Education, US Department of Education, under contract no. 400-81-0031.
Contractors undertaking such projects under government sponsorship are
encouraged to express freely their judgment in professional and technical
matters. Prior to publication the manuscript was submitted to The Council for Exceptional Children for critical review and determination of professional competence. This
publication has met such standards. Points of view, however, do not necessarily represent the official view or opinions of either The Council for Exceptional Children, the
National Institute of Education, or the Department of Education.

Printed in the United States of America.

CONTENTS

CONTENTS (continued)

CONTENTS (continued)

CONTENTS (continued)

CONTENTS (continued)

About the Authors

John Ardizzone completed his doctorate in the Combined Program in Education and Psychology at the University of Michigan with specialization in school psychology and education of emotionally disturbed children. Prior to entering the doctoral program he completed a masters degree in counseling pyschology and worked with emotionally disturbed children and their families in the Washington DC area. Currently he is a psychotherapist and school consultant in the Detroit area.

Robin L. Brown is completing her doctorate in the Combined Program in Education and Psychology at the University of Michigan. She holds a masters degree in counseling and human development from the University of Georgia and a masters degree in psychology and clinical social work from the University of Michigan. She has worked with emotionally disturbed and developmentally disabled children and their families in a variety of settings. Currently she is a part-time instructor in the psychology department at the University of Michigan and works in a private clinic, where she does diagnostic assessments and psychotherapy with children, adolescents, and families.

Paula Elitov works as a psychologist at Hawthorn Center, a residential treatment facility for emotionally disturbed children in Northville, Michigan. She completed her doctorate in the Combined Program in Education and Psychology at the University of Michigan. She received a masters degree in early childhood education from the University of Rochester. Her professional interests have focused on assessment and psychoeducational interventions with preschool and elementary school children. She is a former director of a preschool special needs project and has conducted workshops on assessment of young children with special needs.

Jody Harrison is a school psychologist with the Wilson County Schools in Wilson, North Carolina. She earned an education specialist degree in school psychology and a masters degree in psychology at the University of Michigan. She was previously employed as a school psychologist with the Calhoun Intermediate School District in Marshall, Michigan. She is a member of the National Association of School Psychologists and the North Carolina School Psychology Association.

Sister Yvonne Mary Loucks is a doctoral candidate in the Speech and Hearing Sciences program in the School of Education at the University of Michigan. Currently she is working as a speech and language pathologist in the early intervention program, Watertown, Connecticut public school system. Previously she worked as a speech and language pathologist in the International School in Jerusalem, Israel and in the Yale-New Haven Hospital. She is a former administrator of a small psychiatric facility in Bethlehem, Connecticut. Her current research is on communicative competence in the dispute processes in very young children.

Eileen Mollen is a clinical instructor in the Department of Pediatrics and Communicable Diseases, Pediatric Psychology, at the University of Michigan Hospital. A major part of her work involves psychoeducational evaluation of children with learning problems. She earned her masters and doctoral degrees in learning disabilities at the University of Michigan and a bachelors degree in special education from the University of Virginia. Her professional experience includes teaching mentally impaired and learning disabled children in the public schools. Currently she is involved in research focusing on learning characteristics among clinical populations, including adults who have dyslexia.

Evelyn R. Oka completed her doctorate in the Combined Program in Education and Psychology at the University of Michigan. She also has earned a masters degree in developmental psychology and an education specialist degree in school psychology from the University of Michigan. Her experience in school psychology has focused on the identification of cultural and motivational influences on learning problems. Currently she is a teaching assistant in child psychology and is conducting research on individual differences in achievement motivation.

Geraldine T. Scholl is professor of education in the special education program of the School of Education, the University of Michigan. She holds a masters degree in special education from Wayne State University and a doctorate in educational psychology from the University of Michigan. She has taught visually handicapped children and emotionally disturbed children. She was also the elementary principal of the Michigan School for the Blind. Her research interests include teacher competencies and program evaluation in the area of education of the visually handicapped.

Amy Swan is a school psychologist for the Burnsville, Minnesota public schools. She holds a doctorate in educational psychology and an education specialist degree in school psychology from the University of Michigan. Her professional experience includes teaching elementary students in a public school in Wisconsin. Her current research interests include studies of the personality characteristics of students enrolled in teacher training programs.

Shauna Tindall is a school psychologist for the Ann Arbor, Michigan public schools. She holds an education specialist degree from the University of Michigan and has done graduate work in developmental psychology at Ohio State University. As part of her work on the Dean's Grant Project at the University of Michigan, she developed a course packet to teach prospective student teachers about systematic observations. She is currently working on a project to develop a multidisciplinary preschool evaluation team in order to provide a more specialized diagnostic/prescriptive approach to preschool evaluations.

Preface

This book grew from the experience of the editor in teaching an introductory course in special education for the school psychology program at the University of Michigan. The special education department was asked to initiate a course for the school psychology students because the existing introductory courses were designed for undergraduate and masters level students preparing to be regular teachers and for undergraduate students in special education. Their orientation was primarily educational. We designed the new course to focus on information about handicapped children that would have the greatest relevance for students in the school psychology program, many of whom have little knowledge about handicapped pupils.

We also found that the content of most of the existing texts were not appropriate to the needs of school psychologists. School psychology students need information about the characteristics and needs of various types of exceptional children that have an impact on the assessment process. Thus, we decided to write this book.

The first drafts of the categorical chapters were written by teams of students. During the following 2 years the book in draft form was used and critiqued by students in the course. Our sincere appreciation goes to the students who read and critiqued the earlier drafts and to the following, who prepared first drafts for some of the chapters or sections of chapters: Elizabeth Brunner, Jan Collins-Eaglin, Sharon Conley, Tim Comfort, Diana DePaemelere, James Kondzida, Ken Newbury, James Rayment, and Richard Reinesmith.

In any edited text portions of chapters are moved to other chapters where the content may be more appropriate. A portion of the content on parents prepared by John Ardizzone for the chapter on mental retardation was moved to Chapter 1; a portion on assessment prepared by Robin Brown for the chapter on emotionally disturbed students was moved to Chapter 2. Robin Brown also prepared the materials included in Appendixes A through E.

We express appreciation to the following colleagues who reviewed and made suggestions for selected chapters: Professors Percy Bates, Calvin Dyer, Susan Ianna, Jeannie Johns, and William C. Morse of the University of Michigan; Mrs. Margaret Singer and Mr. John Higgins of the Washtenaw, Michigan Intermediate School District; and Dr. Susan Spungin and Ms. Zofja S. Jastrzembska of the American Foundation for the Blind. Finally, we thank the reviewers who made valuable comments and suggestions for improving the manuscript.

The audience for this book includes school psychologists in training and those in the field who have little or no background in special education. We trust they will find the book useful in their future assessment work with exceptional children.

Geraldine T. Scholl

Introduction

"A deaf child? Will I need an interpreter? How can I establish contact with her?"

"Cerebral palsy? How can I test him if he can't speak understandably or use his hands?"

"Don't I need special norms when I test handicapped children?"

"How do they expect me to assess a child who has neither verbal nor written communication skills?"

These are typical questions school psychologists ask when requested to assess a handicapped child. Public Law 94-142, the Education for All Handicapped Children Act of 1975, requires assessment of handicapped pupils as a prerequisite to placement in the least restrictive environment. School psychologists are expected to participate in identification and placement decisions about various types of handicapped children. Further, they are often asked to make recommendations regarding appropriate educational strategies for remediation within the classroom. To perform this function, they must be knowledgeable about the needs and characteristics of all types of exceptional children so that they will be able to select the appropriate instruments and strategies to use in the assessment process. They must be able to interpret the results they obtain from these instruments and strategies to parents and professionals in a meaningful way so that the best possible placement decision may be made, and they must have the background necessary to make recommendations for educational intervention. They must also be knowledgeable about the process of education, particularly about the roles of teachers in facilitating learning. All these expectations growing out of the legislation are expanding the role of the school psychologist.

Although skilled in the administration and interpretation of a wide variety of assessment measures, many school psychologists have limited knowledge of the nature and needs of handicapped children, of their likenesses and differences as compared with nonhandicapped children, and of how the results of an assessment should be interpreted because of these differences. In their survey of 303 colleges and universities with state-approved school psychology training programs, Sullivan and McDaniel (1982) found that 42 or 25% of the 172 colleges and universities responding required no courses in handicapping conditions, and an additional 40 or 23% required one course. There was no indication whether or not these programs met the standards of the American Psychological Association or the National Association of School Psychologists, both of which do require course work related to handicapped children. Even in programs requiring course work in various exceptionalities, the emphasis tends to be on mentally retarded, emotionally disturbed, or learning disabled children, the high incidence categorical groups. Low incidence handicapping conditions such as hearing impairment (Schoenwald, 1980) and visually handicaped (Ward, 1982) are neglected. To meet the intent of P.L. 94-142, school psychologists need information about the nature and needs of *all* handicapped children, including those from low incidence areas.

This book is intended to be a resource guide to help school psychologists, especially those in preservice programs, understand various types of exceptional children and to apply that knowlege in their professional role. The book assumes that the reader has little or no previous background or knowledge in the psychology or education of exceptional children or youth.

The book is divided into two major parts. Part I, "General Considerations," includes a brief discussion of the changing role of the school psychologist, an overview of assessment, and a description of the use of informal procedures as assessment tools. Part II, "Areas of Exceptionality," reviews the specialized characteristics and needs of each group among the commonly accepted categories of exceptional pupils.

Informal and formal assessment instruments are mentioned in various chapters. Appendix H includes a listing of all these instruments together with the addresses of the publishers.

REFERENCES

Schoenwald, B. (1980). The great training default. *The Directive Teacher, 2,* 19, 30.

Sullivan, P.D., & McDaniel, E.A. (1982). Survey of special education coursework in school psychology training programs. *Exceptional Children, 46,* 541-543.

Ward, M.F. (1982). Attitudes and concerns of school psychologists toward assessment of visually handicapped children. *DVH Newsletter, 27,* 29-43.

PART I

GENERAL
CONSIDERATIONS

Part I includes general background information for understanding the role and function of psychologists who work in the school setting with handicapped children.

The first chapter focuses on selected sections of Public Law 94-142, the Education for All Handicapped Children Act of 1975, and Section 504 of Public Law 93-112, the Rehabilitation Act of 1975. These laws include important regulations regarding the parameters in the assessment of handicapped persons, with special emphasis on non-discriminatory evaluation, due process, parental rights, and confidentiality of records. The first section of Chapter 1 focuses on these requirements. The next section discusses some of the issues related to assessment that are an outgrowth of judicial and legislative actions. The third section suggests ways of developing and maximizing interdisciplinary team relationships as an approach to arriving at decisions regarding placement and educational planning. The final section in this chapter outlines some leadership roles and responsibilities that should be assumed by school psychologists.

The second chapter presents a five-step model for the process of assessment from the time of referral to the formulation of an individualized education program to meet the needs of the handicapped child and provide him or her with a free appropriate education, which is the ultimate goal of the assessment process.

The third chapter includes two major sections. The first section discusses theoretical and practical issues related to employing an ecological approach to assessment. This section responds to the increasing focus in the field of school psychology on looking at the child in the natural setting, particularly the classroom. The second section discusses some non-test-based assessment procedures, including classroom observation, that may be useful techniques for studying the child in the natural setting.

CHAPTER 1

The Role and Function of the School Psychologist in Special Education

Geraldine T. Scholl

The roles performed by school psychologists are diverse, with variations even among those who are employed within the same school district. This diversity results in part from the interaction between school psychologists who come from a variety of training and experiential backgrounds and the wide variety of the school settings in which they function (Monroe, 1979). Monroe (1979) identified five roles performed by school psychologists along a continuum from those with the most direct influence to those with indirect influence on the child:

1. Counseling or therapy on either an individual or group basis to improve the school adjustment of the individual child,
2. Psychoeducational assessment through formal and informal procedures to use in making educational decisions,
3. Consultation with parents or teachers to facilitate the adjustment of the child,
4. Inservice training of school personnel, usually to effect some needed change within the school program,
5. Research through the systematic collection and analysis of information to improve educational programs.

Monroe concluded that few "school psychologists provide all of these services to the public schools; some provide only one, while most offer the services contained in two or three of the roles" (p. 33). Although the expectations of administrators, the type of school setting and community, and the training and experience of the school psychologist have an impact on the selection of a particular role or roles to be performed, outside forces also have an influence.

The passage of Public Law 94-142, the Education for All Handicapped Children Act of 1975, has had a great impact, both positive and negative, on the role of the school psychologist. In implementing the law, some states now restrict the services of school psychologists to identification and assessment of pupils in special education or those suspected of being in need of special education services. Thus, their prior role in working with regular education teachers and pupils has been curtailed. Some provisions in P.L. 94-142, for example, due process, nonbiased assessment, and confidentiality of records, place restrictions on how the school psychologist assesses and works with special education students. These issues have led to concern in the field regarding the appropriate role of the school psychologist. However, it is not within the scope of this book to explore in depth the issues related to role definition that abound in the field today. The reader is referred to Hynd (1983) and Ysseldyke and Weinberg (1981) for such information. The focus in this book is on the school psychologist's role in special education with pupils and their parents and with teachers and other staff who work in special education. The emphasis is placed on what that role *should* be, which may not be the way it is currently defined in some school districts.

One intent of P.L. 94-142 is to improve assessment and placement procedures so that handicapped children can receive their free appropriate education in the least restrictive environment. Decisions are expected to be made from an interdisciplinary team approach. The various members of the interdisciplinary team are charged with different tasks or duties in the processes of identification, diagnosis, or certification of a need for special education and selection and interpretation of results from formal and informal assessment measures. Recommendations for appropriate placement and education program plans for handicapped pupils are to result from sharing information among team members. Participation on the team calls for an expanded role for the school psychologist from routine "testing" to "assessment," and for a different relationship with teachers, other school personnel, parents, and particularly the pupil. Frequently the school psychologist becomes an advocate who at times is viewed as an adversary of the school district.

This chapter presents an overview of influences and issues related to the role of the school psychologist in special education. It is divided into four sections: legislative forces, issues related to testing/assessment, interdisciplinary team relationships, and finally, the school psychologist in a leadership role in the school setting.

LEGISLATIVE FORCES

Public Law 94-142

During 1982 the U.S. Department of Education proposed a comprehensive revision of the August, 1977 regulations governing implementation of P.L. 94-142. However, at present it appears that major revisions will not be made. We include here a summary of the intent of sections in the current rules and regulations that have particular relevance for the school psychologist.

Definition of Psychological Services

Section 121a.13 of P.L. 94-142 (DHEW, 1977a) includes "Psychological services" under "Related services" and defines them as follows:

(8) "Psychological services" include:
(i) Administering psychological and educational tests, and other assessment procedures;
(ii) Interpreting assessment results;
(iii) Obtaining, integrating, and interpreting information about child behavior and conditions relating to learning;
(iv) Consulting with other staff members in planning school programs to meet the special needs of children as indicated by psychological tests, interviews, and behavioral evaluations; and
(v) Planning and managing a program of psychological services, including psychological counseling for children and parents.

This definition expands the role beyond test adminstration and interpretation to include consultation with other staff members and psychological counseling for children and parents.

Evaluation Procedures

The rules specifying evaluation procedures are of particular interest for several reasons: the kinds of assessment instruments to be used are described in some detail; the assessment must be multidisciplinary and include more than a single measure; and all areas relevant to the child's suspected disability must be assessed.

§ 121a.532 Evaluation procedures.
State and local educational agencies shall insure, as a minimum that:

(a) Tests and other evaluation materials:

(1) Are provided and administered in the child's native language or other mode of communication, unless it is clearly not feasible to do so;

(2) Have been validated for the specific purpose for which they are used; and

(3) Are administered by trained personnel in conformance with the instructions provided by their producer;

(b) Tests and other evaluation materials include those tailored to assess specific areas of educational need and not merely those which are designed to provide a single general intelligence quotient;

(c) Tests are selected and administered so as best to ensure that when a test is administered to a child with impaired sensory, manual, or speaking skills, the test results accurately reflect the child's aptitude or achievement level or whatever other factors the test purports to measure, rather than reflecting the child's impaired sensory, manual, or speaking skills (except where these skills are the factors which the test purports to measure);

(d) No single procedure is used as the sole criterion for determining an appropriate educational program for a child; and

(e) The evaluation is made by a multidisciplinary team or group of persons, including at least one teacher or other specialist with knowledge in the area of suspected disability.

(f) The child is assessed in all areas related to the suspected disability, including, where appropriate, health, vision, hearing, social and emotional status, general intelligence, academic performance, communicative status, and motor abilities.

A subsequent section (121a.534) stipulates that a reevaluation must take place at least every 3 years.

Placement Options

One of the important provisions in P.L. 94-142 is placement of the handicapped child in the least restrictive environment (LRE). Section 121a.550 requires that handicapped children be placed with those who are not handicapped to the maximum extent appropriate. Section 121a.551 requires that a continuum of alternate placements be available so that children are placed where their educational needs can be met most effectively. These alternate placements should range from regular classes to segregated schools, residential or day. The intent of this section in the regulations was to ensure that handicapped children would be placed in the best setting for obtaining an appropriate education. Many school districts do not provide such a continuum either within their district or through cooperative arrangements with other districts.

This is especially true of programs for low incidence handicapped children: those with hearing or visual impairments and those with physical handicaps.

There is no easy solution to how school districts, especially small districts or those in rural areas, can provide a full continuum of services. Several models have been proposed, each with disadvantages. Some initiate cooperative arrangements with neighboring districts. For example, one district provides a program for visually handicapped children, another for the hearing impaired, and a third for physically handicapped children, with each serving pupils from all three districts. This solution may increase transportation costs, cause problems related to operational costs when one district's assigned program is more expensive than another's, and create issues related to varying teacher salary schedules across districts. A regional or intermediate school district organization for all special education programs provides another model. The program becomes centralized, and local districts may lose control over monitoring the quality of services provided to children from their district. Some districts place several categorical groups into one program; for example, combining emotionally disturbed, learning disabled, and educable mentally retarded pupils or pupils from all the low incidence categories. This model has distinct disadvantages. Teachers often are not certified in all categorical areas, and there are extraordinary challenges in attempting to meet the heterogeneous educational needs of several distinctly different types of pupils within a single program. The children themselves, because of their particular impairments, may not be able to communicate with their peers; for example, a blind child in the same program with hearing impaired children.

The lack of options within a continuum of services presents one of the most critical problems in special education, but it is one that few small- to medium-sized school districts have been able to resolve to any satisfactory degree. Great ingenuity is required to ensure implementation of this section of the law. School psychologists face a dilemma when the only available placement in the school district may not be the one most appropriate for the child's educational needs. It may be necessary to function as an advocate with the school administration on behalf of the child and his or her parents to secure the most appropriate placement (Frith, 1981; Heshusius, 1982).

Due Process Procedures

Subpart E of P.L. 94-142 Sections 121a.500-.574 outlines in some detail the due process procedures for parents and children. School psychologists must be familiar with their state and local procedures for implementing this subpart, particularly those related to notice and consent and to due process. Under the provisions of Section 121a.503 in this part, parents have a right to secure an independent educational evaluation, at public expense, if they disagree with the evaluation by the school district and if the hearing officer is in accord.

Because of their critical role in the placement and planning process, school psychologists should become thoroughly familiar with these sections since they may be called upon to justify their recommendations to the parents or the school district or both during a due process hearing.

Confidentiality of Information

The confidentiality of information is spelled out in Sections 121a.560-.575. Because the school psychologist needs to keep detailed notes, he or she should become thoroughly familiar with the regulations in these sections as well as with the school district's implementation of the regulations. Some questions that may arise include the following: Do parents have a right to see test protocols with raw data? Can parents demand to be present and observe the assessment? Can parents decide which assessment instruments are to be used?

For additional details about these provisions as well as other provisions of importance for school psychologists, the reader is referred to Ballard (1977), Reschly (1983), and Reynolds and Birch (1982).

Section 504

Section 504 of Public Law 93-112, the Rehabilitation Act of 1975, has been called the "Civil Rights for the Handicapped Act" (Ballard, 1977). The following sections of the rules and regulations are relevant for school psychologists.

Definitions

A handicapped person is more broadly defined under the provisions of this law to include not only those who currently have a physical or mental impairment but also those who have a record of having had or are regarded as having an impairment (DHEW, 1977b, Section 84.1j). Such impairments must be considered as limiting the person in one or more of the major life activities. Several impairments included under this act, such as some physical handicaps described in Chapter 8, typically have no educational implications. The role of the school psychologist in such instances may be minimal until it is time for a referral to an appropriate agency outside the school setting, such as vocational rehabilitation.

Education-Related Provisions

The regulations also include provisions for a free appropriate public education (Section 84.33); placement in a setting with nonhandicapped persons (Section 84.34); evaluation and placement procedures (Section 84.35); and procedural safeguards (Section 84.36); all of which are similar to those under P.L. 94-142.

State and Local Regulations

Each state has developed its own guidelines or rules and regulations within the framework of the federal legislation. School psychologists should obtain a copy of and become familar with their state regulations for special education programs and services. There is variation among states, especially on criteria for eligibility for special education programs and services.

Under the provisions of P.L. 94-142 each state submits to the U. S. Department of Education a plan for implementation. This plan may be a good resource for obtaining information about state-wide implementation of special education legislation. A request for both the state regulations and the implementation plan should be made through the director of special education in the state department of education.

Procedures followed by local districts may also vary within the framework of state and federal guidelines. Some states require the submission of local or intermediate/regional plans for the delivery of special education programs and services. If it is available, the school psychologist should obtain a copy from the local or intermediate/ regional special education director. In any event, it is important for the school psychologist to be familiar with the rules and regulations at all levels as they pertain to identification, placement, and educational programming for handicapped pupils.

ISSUES RELATED TO TESTING/ASSESSMENT

Federal and state legislation as well as judicial rulings have raised questions related to the use of standardized tests with minority pupils for placement purposes. The first part of this section summarizes some of these issues and reviews a few proposals for modification. Since these kinds of tests are frequently questionable when used with handicapped pupils, the use of such instruments in nonstandardized ways for these pupils is discussed.

Standardized Tests

The traditional tools of the school psychologist have been standardized tests of intelligence. Typically these tests have norms derived from their use on a specific population that may or may not be representative of the population as a whole. This issue of bias is not new (Haney, 1981) but it has become more prominent in recent years, partly because of the involvement of the courts in determining whether the use of standardized tests of intelligence has resulted in the disproportionate placement of minority pupils in special education classes, especially those for educable mentally impaired students (cf. Bersoff, 1981; Haney, 1981; Lambert, 1981; Reschly, 1981). P.L. 94-142 requires the use of nondiscriminatory instruments. This means that the school psychologist must be familiar with a wide variety of instruments and know the procedure for selection as well as characteristics of their standardization populations and data on their validity and reliability.

The controversy over the use of standardized tests should lead school psychologists to view these instruments with caution, but this does not necessarily mean that they should be discarded. Banning the use of standardized tests in California, for example, has not led to the anticipated decrease in the number of Black students placed in special classes for the educable mentally impaired (cf. Lambert, 1981; Reschly, 1981). In fact, it is possible that avoiding the use of such standardized measures may result in a child's not receiving the needed special education services (MacMillan, 1982). Instead of banning the use of tests, the way in which the results are applied should be examined. For example, school psychologists could abandon the use of the term *IQ*; employ multifactored assessment; explore the use of other instruments such as criterion-referenced tests; and use behaviorial consultation methods that emphasize assessment, intervention, and evaluation of outcomes in the natural setting (Reschly, 1981).

Glaser (1981) recommended an agenda for research leading to the development of instruments that will assist in making instructional decisions. He suggested that there be less emphasis on tests as selection tools and more on how to assist children to take full advantage of their educational opportunities. Other factors also need to be considered, such as the assessment of the role of motivation and adjustment in determining intellectual competence and in planning intervention programs (Scarr, 1981).

If standardized tests are viewed as observations in a controlled setting, then school psychologists should pick and choose appropriate tests and parts of tests that will yield the most useful information for a particular child and augment these with informal assessment procedures such as classroom observation. The results of these multiple sources of information will lead to more effective recommendations for intervention within the school setting. Some informal assessment procedures are discussed in Chapters 2 and 3.

The National School Psychology Inservice Training Network has developed two training modules that relate to these problems. *Non-biased Assessment* (Oakland, n.d.) includes the topics of basic considerations, legal principles, sociocultural considerations, understanding language characteristics, educational assessment, assessment and the mentally retarded student, and assessment and the emotionally disturbed student. *Non-Test-Based Assessment* (Tucker, n.d.) includes an introduction and overview and deals with the topics of observation-based assessment, interview-based assessment, and curriculum-based assessment. Although the modules are designed for a workshop presentation, individual school psychologists will find in them information that will be helpful in determining how to assess and interpret data obtained from various tests and instruments in light of the varying backgrounds of the pupils.

Nonstandardized Use of Standardized Instruments

The controversy over the use of standardized tests has revolved primarily around the disproportionate numbers of minority pupils placed in special classes, most often classes for educable mentally retarded children. In judicial rulings, courts have viewed the tests as being biased and unfair to minority groups.

This same criticism of standardized tests may be applied to handicapped pupils. Some pupils, because of the nature of their impairments, have restricted access to their environment for learning experiences and are truly disadvantaged; some lack fine motor skills needed to manipulate test materials quickly and efficiently. The use of the recommended standardized procedures for administration and scoring as well as the application of test norms for such pupils might be seriously questioned. For example, a number of years ago a 5-year-old child who wore prostheses because her own eyes had been removed when she was a toddler, responded to the Stanford-Binet question "What do we do with our eyes?" with "In the morning my mother puts them in and at night she takes them out." Obviously the life experiences of this 5-year-old differed from those of the typical child her age. When asked what *other* people did with their eyes, she gave the correct response. School psychologists face similar situations almost daily in assessing handicapped children, and they must ask themselves to what extent they should modify the tests used in such situations.

The answer to this question will depend in large measure on the purpose of the test administration: Is it for "testing" or for "assessment''? If the school psychologist is interested in determining the learning potential of the child in order to recommend appropriate placement and intervention, then modifications in administering and scoring are appropriate. If, for a particular purpose, the school psychologist must determine how this child's ability compares with that of his or her peers, then modifications should probably not be made. The reader is referred to Scarr (1981) and Glaser (1981) for a more detailed discussion regarding the question of ''Why test?''.

To fulfill the teacher's need for information relevant for planning an appropriate educational program, the school psychologist should use a variety of assessment procedures. Standardized tests and subparts of tests, modified as necessary so as not to penalize the child because of the nature of the disability, should be used to assess potential and for comparative purposes as well as for determining eligibility for services. Criterion-referenced instruments and standardized tests of achievement should be used in whole or in part to assess the child's current level of functioning relative to chronological age and grade level. Observation and other informal assessment techniques should be used for obtaining data on other variables that have an impact on the child's functioning in the classroom, home, and community settings. With data from a variety of sources, the school psychologist can make recommendations for appropriate placement and educational planning.

Guidelines for assessment of pupils with various disabilities are provided in the chapters in Part II. In addition, school psychologists should become familiar with the variety of procedures, including classroom observation, that can be used for informal assessment (Chapters 2 and 3).

INTERDISCIPLINARY TEAM RELATIONSHIPS

Professionals concerned with the education of handicapped children are now frequently working together in an interdisciplinary team relationship. Included on the team are parents and pupils themselves, when appropriate, as well as other school personnel. A well functioning team relationship requires that each member know and appreciate the role of others in the process and their potential contribution. The following sections provide information that may help school psychologists work more effectively with teachers, parents, and other school personnel, particularly other members of the interdisciplinary team.

Teachers

The special educator and the regular teacher can be invaluable resources to the school psychologist in preparing for the assessment. The regular teacher can provide specific referral questions and information about the child's areas of strengths and weaknesses in educational and social functioning; the steps already taken to assist the child in areas of deficiency and the results of that assistance; and summaries of parent conferences and consultations with other teachers, both regular and special. The referring teacher can also provide descriptions of the school program expectations, academic standards, and how the child functions in relation to them in the classroom, as well as observations of the child's emotional and social functioning, particularly reaction to success and failure, peer relationships, and attitudes. Frequently, the referring teacher may also provide pertinent family information based on personal contacts. Unfortunately, regular teachers seem to be under utilized as members of the interdisciplinary team. (Ysseldyke, Algozzine, & Allen, 1982).

Special education teachers can provide data about the child's developmental level from their informal observations and assessments. The special educator's knowledge of current programming can be invaluable in assisting the school psychologist in formulating a recommendation for placement. Special education teachers have been found to be the most important and influential contributors to individualized education program (IEP) meetings (Gilliam & Coleman, 1981). In addition, the special educator (particularly the receiving teacher) plays an essential role in reevaluation. By addressing the specific concerns in the initial referral and subsequently reported strengths, weaknesses, and results of recommended programming, the special educator provides a profile of the child's progress and changes that the school psychologist can then use in reevaluation.

Teachers expect a report to tell them more than they already know about the child, and they want concrete suggestions for teaching strategies. It is frustrating to get a report that speaks only in terms of test scores and personality dynamics, with no hint of how they relate to the classroom setting.

As part of the assessment, the school psychologist could do trial teaching in order to ascertain cognitive styles and provide specific suggestions to the teacher for behavioral and instructional management.

The school psychologist should also know about the curriculum and instructional resources of the school. It is of little value to suggest that a teacher use materials that are not readily obtainable. Teachers sometimes need guidance in using available materials or in making or obtaining appropriate materials. The school psychologist's knowledge of the school and its resources will enable him or her to assist the teacher in utilizing them. Further, the assessment should be conducted with full knowledge of the curriculum employed in the particular classroom. This knowledge may be gained most effectively through classroom observation (see Chapter 3).

In order to build a good relationship with teachers, school psychologists need both training and experience. Course work in curriculum development is a typical requirement in school psychology preparation programs. Although teaching experience is not usually required, many school psychologists bring to their preparation programs some experience in regular or special education teaching. Those who have that background can often make recommendations that are more acceptable, especially to teachers who are reluctant to have someone without practical experience offer to help them. School psychologists with no prior teaching experience should complete a program of planned observation at various grade levels as part of their preparation program so they become familiar with the dynamics of the classroom.

The Family

Parents

The birth of a baby is traditionally a happy occasion, but in some instances even a healthy baby may be perceived as an intruder in the marriage relationship, as attention focuses on the helpless infant who is causing an imbalance in family priorities and a shift in the dynamics of the family system. Sometimes the child either draws parents together or becomes a source of discord. The arrival of a handicapped child brings even greater elements of imbalance, intrusion, uncertainty, and anxiety. Parents may find few of the joys usually associated with child rearing; instead, they may find dreams shattered and in their place guilt, recriminations, and an exacerbation of marital conflict. Our culture fosters the myth that all parental feelings toward a child should be positive. Some parents may not be able to recognize or accept their disappointment and feelings of rejection (Waterman, 1982; Watson & Van Etten, 1976).

School psychologists may find parental reactions to be a major issue. Since the child is viewed as an extension of self, parents may resort to one or more defensive mechanisms: denial, projection of blame, or repression of real anger. At the base of these reactions may be feelings of guilt or fear. Most parents are naturally concerned about their possible responsibility for the handicapping condition. This concern is grounded in reality in those cases where the condition is hereditary; but even in cases where there are no hereditary factors, rudimentary knowledge of chromosomal or genetic factors or simply superstition and misinformation may lead some parents to feel that their child's condition has been "passed on" by them. Further, guilt about bringing the child into the world, concern about any future children, and worry about what other people will say are intertwined. Often accompanying the anxiety is fear about the uncertainties that lie ahead. Not only is the child's potential very uncertain, but so is the parent's ability to maintain emotional strength. Unspoken shame and disappointment add to the problem. It is little wonder that parents usually need careful counseling and accurate information. The school psychologist should be aware that professional counseling might be necessary not only for the parents but for the entire family (Waterman, 1982).

How can the school psychologist respond to parents' needs and expectations? McLoughlin, Edge, and Strenecky (1978) have suggested that an informal conference in an atmosphere of warmth, understanding, assurance, and trust can be the basis of a productive and helping relationship. Effective parent training involves a combination of education and counseling (Kronick, 1978). The first role of the school psychologist may have to be that of a listener trying to ascertain where the parents need support. Are they denying the existence of their child's disability, feeling guilty about it, or wondering what the future holds? The school psychologist must meet parents at their level with acceptance and understanding before beginning any "re-education."

As parents begin to move toward an acceptance level, the school psychologist can increase the amount of information about the child's specific problem; the handicapping condition in general, including etiology and prognosis; potential school services; and community, state, and national resources. Later, parents need more specific information about the nature of the handicapping condition and realistic expectations for their child's future. Such information should be given clearly, directly, and compassionately. False hopes should not be raised. Parents must be told frankly about the facts regarding "cures." Often parents will use the false hope of some "cure" to delay recognizing the dimensions of the problem.

The school psychologist should be acquainted with the services available in the community, such as parent groups and respite care, so that use of these resources can be recommended when needed. Parents often feel they must care for their handicapped child without outside assistance, and they may have guilt feelings when they leave the child in the hands of another caregiver. The 24-hour-a-day care of a handicapped child can be emotionally as well as physically draining, and at times parents may neglect either their other children or each other. Parents need counseling to accept respite care when appropriate in order to allow them an opportunity to meet their own needs and those of other family members.

Parents need time to absorb and evaluate information and to integrate the new knowledge and formulate their next questions. They may need to receive information repeatedly over a period of time. Furthermore, they also need affirmation, encouragement, and understanding about their own abilities as parents (McLoughlin, et al., 1978; Schnell, 1982).

Parents are a vital part of the interdisciplinary team. They should have a voice in determining the most appropriate placement, they should be encouraged to visit possible sites, and they should be included in developing the educational plan for their child.

The Handicapped Child

Handicapped children need a sense of being loved, wanted, and part of the family. Like nonhandicapped children, they must learn that there are limits to demands and be reassured that they will be given the same limits as well as the same love as their brothers and sisters. They must have the opportunity to develop their potential, neither pushed beyond their capabilities nor "helped" beyond what is necessary. Parents should accept limitations but should not be satisfied with performance that is less than the child's capabilities allow.

Other Family Members

Frequently, needs of nonhandicapped siblings are overlooked in the process of parental concern with the handicapped child. Siblings may have concerns about telling their friends about the child and explaining what the problem is. They need information on a level appropriate to their stage of development and understanding so that they in turn can explain it appropriately to their friends. Often siblings sense the burden of tension that caring for the handicapped child places on their parents. Open lines of communication with their parents can help relieve the anxiety that nonhandicapped siblings may acquire. The extra effort required for coping with the handicapped child should not deprive the other children in the family of caring attention from their parents.

Siblings often need help in coming to terms with their own resentment, fear, and shame about the handicapped child. Such feelings are difficult to admit without guilt. The school psychologist should know that siblings often have nowhere they can turn in attempting to resolve their concerns. If the school system is open to the practice, the school psychologist might provide a valuable service by offering discussion groups for nonhandicapped siblings. Such groups could provide an outlet for feelings and go a long way in relieving some of the burden siblings carry.

The presence of an extended family in the home, such as grand-parents, should also be acknowledged. These persons should be included in any family counseling, especially if they are the primary caregivers for the handicapped child. Extended family members often have needs similar to those of the parents and siblings. Their attitudes and feelings toward the handicapped child may influence the ecological setting in which the child lives, and thus their role in that setting must be recognized. Extended family members can often provide respite care for the child when a break is needed by the parents. They may lend objectivity to the family's perception and treatment of the child.

Waterman (1982) listed ten questions that provide guidance for understanding the family with a handicapped child:

1. Do both parents participate with the children and share in discussing the children?
2. Is one parent—or both parents—unusually overprotective or rejecting toward the handicapped child?
3. Is either parent blaming the other (or himself or herself) for the handicapping condition?
4. Does the handicapped child seem to have access to the parents similar to that of the other children in family? Is he or she heard by them but not stifled or prevented from growing?
5. Do siblings receive appropriate time and attention from the parents?
6. Do siblings seem secure, or do they need to seek attention from their parents or others in negative ways?
7. Are family members allowed to express negative feelings toward the handicapped child? Is this done in a nondestructive way?
8. Do the parents support and nurture each other?
9. Do the parents spend some time together away from all the children?
10. Do family members have some sources of support to fall back on outside of the nuclear family (extended family, friends, and so on)? (p. 178)

Other School Personnel

The interdisciplinary team frequently includes other school personnel with whom the school psychologist must work: the speech and language pathologist, school social worker, administrative personnel, school counselor, school nurse, and the rehabilitation counselor for older pupils. The relationship with the speech and language pathologist is described in Chapter 11.

School social workers, when available in the school district, can provide valuable assistance in case work with the child and the family and in obtaining and interpreting information about the home situation. Overlapping skills of these two professionals, especially in counseling, may cause some conflict. It can usually be resolved through clearly delineated roles in job descriptions and through developing a working relationship based on mutual trust and respect. The two should work closely together, particularly in the identification and diagnostic stages of the assessment process.

Administrators, primarily the principal and the director or supervisor of special education, are other school personnel who are involved on the interdisciplinary team. The fiscal role of these professionals may sometimes precipitate conflicts, especially when needed services are not available within the school district and financial constraints preclude the addition of such resources. Working through these problems may require considerable understanding and compromise on all sides.

Other school personnel are included on the interdisciplinary team when appropriate. The school guidance counselor is often present for secondary level pupils especially, to help in selecting appropriate courses. Guidance counselors can often provide input about the school climate, curriculum, and teachers that may be helpful in developing the individualized education program. The school nurse has a special contribution to make in planning for children with physical impairments, including vision and hearing, and is also a resource person for interpretation of medical reports. The rehabilitation counselor is an important addition to the team when plans are made for the transition to a postsecondary placement.

All involved personnel need to understand and respect the responsibilities and potential contributions of each team member in order to develop a truly interdisciplinary team relationship.

LEADERSHIP ROLES

Within the school system, the school psychologist often is called upon to play vital leadership roles in curriculum development, advocacy, and research.

Curriculum Development

The school psychologist can perform several important functions in curriculum development. The responsibilities of identifying, assessing, educational planning, and placement for handicapped pupils provide a unique overview of the educational system with all its assets and limitations. An "epidemic" of referrals from one particular teacher, of children from the same grade levels but different schools, or of similar problems in the same school should alert the school psychologist to the possibility that the problems may be due to something within the school or school district. When referrals within a school come primarily from one teacher, the school psychologist may discuss the situation with the principal in an attempt to discover the underlying cause. If the referrals are from similar grade levels, the school psychologist might discuss the problem with the curriculum consultant or with an appropriate administrator to determine whether the curriculum for that particular grade level is too difficult or not sufficiently challenging for the pupils. A rash of similar problems in a school might be attributed to the atmosphere, morale of the staff, relationship between principal and teachers, or other factors within the ecology of the school (see Chapter 3). The school psychologist can discuss freely with both teachers and administrators the problem areas he or she has observed and can work with them to remediate or eliminate the underlying causes.

Many school districts have curriculum review committees charged with the responsibility to recommend curriculum changes. Again, the school psychologist can play a significant role on such committees through interpreting the growth and developmental needs and characteristics of pupils at various age levels, recommending changes to make the curriculum more responsive to societal and community needs, and providing input based on referrals of students with problems where modification in the curriculum may alleviate the problems.

Advocacy Role

The handicapped child can have no more powerful advocate than the school psychologist. Through the assessment process, the psychologist identifies the educational needs of the child and must now work to assure the child an appropriate placement with an appropriate curriculum. This should be a major commitment. One school psychologist described herself as "scrappy" when she advocates for appropriate services.

This advocacy role must also be carried out when problems arise between parent and child and between teacher and child. When tensions arise among other school personnel, for instance, teachers and principals or principals and administrators, the school psychologist again may function as an advocate. The training of school psychologists in consultation skills should help them prepare for these roles (Martin, 1983).

School Psychologists and Research

Because of their training and assigned roles, school psychologists may be the professionals in school systems who are best equipped to be involved in research. This involvement includes making a contribution to the research literature, bridging the gap between research findings and their application to school improvement, and program evaluation. In recognition of this potential role an increasing number of graduate programs now require a research component for their school psychology trainees (Brown, 1979).

School psychologists are in a unique position to make a contribution to the research literature. By virtue of their role and their work setting, they have access to a subject pool of special education students, with data on these subjects available from a variety of sources including assessment instruments. Comparative data on the total school population are usually also readily accessible from the school district's routine record-keeping and assessment program. Teachers and administrators usually have numerous questions about pupils, their educational needs and problems, and how their individualized education programs may be made more effective. Such questions lend themselves to field-based research. From them, school psychologists can formulate educationally relevant research questions and design appropriate methods for shedding light on the problem areas. Computers are often used routinely in the administrative operation of the school and thus are readily available for data analysis.

There is some evidence that practicing school psychologists, especially those with doctoral degrees, have the desire and ability to conduct research. Medway, Delp, Ierace, Lazarus, and Westphal (1978) found that, among those who hold a doctorate, practicing school psychologists produce as much research as do academic school psychologists. With all the critical problems in schools today, school psychologists may play a key role in finding solutions through their research efforts.

Applying Research Findings

Another aspect to the research role is that of translating research findings into practice. Although the preparation of special education teachers, counselors, and educational administrators usually emphasizes the application of research to the improvement of educational practice, many remain suspicious of research and skeptical of the relationship between specific findings and actual practice. School psychologists can play a role in attempting to remove such resistance by showing practitioners how the findings of a particular study may have applicability to problems they identify in their settings. School psychologists may be the most influential professionals within the school district in bridging the gap between research and practice. Miller (1981) described this role as that of a "knowledge-linker" between the researcher who needs assistance in facilitating the application of research findings and the administrators, teachers, and pupils who need the information for achieving greater academic growth through enriched educational experiences resulting from the application of research findings.

Evaluating Program Effectiveness

Finally, school psychologists with their professional knowledge and skills may be the most appropriate professionals in the school to manage the program evaluation mandate of Public Law 94-142. By assessing systematically the outcomes of their efforts in assessment and educational planning for individual students and through monitoring the implementation of the individualized education programs, they are in a position to facilitate better educational opportunities for handicapped pupils (Phye, 1979). Further, with their role firmly based within the ecology of the school they are in a good position to evaluate the effectiveness of various segments of the total school program, such as the special education component. Maher (1981) identified four dimensions to program evaluation: evaluative information "that describes the nature, scope or impact of a program"; evaluative methods employed "to acquire the information"; the evaluative process that communicates the relevant information to decision makers; and finally the use of the information for decision making purposes (p. 115). He viewed school psychologists, particularly those who function in the smaller districts, as appropriate personnel to be assigned responsibility for organizing information along these four dimensions in implementing program evaluation for special education.

SUMMARY

This chapter presented a brief overview of the role of school psychologists in the school setting. The impact of P.L. 94-142 and other legislative and judicial actions on the performance of that role was discussed. Issues surrounding "testing" were summarized including the controversy over use of standardized tests with atypical populations. Some guidelines were presented for using such tests in nonstandard ways with handicapped children. Finally, the roles of the school psychologist as a member of the interdisciplinary team and as a leader in the school district were described.

REFERENCES

Ballard, J. (1977). *Public Law 94-142 and Section 504 — Understanding what they are and are not.* Reston VA: The Council for Exceptional Children.

Bersoff, D. N. (1981). Testing and the law. *American Psychologist, 36,* 1047-1056.

Brown, D. T. (1979). Issues in accreditation, certification, and licensure. In G. D. Phye & D. J. Reschly (Eds.), *School Psychology: Perspectives and issues.* pp. 49-82. New York: Academic Press.

DHEW. (1977a, August 23). Education of handicapped children. Part II. *Federal Register.*

DHEW, (1977b, May 4). Section 504 rules and regulations. *Federal Register.*

Frith, G. M. (1981). "Advocate" vs. "Professional Employee": A question of priorities for special educators. *Exceptional Children, 47,* 486-492.

Gilliam, J. E., & Coleman, N. C. (1981). Who influences IEP committee decisions? *Exceptional Children, 47,* 642-644.

Glaser, R. (1981). The future of testing. *American Psychologist, 36,* 923-936.

Haney, W. (1981). Validity, vaudeville, and values. *American Psychologist, 36,* 1021-1034.

Heshusius, L. (1982). At the heart of the advocacy dilemma: A mechanistic world view. *Exceptional Children, 49,* 6-13.

Hynd, G. W. (Ed.). (1983). *The school psychologist: An introduction.* Syracuse NY, Syracuse University Press.

Kronick, D. (1978). Educational and counseling groups for parents. *Academic Therapy, 13,* 355-359.

Lambert, N. M. (1981). Psychological evidence in Larry P. V. Wilson Riles. *American Psychologists, 36,* 937-952.

MacMillan, D. L. (1982). *Mental retardation in school and society.* Boston: Little, Brown.

Maher, C. A. (1981). School psychologists and special education program evaluation: Contributions and considerations. In J. L. Carroll (Ed.) *Contemporary school psychology: Selected readings from Psychology in the Schools* (2nd ed.) (pp. 114-119). Brandon VT: Clinical Psychology Publishing Co.

Martin, R. P. (1983). Consultation in the schools. In G. W. Hynd (Ed.), *The school psychologist: An introduction* (pp. 264-292). Syracuse NY: Syracuse University Press.

McLoughlin, J. A., Edge, D., & Strenecky, B. (1978). Perspective on parental involvement in the diagnosis and treatment of learning disabled children. *Journal of Learning Disabilities, 11,* 32-37.

Medway, F., Delp, P., Ierace, C., Lazarus, S., & Westphal, K. (1978). Research activities of doctoral school psychologists. *Journal of School Psychology, 16,* 34-41.

Miller, W. E. (1981). A new role for the school psychologists—Who needs it? In J. L. Carroll (Ed.), *Contemporary school psychology: Selected readings from Psychology in the Schools* (2nd ed.) (pp. 48-52). Brandon VT: Clinical Psychology Publishing Co.

Monroe, V. (1979). Roles and status of school psychology. In G. D. Phye & D. J. Reschly (Eds.), *School psychology: Perspectives and issues* (pp.25-45). New York: Academic Press.

Oakland, T. (n.d.). *Nonbiased assessment.* Minneapolis: University of Minnesota National School Psychology Inservice Training Network.

Phye, G. D. (1979). School psychologists as consultants in the evaluation of learning and intervention outcomes. In G. D. Phye & D. J. Reschly (Eds.), *School psychology: Perspectives and issues* (pp. 257-280). New York: Academic Press.

Reschly, D. J. (1981) Psychological testing in educational classification and placement. *American Psychologist, 36,* 1094-1102.

Reschly, D. J. (1983). Legal issues in psychoeducational assessment. In G. W. Hynd (Ed.), *The school psychologist: An introduction* (pp. 67-93). Syracuse NY: Syracuse University Press.

Reynolds, M. C. & Birch, J. W. (1982). *Teaching exceptional children in all America's schools.* Reston VA: The Council for Exceptional Children.

Scarr, S. (1981). Testing *for* children. *American Psychologist, 36,* 1159-1166.

Schnell, R. R. (1982). The psychologist's role in the parent conference. In G. Ulrey & S. J. Rogers (Eds.), *Psychological assessment of handicapped infants and young children* (pp. 179-187). New York: Thieme-Stratton.

Tucker, J. A. (n.d.). *Non test-based assessment.* Minneapolis: University of Minnesota National School Psychology Inservice Training Network (1982).

Waterman, J. (1982). Assessment of the family system. In G. Ulrey & S. J. Rogers (Eds.), *Psychological assessment of handicapped infants and young children* (pp. 172-178). New York: Thieme-Stratton.

Watson, B. L. & Van Etten, C. (1976). Programs, materials, and techniques. *Journal of Learning Disabilities, 9,* 6-11.

Ysseldyke, J. E., Algozzine, B., & Allen, D. (1982). Participation of regular education teachers in special education team decision making. *Exceptional Children, 48,* 365-366.

Ysseldyke, J. E., & Weinberg, R. A. (1981). The future of psychology in the schools: Proceedings of the Spring Hill Symposium. *The School Psychology Review, 10,* 116-318.

ADDITIONAL RESOURCES

Bailey, D. B., Jr., & Harbin, G. L. (1980). Nondiscriminatory evaluation. *Exceptional Children, 46,* 590-596.

Buscaglia, L. (1975). *The disabled and their parents: A counseling challenge.* Thorofare, NJ: C. B. Slack.

Conoley, J. C. (1981). *Consultation in schools: Theory, research, procedures.* New York: Academic Press.

Jensen, A. R. (1981). *Straight talk about mental tests.* New York: The Free Press.

Kroth, R. L. (1975) *Communicating with parents of exceptional children.* Denver: Love.

Kroth, R. L., & Scholl, G. T. (1978). *Getting schools involved with parents.* Reston VA: The Council for Exceptional Children.

Losen, S., & Diament, B. (1978). *Parent conferences in the schools.* Boston: Allyn & Bacon.

Meyers, C. E., Sundstrom, R. E., & Yoshida, R. K. (1974). The school psychologist and assessment in special education. *School Psychology Monograph, 2,* 3-57.

Phye, G. D., & Reschly, D. J. (Eds.) (1979). *School psychology: Perspectives and issues.* New York: Academic Press.

Seligman, M. (1979). *Strategies for helping parents of exceptional children: A guide for teachers.* New York: The Free Press.

Sherman, S. W., & Robinson, N. M. (Eds.) (1982). *Ability testing of handicapped people: Dilemma for government, science, and the public.* Washington DC: National Academy Press.

Sherrer, C. W. & Sherrer, M. S. (1980). *Ethical and professional standards for academic psychologists and counselors.* Springfield IL: Charles C Thomas.

Swanson, H. L., & Watson, B. L. (1982). *Educational and psychological assessment of exceptional children* (Chap. 4). St. Louis: C. V. Mosby.

Webster, E. J. (1977). *Counseling with parents of handicapped children.* New York: Grune & Stratton.

CHAPTER 2

The Process of Assessment

Paula Elitov

The emphasis of this chapter is on the *process* of assessment, that is, how the school psychologist proceeds step by step from the initial referral through developing an appropriate educational plan and arranging for placement in a program. Children with problems usually first come to the attention of parents or teachers and are then referred to another person for help. Most school districts have a formal procedure for handling referrals and school psychologists should be familiar with all local policies and procedures.

Step one in the assessment process is a determination of the referral concerns, which includes collecting descriptive and anecdotal information that helps to clarify the problem. Step two is the collection of all relevant historical and behavioral data that will enable school personnel to determine whether this is an appropriate referral and, if so, to formulate questions to be answered by means of assessment. In step three the school psychologist selects and administers appropriate instruments. In step four, the psychologist uses the information thus obtained and input from other members of the interdisciplinary team to prepare a report that integrates and interprets the available data. Finally, in step five, strategies for educational planning and intervention are developed, typically in a team meeting.

The approach described here emphasizes consideration of how the child functions in relation to peers, how good a match there is between the child and the learning environment, and how the child goes about learning new tasks. This approach encourages the school psychologist to use clinical skills and knowledge of the learning process as primary evaluation tools and to use norm-referenced tests, criterion-referenced tests, diagnostic teaching episodes, and informal observation as sources of particular types of diagnostic information.

DESCRIPTION OF THE PROCESS

Step One: Determining the Referral Concerns

The first step is to understand as completely as possible why the child is being referred. The school psychologist should ascertain what interventions have been attempted within the framework of regular education. This is critical, especially for children with mild handicapping conditions, since there appears to be increasing concern about the over-identification of such children—especially those with learning disabilities—for special education programs and services (see, for example, Madden & Salvia, 1983; Shepard, Smith, & Vojr, 1983). School psychologists should determine from the regular teacher and other appropriate school personnel what options in regular education have been attempted and how they have been evaluated.

If alternatives have not been explored, then the school psychologist should work with regular school personnel to identify what intervention strategies might be attempted prior to initiating a formal referral for assessment. The next chapter includes suggestions for studying the child within the school setting as part of an ecological approach and for conducting classroom observations, both of which can provide useful tools for identifying alternatives. Possible alternatives that might be employed within regular education include the use of cross-age tutors, volunteers for tutoring in particular subject matter areas, placement for part of the school day in another classroom for a specific purpose, suggestions for parents to work on at home, structuring the classroom to maximize the learning environment, and individualizing instruction. A case conference with the school principal and regular teacher might help to determine the most appropriate strategy to enable the child to remain in the regular classroom.

If it appears that options within regular education have been exhausted, then the school psychologist should interview the referring person to identify specific questions that person would like answered. From this information assessment strategies can be determined. A suggested format for this purpose is included in Appendix A.

If specific referral concerns have not already been presented, it is useful to discuss in detail with the parent or teacher the behaviors or attributes of the child that are a source of worry. In this way, specific questions can be formulated to assist the assessment process. The process of coming to a consensus about the essential questions serves several useful purposes. First, asking parents and teachers for specific questions helps them pinpoint their concerns and helps the school psychologist to focus the assessment and the feedback to address these concerns. Second, it provides an opportunity for the school psychologist to call the attention of the teacher or parent to additional questions that may be suggested by the data provided, but that did not occur to the person referring the child. Third, it provides an opportunity for the school psychologist to set realistic expectations for what the evaluation can and cannot accomplish.

Specific questions will also help the school psychologist determine the most appropriate type of assessment. Some questions are best answered by observation in the classroom; other information is best gathered by observing the child on a playground with peers. Contrasting the child's level of functioning in a one-to-one session and in a large, noisy classroom can provide information about which environments are optimal.

As the school psychologist talks with the parent or teacher about expressed concerns, it is also important to listen for hidden fears and concerns. For example, a parent's most pressing question may be what caused the child's disability. This question will most likely not be answered by the assessment and, if a parent is waiting for such an answer, the results of the assessment may be disappointing. It is useful at the outset to clarify for parents what questions can be answered and, if there are some unanswerable ones, to acknowledge the frustration of not having these answers. A teacher may refer a child because he or she really wants the child transferred to another class. For this teacher, a long list of suggestions for remediation is likely to be poorly received. Knowing at the outset what the real issues are can make the assessment process more helpful to the child, the teacher, and the parent.

It may be useful for the school psychologist to summarize this initial period of sharing concerns and behavioral observations by listing the referral questions with the teacher or parent and developing a plan and a timetable for answering each question. This plan may include what types of assessments are needed, who will carry out each one, where the assessments will take place, and what question each assessment will attempt to answer. The school psychologist may want to serve as a central "case manager" who integrates the findings of a number of evaluations and provides the feedback to the parent or teacher.

Step Two: Gathering Historical and Behavioral Data

Time used to find out what is already known about the child is time well spent. This procedure should include obtaining a detailed developmental history from the parents. The level of detail in the developmental history will vary depending on the nature of the setting in which this information is collected and the type of problem the child seems to evidence. A typical basic developmental history should include information about the mother's pregnancy; the prenatal, perinatal, and postnatal periods; the child's early development and affect; information about the child's temperament; and early sleeping and eating patterns. Parents should be asked about any medical problems the child has had including allergies, hospitalizations, and accidents. It may also be useful to ask about any separations or traumatic experiences the parent remembers as being significant to the child.

The developmental history should continue through the preschool period with questions about the child's early learning in the area of language, gross and fine motor development, interaction with peers, and reactions to early school experiences. The style of discipline that the parent has found to be effective and any difficulties with discipline should be noted.

For school-age children, the history should continue with questions about growth and development in three areas: school, home, and community. Questions about school progress should focus on areas of strength and weakness in academic subjects; nonacademic subjects such as art, music, or sports; and, interactions with peers and teachers. Questions about interactions of the child within the family should stress how the child plays in the family, and relationships with various family members. Finding out about how the child functions within the community can reveal the degree of personal independence the child has from the family and may point out community activities and resources that might be used on the child's behalf. For school-age children, the inquiry would include questions about any involvement with the law and with drugs.

It is also helpful to know as much as possible about the setting in which the child is currently placed, what approaches have already been tried, and what has or has not been successful. This information helps focus the assessment on obtaining new information rather than telling parents and teachers what they already know. The school psychologist, in talking with the teacher and/or observing the child in the classroom, should consider the size of the classroom, the skills and characteristics of the other children, the curriculum being employed, the teacher's style, the tasks the child is asked to do, and the competencies necessary to be successful in the classroom.

After obtaining this overview, it is useful to look more carefully at the child's academic work and history of successes and failures. As the student moves from individual to small group to large group activities during the school day, what differences are noted in his or her ability to attend to and to profit from these experiences? How does the child seem to fit in with the social scene of the classroom? Is the child a central member of the class social structure, a scapegoat, or an isolated member of the classroom? It is also useful to ask the teacher what specific approaches work best with the child and what has already been tried. Acknowledging and using the wealth of information the teacher already has can create a feeling of partnership with the teacher and help focus the assessment on providing genuinely new information.

Throughout this process of information gathering, the school psychologist should be looking for "red flags," bits of information about the child's behavior that can help in the formulation of tentative hypotheses about the child's learning. These can suggest questions to explore further and help determine the most effective assessment tools to use. Some "red flags" may be:

1. Inconsistencies in reports of the child's behavior, particularly in different settings.
2. Patterns of strengths and weaknesses.
3. Behaviors that suggest which a particular type of learning problem.
4. Patterns that suggest which approaches seem to be effective or ineffective in working with the child.
5. Relationships between behavior and learning problems.
6. Aspects of the developmental history that are suggestive of specific developmental disabilities.
7. Poor attendance record.

Step Three: Conducting the Assessment

Once objectives for the assessment are established, the school psychologist must determine what tools to use in order to answer the referral questions. Depending on the concerns, one or more of the following types of assessment instruments may be used.

Intelligence Tests

IQ tests can be useful in giving a global picture of a child's learning ability in relation to a normative group, but they do not tell why a child obtained a certain score nor whether the child would obtain a different score following intervention. The preceding chapter included a discussion of the difficulties of using standardized tests of intelligence with atypical groups. School psychologists are cautioned to interpret results of such tests with an awareness of their weaknesses. Frequently, it is wise to use only those subtests that will answer the referral questions rather than to administer a complete test for the sake of obtaining an IQ score.

Ordinarily, an effort is made to select an intelligence test that will minimize a child's area of disability. For example, a nonverbal IQ test such as the Leiter International Performance Scale might be chosen as most appropriate for a child who has a severe language or hearing disability. The Wechsler Intelligence Scales are also popular because the tests give a profile of subtest scores in specific areas of intellectual functioning. Suggestions for standardized tests of intelligence appropriate to specific disability groups are included in the chapters in Part II. With some handicapped children, school psychologists may wish to employ a particular test or subtests in nonstandardized ways as described in Chapter 1. School psychologists should be aware of the pitfalls and limitations of standardized tests of intelligence and use them as only one source of information in the assessment process.

Standardized Achievement Tests

Achievement tests are another form of norm-referenced tests that compare a child to peers within academic subject areas such as reading and mathematics. They may be helpful in pinpointing levels at which criterion-referenced or diagnostic testing should begin. Generally, achievement tests will suggest areas of strength and weakness, but the scores will not provide information about *how* the child learns or which subskills present the most difficulty.

Criterion-Referenced Tests

The purpose of criterion-referenced instruments is to determine particular patterns of skill acquisition within a curriculum area. For example, in mathematics, one could assess subskills such as numeration, geometry, or measurement; in reading, one could measure subskills such as sound-blending, comprehension, or decoding. Criterion-referenced assessment does not compare the child with peers but rather looks at what specific skills the child has or has not acquired. Educational recommendations for where to start and what to work on usually grow out of this type of assessment.

Adjusted Conditions Testing or Trial Teaching

Trial teaching is an attempt to assess under what conditions the child is able to learn specific tasks. It is the most individualized of all assessments discussed so far because the student is used as the reference (Cruickshank, Morse & Johns, 1980). In order to carry out a trial teaching episode, the school psychologist must understand both task and learner analysis, know a variety of teaching methods, and understand the learning process. This is a time to experiment with altering task variables and carefully observing the effect on the child's ability to learn. Some task variables to consider include:

1. Types of materials (concrete, abstract, sensory, etc.).
2. Mode of presentation of tasks (verbal directions, demonstration, multisensory, etc.).
3. Sequencing, pacing, and timing of instruction.
4. Nature of the output required.
5. Level of stimulation.
6. Amount of supervision and feedback required.

For example, the school psychologist may give the child some arithmetic tasks to perform, such as addition, and make available concrete teaching aids, such as blocks. By observing how the child performs with and without the concrete aids, the school psychologist may be able to offer the teacher specific suggestions for remediation in the classroom.

The highly individualized nature of trial teaching makes it a time-consuming and therefore costly procedure. It requires the school psychologist to have intimate knowledge of school learning tasks and how they can be modified and creativity to vary procedures for specific purposes. After some experimentation, however, the school psychologist should be able to use trial teaching as an effective means of finding out about a child's learning style.

Classroom Observation

Observing a child within the classroom setting can provide valuable information for the assessment process as well. This technique is discussed in greater detail in Chapter 3.

Rating Scales

Rating scales may be useful tools for quickly gathering impressions from teachers and/or parents about the child's everyday behavior in settings where the school psychologist seldom can do extended observation (Connors, 1969). Teachers and parents have considerable knowledge about the child that is sometimes difficult to articulate or organize. Rating scales that ask a wide variety of questions about the child's behavior can provide a format for teachers and parents to use in organizing their observations.

Teacher-rated behavior scales typically ask about school-related problems and can be used by the school psychologist to assess how the child's difficulties interface with the demands of the school environment. Such questionnaires may also clarify for the school psychologist what behaviors are most bothersome for the teacher. Typically, behavior rating scales contain a variety of questions grouped in clusters that tap the same underlying dimension of behavior. Some scales provide a profile of factor scores that can be useful in summarizing the teacher's ratings.

Parent-rated behavior scales provide the school psychologist with an opportunity to get a sense of the child's behavior at home and in the community. From the parents' perceptions of the child, the school psychologist can begin to piece together similarities and differences in the parents'and the teacher's perceptions and to evaluate in which settings the child's behavior is "disturbing."

Behavior rating scales may sometimes be used instead of an interview, if it is not possible to meet in person with the parent or teacher. Some school psychologists ask the parent or teacher to fill out the rating scale ahead of time and then use it as a focal point for the interview. It can be useful to sit down with the parent and the teacher and compare observations as a basis for beginning a dialogue between them. Rating scales can also be used to evaluate the progress of intervention strategies by providing a baseline description of behavior that can then be compared with a second rating at the end of treatment.

As with any shortcut method, rating scales do not substitute for a good clinical interview conducted by a trained clinician, but they can add a quantitative enhancement to it. Because they consist of many specific questions, it is sometimes difficult to get a total picture of the child without some summary data or general impressions from the teacher or parent. It also happens that very significant dimensions of a child's behavior are not tapped by the particular rating scale.

The school psychologist should be sensitive to the reading level and sophistication of parents. For some parents a 50- or 100-item questionnaire is overwhelming, and for some it is too difficult to read. Nevertheless, the school psychologist can often quickly obtain more specific information about the child's behavior with a rating scale than can be obtained from simply getting a teacher's global impression of a child. Teachers and parents are often more willing to respond to a questionnaire by checking off or circling items than by answering long, open-ended questions.

Some of the more current teacher behavior rating scales are the Behavior Problem Checklist (Peterson & Quay, 1979); the Hahnemann High School Behavior Rating Scale (Spivack & Swift, 1975); and the Devereaux Behavior Rating Scales (Spivack & Swift, 1967). Some examples of parent behavior rating scales include the Louisville Behavior

Checklist (Miller, 1967) and the Child Behavior Rating Scale (Achenback & Edelbrock, 1978).

Ecological Evaluation

After determining effective teaching strategies in a one-to-one setting under favorable circumstances, it is important to evaluate the classroom settings where the child is or could be placed. In what ways are these natural settings different from the assessment setting? What skills does the child need to be able to function in this class? To what degree is the child able to work alone, get materials himself or herself, and so forth? How will the child fit in with the other children socially? What expectations exist in this classroom for academic and social performance? How flexible is the teacher in accepting and implementing the suggestions the school psychologist might make? Will the teacher need modeling or instruction to be able to implement the school psychologist's suggestions? What are the specific dynamics within the classroom that may help or hinder the child's learning?

These considerations are extremely important in working toward meaningful educational planning. The value of the school psychologist's report to the teacher and parent often depends on the feasibility of carrying out suggestions for remediation in the natural setting where the child will spend most of his or her time.

A more extensive discussion of ecological evaluation is included in Chapter 3.

Step Four: Integrating and Interpreting the Results

After the assessment process, the school psychologist's greatest challenge is to integrate the information gathered using his or her best clinical judgment and knowledge. This requires a careful review of the results of the total assessment in relation to the original referral questions and a synthesis of these results into a meaningful, comprehensive report. Parents and teachers expect to learn more about the child at the conclusion of an assessment than they knew at the time of referral. They also want a report that addresses their original concerns and provides them with specific suggestions for how to manage the child and the setting to facilitate learning. Finally, they want a report they can read and understand, one that is free of jargon.

All categories of exceptional children may show uneven patterns in skill development. It is useful to describe the child's current skill level and provide suggestions for instruction to build on the current level.

There is also a need to discuss how a specific disability relates to other aspects of learning or social development. For example, how might dyslexia affect the child's self-esteem and feelings of competence? Could it interfere with completion of assignments in areas where the child is otherwise competent, such as math or science, and if so, how? Gliedman and Roth (1980) have challenged professionals to create a new developmental psychology of handicapping conditions from which we can come to appreciate the unique developmental tasks facing children with handicaps and from which mental health professionals can begin to evaluate the adaptive potential of a variety of behaviors that might ordinarily be construed as maladaptive.

It is important to integrate the findings and create a picture of the whole child, including strengths and weaknesses within the child and within the ecology. To do this, the school psychologist must move beyond findings on tests to essential issues, needs, and difficulties as well as strategies that work.

Finally, it is helpful to tie together evidence from the assessment data with observations from parents and teachers. To do so makes the process more relevant and conveys to parents and teachers the value placed on their input. Original referral questions must be addressed in the comments.

Step Five: Recommending Strategies for Educational Intervention

The recommendations for remediation should follow logically from the conclusions drawn in Step four. For maximum usefulness the suggestions should be as specific as possible. If particular remediation techniques are recommended, it is helpful to list sources of information about these techniques for parents or teachers who may be unfamiliar with them. If suggestions are made that might be unrealistic for the classroom teacher to implement, a strategy should be offered for providing extra services to the child. Listing specific available community resources may facilitate the process.

Writing the Report

Frequently, the written report represents to the teacher and/or parent the end point of the assessment process. All of the clinical observations; test results; and evaluations of the child, the family, and the school setting must be woven together to make a succinct statement about the nature of the child's strengths and weaknesses, the child's needs, and the plan for remediation.

A typical report includes the following sections:

1. A summary of demographic information: name, date of birth, name of parent or guardian, name of school and grade, etc.

2. A statement of the problem or referral questions including any differences in the perception of the problem on the part of parents, teachers, the child him/herself, etc.

3. A section on behavioral observations. This part of the report should include a description of how the child related to the examiner; general impressions of language and gross motor functioning; how the child approached the tasks involved in the assessment; how the child reacted to stress, to difficult tasks, to success; the amount of support the child required; the types of feedback that helped the child to focus on the tasks presented. If the school psychologist observed the child in the home or in the classroom, impressions of how the child related in these settings should also be included.

   It should be noted that the same behavior may have different meanings in different children and in different settings. For example, a hyperactive child may be expressing his/her immaturity, be overly anxious or have some neurological impairment. It is important, therefore, to view each child's behavior in relation to the child's developmental history and in terms of the frequency of the behavior and the context in which it occurs. Appendix B describes a variety of common behaviors and suggests some alternative hypotheses about the nature of these behaviors that the school psychologist may want to consider. Appendix C provides some guidelines for the school psychologist to use in writing behavioral observations.

4. A description of the child's current developmental level. Depending on the nature of the assessments completed in Step three, this section of the report should describe and integrate the results. All formal tests administered should be listed along with appropriate information to help the reader interpret the test findings. It is useful to move beyond describing test scores to describing how the child learns, what it is like for the child in the school setting, and generally what is the nature of the child's needs. Attempting to describe what it feels like to be this child is often a useful way to explain test findings to teachers and parents and to help them appreciate the child's needs. Integrating the information gathered during formal testing with the behavioral observations gathered from teachers and parents in a variety of contexts helps create a picture of how the child functions differently in different settings, depending on the stressors and supports that each setting presents.

5. A description of what techniques appear to work well for the child in facilitating learning or enhancing social and emotional growth. At this point, it may be useful to acknowledge the limitations parents or teachers may have in meeting the child's needs and to discuss added support that may be useful. If the school psychologist has had the opportunity to assess strengths and potential resources within the family and the community, he or she may want to discuss ways in which these resources might be mobilized on the child's behalf.

6. A summary statement that briefly underscores the child's current level of functioning, the child's needs, and recommendations for remediation.

The writing of the report reflects the process of the assessment itself. Clinical assessment is a creative process that challenges the school psychologist to utilize knowledge of child development, skills in engaging and relating to children, and abilities to develop and test out hypotheses, so that assessment information can be pieced together into an individualized education program that will enable the child to meet success in the school setting.

SUMMARY

This chapter described the process of assessment from the time of initial referral to placement in a special education program or service and formulation of an individualized education program. Although policies and procedures vary among school districts, the steps in the process are similar across districts.

The school psychologist first determines why the child is being referred. This typically involves an interview with the person referring, such as the teacher or the parent. The school psychologist next collects existing data from appropriate sources, including the child's teacher and parents, that will help clarify the problem and determine whether or not the referral is appropriate.

On the basis of these data and the referral questions, the school psychologist selects appropriate formal and informal assessment instruments that will best address the identified problems. With the results from the preassessment and from the instruments employed in the assessment itself, the school psychologist, in concert with other members of the school team, integrates the findings and prepares a report that addresses the referral questions. Finally, a program of remediation is planned by the interdisciplinary team including recommendations for placement and teaching strategies to address the child's problems.

REFERENCES

Achenbach, T. M., & Edelbrock, C. S. (1978). The classification of child psychopathology: A review and analysis of empirical efforts. *Psychological Bulletin, 85,* 1275-1301.

Connors, C. K. (1969). A teacher rating scale for use in studies with children. *American Journal of Psychiatry, 126,* 884-888.

Cruickshank, W. M., Morse, W. C. & Johns, J. (1980). *Learning disabilities.* Syracuse NY: Syracuse University Press.

Gliedman, J. & Roth, W. (1980). *The unexpected minority.* New York: Harcourt, Brace, Jovanovich.

Madden, N. A., & Salvia, R. E. (1983). Mainstreaming students with mild handicaps: Academic and social outcomes. *Review of Educational Research, 53*(4), 519-569.

Miller, L. C. (1967). Louisville Behavior Checklist for males 6-12 years of age. *Psychological Reports, 21,* 885-896.

Peterson, D. R., & Quay, H. C. (1979). Behavior Problem Checklist. Unpublished manuscript. (Available from D. Peterson, 39 North Fifth Ave., Highland Park NJ 08904).

Shepard, L. A., Smith, M. L., & Vojr, C. P. (1983). Characteristics of pupils identified as learning disabled. *American Educational Research Journal, 20* (3), 309-331.

Spivack, G., & Swift, M. (1975). *Hahnemann Elementary School behavior rating scale (HESB).* Hahnemann Community Mental Health/Mental Retardation Center, 314 North Broad Street, Philadelphia, PA 19102.

Spivack, G., & Swift, M. (1967). *Devereaux Elementary School Behavior Rating Scale Manual.* Devon PA: Devereaux Foundation Press.

ADDITIONAL RESOURCES

Salvia, J., & Ysseldyke, J. E. (1981). *Assessment in special and remedial education* (2nd ed.). Boston: Houghton Mifflin.

Swanson, H. L., & Watson, B. L. (1983). *Educational and psychological assessment of exceptional children: Theories, strategies, and applications.* St. Louis: C. V. Mosby.

Taylor, R. L. (1984). *Assessment of exceptional students: Educational and psychological procedures.* Englewood Cliffs NJ: Prentice-Hall.

Tucker, J. (n.d.). *Sequential stages of the appraisal process: A training module.* Minneapolis: National School Psychology Inservice Training Network, University of Minnesota.

Zigmond, N., Vallecorsa, A., & Silverman, R. (1983). *Assessment for instructional planning in special education.* Englewood Cliffs NJ: Prentice-Hall.

CHAPTER 3

Non-Test-Based Approaches to Assessment

Evelyn Oka
Geraldine T. Scholl

As noted in Chapter 1, recent changes in education have led to a re-examination of the role of school psychologists. The demands and challenges of Public Law 94-142 and recent court decisions that call into question the use of standardized instruments with certain populations for whom such tests may not be appropriate necessitate a reconsideration of employing those instruments in the assessment process. Although standardized tests have traditionally been used by school psychologists to obtain information about a child's skills and abilities, they are not adequate to answer questions about how the child uses those skills and abilities in a group setting (Carlson, Scott, & Eklund, 1980). Children usually behave differently in a one-to-one situation, and problem areas may not be identified by the school psychologist from an assessment using standardized instruments. The critical question in the referral concerns expressed by teachers and parents, therefore, may not be addressed.

To respond effectively to these needs, many school psychologists are adopting another perspective, studying the child as a functioning being within the total environmental system, that is, the child's ecology (Wallace and Larsen, 1978). Drawing from the biological sciences, the school psychologist uses non-test-based or informal assessment methods to study the child as an organism interacting with his or her environment.

This chapter is divided into two sections. The first section describes the background of the ecological approach and its application to psychology and to the assessment process. The second section describes three non-test-based procedures that may be useful for studying the child in his or her ecological or natural setting: interviews, observation, and consultation.

DESCRIPTION OF THE ECOLOGICAL APPROACH

Background

School psychologists are charged with the two-fold responsibility for assessment and intervention: They seek ways to measure the abilities and behaviors of children so they can recommend appropriate interventions. They may use one or more approaches: behavioral, psychodynamic, biophysical, and sociological frameworks (see Long, Morse, & Newman, 1980, pp. 82-83 for a brief description). Despite this wide array of orientations and their associated techniques, factors such as the imprecise nature of the instruments, the multitude of variables beyond control, and the ambiguous conditions under which judgments are made make the realization of the school psychologists' goal difficult.

Part of the solution to these problems is to base decisions on as wide a range of information as possible and to view the child as embedded in a system, as part of a whole. An ecological approach is representative of this holistic view, regarding the child and the environment in totality rather than as discrete and separately functioning entities.

An ecological view has been discussed in the literature for many years (Barker, 1965, 1968; Gump, Schoggen, & Redl, 1963; Hobbs, 1966; Rhodes, 1967; Rhodes & Tracy, 1972). In *Ecological Psychology*, Barker (1968) reported a landmark project in which he and his associates surveyed and documented the environment of a midwestern town in terms of behavior settings. On the basis of their systematic description of the environment and its behavioral output, they concluded that:

> The environment provides inputs with controls that regulate the inputs in accordance with the systematic requirements of the environment, on the one hand, and in accordance with the behavior attributes of its human components, on the other. This means that the same environmental unit provides different inputs to different persons, and different inputs to the same person if his behavior changes; and it means, further, that the whole program of the environment's inputs changes if its own ecological properties change; if it becomes more or less populous, for example. (p. 205)

This work was critical in establishing the importance of viewing the individual in relation to the environment in order to understand behavior. What Barker pointed out then is especially relevant to assessment today. If behavior is the outcome of an interaction between the characteristics of the individual and the features of the setting, similar environments may be expected to produce different behaviors among different individuals. More importantly, for the purposes of assessment, the same individual may be seen to react differently in different settings. Thus, caution is required when making generalizations based on observing behavior in one setting.

From 1972 to 1974, the Child Variance Project at the University of Michigan delved into the application of the major theoretical positions to the assessment of disturbed children. In a report from this project Feagans (1972) provided a comprehensive introduction to the concept of ecology and its application and development in the social sciences. In its original biological use, ecology was defined as the study of *structure*, that is, the organism and environment, and *function*, that is, the exchange of energy or interaction (Feagans, 1972). This section is concerned with the psychological application of ecology and focuses on the effects of the ecosystem on behavior.

Ecological Approach Applied to Psychology

An *ecosystem* in biology denotes the interaction between the organism and its environment. Similarly, in psychology, the term is used to refer to the relationship between the individual and the setting. Its application in psychology is represented by a merger between environmental and developmental psychology. The study of the classification and measurement of environments is combined with the study of individual differences in growth and development.

A second concept borrowed from ecology is that of the *ecological niche*. This refers to the organism's role in an ecosystem. To the extent that ecosystems are perceived as being different, one's ecological niche will also be different.

The third concept is *niche breadth*, which indicates the range of roles the individual plays. As in biology, where the organism may assume a number of functions in response to the ecosystem's demands, so in psychology an individual may have a variety of response patterns or roles.

Conventional assessment procedures are child-centered; they focus on isolated aspects of the individual's functioning and attempt to identify deficits within the child (Carlson, et al., 1980). On the basis of a single 2-hour session, an examiner describes the child's ability to think abstractly, use language, or reproduce designs. It is upon these brief encounters that placement decisions are often made, admission to a special education program is granted or denied, and a specific label is determined for the child. Misdiagnosis may result from such an approach because the functioning of the child in his or her total environment is not considered.

An ecological approach recognizes the importance of taking the environment into account. Evaluating abilities is only part of the process; the situational factors that initiate and maintain behavior must also be examined. The ecological approach assumes that the individual does not act independently of external influences; rather he or she is viewed as operating in a setting that provides both benefits (satisfactions) and harms (obstructions) with varying degrees of pressure or "environmental press" (Murray, 1938). By analyzing the environments from the perspective of what pressure they apply or offer the individual, the interaction with external factors can be assessed.

Numerous studies have investigated the impact of variables such as birth order, teacher style, class size, learning patterns, parenting, home environment, and instructional strategies, on achievement, adjustment, behavior, and other outcome variables. Although important, they cannot be interpreted in isolation. Child-centered variables (attitude, motivation, and self-concept) and environmental variables (reaction of others, home, school, and peer relations) need to be integrated to obtain a more precise picture of an individual's functioning that will yield greater insight into the nature of the problem and the formulation of more effective remedial strategies (Wallace & Larsen, 1978).

Whereas the assessment of individuals has been longstanding and a countless number of instruments have been made available, only recently have the psychological features of environments been investigated. To balance the dominance of methods of individual evaluation, this section focuses on presenting concepts and techniques for measuring environments. In practice, both approaches should be used in order to view the child in the context of the setting.

Measuring Social Environment

Inherent in an ecological approach is the assumption that different types or dimensions of social environments can be distinguished. Moos (1974) contended that environments, like people, have unique personalities, which he called "social climates." As people can be characterized as supportive, controlling, clear, organized, and directive, so can environments be described and measured in their degree of support, rigidity, order, organization, and regulation and direction of behavior. Moos further assumed that the social climate within which an individual functions has an important impact on attitudes and moods, behavior, health, and the individual's overall sense of well-being. To evaluate environments he developed a three-part scheme with the following dimensions: Relationship, Personal Development (Growth), and System Maintenance and Change.

The Relationship dimension refers to the nature and intensity of personal relationships within the environment; it is concerned with a person's degree of involvement in the environment. Depending upon the specific setting, the aspects being assessed will vary among emotional support, affiliation, teacher support, cohesion, expressiveness, conflict, peer cohesion, staff support, and spontaneity. In the classroom setting, the Relationship domain refers to involvement, the amount of interest, attentiveness, and participation of students in the classroom activities. It also concerns affiliation, the extent to which friendships are fostered and a cooperative spirit characterizes the interactions. Finally, the amount of teacher support is considered, as indicated by the personal interest and friendliness the teacher displays toward students.

The dimension of Personal Development includes those basic areas in which personal growth and self-enhancement occur, such as independence, competition, traditional social orientation, moral-religious emphasis, and academic achievement. This aspect is sensitive to the basic goals in a setting and gives an indication of what the environmental demands are. These may range from scholarly achievements to diversity in behavior to cultural activities to competition for recognition or grades. In a classroom, they may be task orientation (the emphasis on achieving specific academic objectives) and competition (the stress on competition among students for recognition and grades).

The System Maintenance and Change dimension taps the organization of the environment. It provides a means of identifying the structure that is present and measuring the degree of control, freedom, clarity of rules and expectations, and response to change in the environments. In a classroom, this can be seen in the degree of formality, presence or absence of democratic governance, disorganization, diversity, and clarity of work schedules and assignments.

The application of this three-part scheme across a variety of relevant environments (family, school, peer interactions, activities, church) is important in assessment because it may help to explain why pupils do well in one environment and not in another. If a child is reportedly performing below average in a reading class but above average in an arithmetic class, this framework can be useful to help characterize each setting. By observing the relationship between the features of the environment and the criterion behavior, the determinants and impacts of each setting may be ascertained. The contributions of the classroom setting may take the form of inadequate or excessive structure, a hostile or cooperative atmosphere, and a creative or prescribed emphasis. When learning is viewed in this way, as an interactive enterprise, failure to learn is not immediately attributed to a deficit in the individual, but rather to a disturbance located in the individual's total environment.

Ecological Mapping

One means of systematically analyzing the impact of different environments is to use the concept of "mapping" (Hobbs, 1966; Prieto & Rutherford, 1977). Ecological mapping estimates the "fit" of an individual into various settings by graphically portraying areas of disturbance within the ecosystem. Figure 3-1 illustrates how a child's world can be represented schematically by focusing on the interactions that take place between the child and family, peers, teachers, and others. Wallace and Larsen (1978) further suggested using solid lines to indicate where few difficulties are observed and broken lines to designate the setting in which they are most prevalent. Such a diagram provides an overview of an individual's involvements and points out areas where assessment can be directed most profitably.

Figure 3-2 shows how refinement of the components may be necessary to further isolate the source(s) of dysfunction. As more data are collected, the factors relating to the child's difficulties can be more precisely identified and interventions can be developed to overcome them.

Ecological Approach Applied to Assessment

An ecological approach has two major advantages. First, it can function as a heuristic framework for achieving the goals of assessment. As a way of thinking, it is a means of broadening the database for decision making. The school psychologist employing this approach gathers information about a variety of variables, compares competencies across situations, and examines the context in which behaviors take place.

When adopting this perspective, the school psychologist may use a number of strategies, even those associated with other models. For example, projective tasks may be administered to elicit information, to establish rapport, and to test reactions to praise and reproof under controlled conditons. An ecological approach does not exclude the use of a wide range of assessment techniques and procedures, rather it considers problems to have a broad locus in the interactive system of the individual and the environment.

To organize the data collected about the environment, Laten and Katz (1975) recommended the following framework (see Appendix F for the unabbreviated form):

FIGURE 3-1.

Ecological Mapping Diagram.

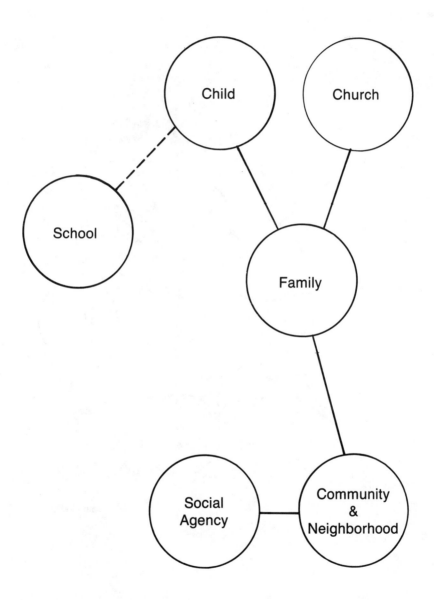

Note. Adapted from Hobbs, 1966.

FIGURE 3-2.

Expansion of School-Child Mapping.

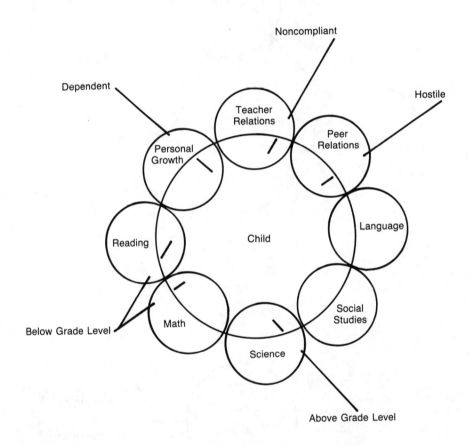

Note. Adapted from Prieto & Rutherford, 1977.

1. Initial descriptions of the environment.

2. Expectations.

3. Behavioral descriptions.

4. Analysis and synthesis of data.

5. Statement of expectations.

Following this outline helps the school psychologist to integrate the frequently disparate data into a manageable and goal-directed format. This framework also incorporates perceptions and expectations of self versus others and allows a comparison among these variables. It should be used to complement the child-centered measures for monitoring the data collection process.

An ecological assessment has a second advantage: a unique set of procedures and instruments for looking at environments and behaviors. A few of these are described in the following paragraphs.

Observation Instruments

Observation is an important basic tool in ecological assessment, and it can take many forms. For a description of a reliable, systematic, and valid technique for observing and coding ongoing behaviors in the natural environment (typically the family), Jones, Reid, and Patterson (1975) have developed a Behavior Coding System. Wallace and Larsen (1978) have also provided an introduction to the use of various types of observation in assessment.

Moos has developed a series of scales, the *Social Climate Scales* (1974, 1975, 1979), which measure environments from the participant's perspective. They include the Family Environment Scale (FES), Classroom Environment Scale (CES), Work Environment Scale (WES), Ward Atmosphere Scale (WAS), Community-Oriented Programs Environmental Scale (COPES), and Group Environment Scale (GES). Each scale measures the three domains of environmental variables: Relationship, Personal Development, and System Maintenance and Change. Each scale is a paper-and-pencil questionnaire consisting of 90 to 100 true-false items requiring 15 to 20 minutes to administer. Pupils, parents, or staff members are appropriate respondents. Each respondent's answers can be translated into seven to ten subscores. Profiles of the environmental characteristics can then be obtained and compared among the various participants. Also available are adaptations of the scales that elicit different perceptions of the same environment (Real, Ideal, and Expectations Forms).

The *Stern Personality and Environment Indexes* provide another series of objective, self-administered measures of personality needs and environmental characteristics. These scales are based on Murray's (1938) need-press conception of behavior. "Needs" are inferred from the individual's daily activities and behaviors, whereas "press" is inferred from the social and physical characteristics of the environmental setting as perceived by the respondent. Of particular relevance are the Classroom Environment Index (CEI), Elementary and Secondary School Index (ESI), High School Characteristics Index (HSCI), College Characteristics Index (CCI), and Organizational Climate Index (OCI) (J. L. Richman & Co., Syracuse, New York). Factor analysis of the scales yields the following kinds of dimensions being measured: intellectual climate, achievement standards, personal dignity, organizational effectiveness, orderliness, impulse control, social form, and peer group dominance.

Another instrument for examining the classroom setting is the *Classroom Interaction Analysis* (Bradfield & Criner, 1975). This is an objective method of measuring interactive behavior in the classroom. It yields three scales which can be used separately or in combination: the Teacher Style Scale, the Teacher Attention Scale, and the Pupil Behavior Scale.

Tools for looking at the home environment include the *Henderson Environmental Learning Process Scale* (HELPS) and the *Home Observation for Measurement of the Environment* (HOME). HELPS is an interview instrument designed to measure characteristics of the home setting that are related to the intellectual and scholastic performance of young children. The 55 items are claimed to tap extended interests and community involvement, valuing language and school-related behavior, providing supportive environment for school learning, attention, and intellectual guidance (Henderson, Bergan, & Hurt, 1972).

The HOME inventories (Bradley & Caldwell, 1976, 1977) were designed to measure aspects of social, affective, and cognitive support available to the child in the home. Two forms are available, an infant and a preschool version. Both forms are completed by interviewing and observing the parent and child in their home. Some of the factors obtained through factor analysis include emotional and verbal responsiveness of the mother; avoidance of punishment; provision of adequate play materials; language stimulation; and pride, affection, and warmth.

These measures represent only a sample of the available instruments for examining the environment. When combined with information gathered through conventional child-centered techniques, the information obtained through the use of these tools has important implications for intervention. Depending on the nature of the problem area, remediation can be developed to induce changes in the individual, in the environment, or in both. If structure is the key element missing in the situation, then steps can be taken to modify the setting. In some cases the locus of the disturbance may be in the environment, but the individual is the one who must accommodate. In any case, the individual is no longer necessarily viewed as being deficient or impaired. Through a broader ecological perspective, factors in either the environment or the individual may be inconsistent and work against each other to create problems for the interaction. The burden of responsibility is expanded to encompasses the total context of behavior and thereby alternatives for intervention are increased.

Conclusion

The legacy of biology provides a compatible framework and structured set of laws for the examination of individual functioning. Ecological assessment is not a new idea, nor has it been an unacceptable one. On the contrary, it has been heralded as a worthy and valuable approach, only to be abandoned and forgotten until the next wave of interest. Part of the reason for the failure to put it into practice, is its crude and abstract form. It lacks the unification and systematic formulation of theory and encompasses a variety of disciplines.

One major disadvantage of the ecological approach is the extensive time demands it makes on all participants. Information must be gathered from a variety of environments and informants, integrated, and formulated into a meaningful statement. Probably such a time commitment is not feasible, and thus its use may be limited to those selected cases who could benefit most from an in-depth analysis.

Efforts to incorporate an ecological perspective in assessment are, however, increasing. Discrete parts of the environment cannot be studied in isolation, but must be assembled to form a complete picture of the individual's functioning. As a result of attempts to translate ecological principles into action by relating the research to comprehensive theory, the widespread past acceptance of the ecological position may develop further into its practical application as well.

NON-TEST-BASED ASSESSMENT

There are several informal assessment techniques that are appropriate to use in an ecological approach. Tidwell (1981) viewed these techniques as providing educationally meaningful information about a child's competencies, strengths, and weaknesses and as helping teachers perceive school psychologists as effective professionals in solving the educational problems of children in their classrooms.

Types of Non-Test-Based Procedures

Three types of non-test-based assessment procedures will be reviewed in this section: interviews, observation, and consultation.

Interviews

Interviews can be useful in all stages in the assessment process (Tucker, n.d.). Unstructured interviews are usually appropriate in the initial stages when the referral concerns are being identified. When the school psychologist has a clearer picture of these concerns, a structured interview with the parents, the teacher and, when appropriate, the child, may be conducted. Suggested forms for this purpose are found in Appendixes D and E. The role of the interview during the preassessment stage was discussed in Chapter 2.

Subsequent interviews may be necessary at varying times during the assessment process, particularly when decisions regarding placement and formulation of the individualized education program are being considered. Interviews with parent and child provide an opportunity for the school psychologist to give support in making the transition to a new placement or educational program. Following placement, interviews with teachers and parents provide evaluative information regarding the success of the decisions.

Successful interviewing requires skills in interpersonal relationships, particularly the ability to establish rapport easily with parents, teachers, and pupils. It requires skills in communication, including listening skills and sensitivity to nonverbal communication. It requires the ability to plan and follow a logical sequence for the interview itself and the ability to analyze and synthesize information obtained in the interview in the diagnosis of the problem area so that appropriate intervention strategies may be identified (Tucker, n. d.). Questionnaires may be helpful in planning and structuring the interview, provided the school psychologist recognizes their utilitiy and limitations in meeting specific needs (Wilson, 1981).

Although interviewing has merit as a non-test-based technique, there are problems areas. Aside from the issues of validity and reliability, Dillon (1981) cautioned that questioning during an interview, especially around sensitive areas, may inhibit expressiveness and increase feelings of defensiveness. School psychologists using this technique should avoid continuous questions and use declarative phrasings and deliberate silence at appropriate times during the interview.

Observation

Many standardized instruments have limited reliability and validity for determining educational strategies for children with special needs, partly because the data gathering occurs outside the classroom and therefore may not be situation specific (Sitko, Fink, & Gillespie 1977). Educational objectives may be established more effectively by employing observational techniques, because they focus on the interactions among the child, teacher, educational materials, classmates, and other situational variables. Sitko, Fink, and Gillespie (1977) viewed diagnosis and remediation as a decision making process based on systematic classroom observation that is continually subject to ongoing evaluation and modification.

Classroom observation is increasingly considered an important component in the assessment process for all types of handicapped children (Nagle, 1983). It provides a better understanding of the child's problems in the natural setting from the teacher's perspective; it serves as a complement to the more formal assessment instruments; it is useful for validating and monitoring recommended intervention procedures growing out of the formal assessment; and it can enhance collaborative consultation among the school staff (Keller, 1980). For some children, such as the autistic, severely and multiply handicapped, and moderately to profoundly mentally retarded, classroom observation is absolutely essential (Berdine & Cegelka, 1980; Bigge, 1976). The typical assessment instruments, both formal and informal, are usually not appropriate, and the school psychologist must rely on observation in order to arrive at some estimate of the child's level of functioning. For other children, such as the hearing, visually, and physically handicapped, classroom observation prior to undertaking a formal assessment is necessary in order to determine the child's sensory, motor, and communication limitations and abilities in the natural setting.

Irwin and Bushnell (1980) listed five reasons for engaging in direct observation: to generate hypotheses or ideas about behavior; to answer specific questions about behavior; to obtain a more realistic picture of behavior or events; to understand the child's behavior better; and to serve as a means of informal evaluation. All these are relevant purposes for classroom observation as a part of the assessment process.

Successful classroom observation depends on several factors. First, the observer must be able to perceive and interpret a variety of verbal as well as nonverbal cues. While the majority of classroom time is considered to be taken up by "teacher talk," there are other forms of communication, mostly nonverbal, going on between and among the teacher and pupils. An analysis of nonverbal cues, including body language, gestures, facial cues, and mannerisms, can often provide the school psychologist with valuable information regarding the cause of the child's problems, and it may provide a frame of reference for making future recommendations for remediation. In making classroom observations, the school psychologist must therefore not only listen to what is going on but also note nonverbal cues.

Second, school psychologists must have a good knowledge base about children and schools. An understanding of normal child growth and development and its many variations is necessary in order to assess whether the observed behavior is beyond the local norm (Keller, 1980). Knowledge of the principles of classroom organization and typical behavioral expectations within the classroom, curriculum activities, and expected performance standards on the part of the school help the school psychologist determine what is different about the functioning of a particular child in his or her classroom situation and to assess to what extent the ecological setting is contributing to the problem. A knowledge of group dynamics as it applies to the classroom setting will help to determine the underlying tenor of the group and whether the child's problem is based in the individual or within the group.

Third, the typical classroom is a complex social system (Good & Brophy, 1978). In order to derive maximum benefit from observation, the school psychologist should focus on a specific problem, preferably the problem identified in the referral questions. Sitting in a classroom without a definite focus will not usually be productive (Tucker, n. d.).

Finally, since a child behaves differently in different settings, the school psychologist should also observe on the playground, in the lunch room, and in any other setting where the child spends the school day in order to obtain a complete picture of behavior and assess the characteristics of and differences between the settings in which the child is successful and those in which he or she is not. Assessment of social skills and initiating a training program for the acquisition of such skills may be helpful in the alleviation of other school problems (Sprafkin, 1980). Observations in the home may also be helpful, especially in assessing social and daily living skills for certain children, for example, the multiply handicapped, and the interaction within the family, especially for children with emotional and behavior problems.

Although the school psychologist has access to the reports and records of the teacher and makes certain observations during the formal procedures, first hand classroom observation should not be overlooked as part of the assessment process.

Although the value of classroom observation cannot be denied, it has one major disadvantage: it is a very time-consuming activity for the school psychologist, particularly for an entire typical case load. Its potential value for a particular child must be weighed carefully against this disadvantage (Keller, 1980).

In selecting or developing an instrument for observation, the school psychologist should consider the following questions:

1. What needs to be observed? The specific problem must be identified and an appropriate instrument developed or selected that will gather data to clarify that problem area (Tucker, n. d.).

2. Will the instrument be acceptable to the teacher and provide immediate constructive feedback? Many teachers fear observation. The instrument must be shared in advance with the teacher, and the results of the observation must be discussed as soon as possible following the observation (Alessi & Kaye, 1983).

3. Will the instrument describe and differentiate clearly the behavior in the classroom situation? The instrument must have face validity in order to be useful for assessing the problem area (Lynch, 1977).

4. Is the instrument easy to use, and can it be administered unobtrusively in the classroom setting? The presence of an observer in the classroom can often have an inhibiting effect on the child in the class. Both observer and instrument must be as unobtrusive as possible (Good & Brophy, 1978).

Alessi and Kaye (1983) described five approaches to recording behavior during an observation:

1. *Interval recording.* This approach ''results in a measure of the number of intervals (time blocks) within which the behavior was observed to occur, (e.g., Mary was on task during 8 of the 40 intervals observed)'' (p.6). The observer first decides on the interval of time and then records whether the behavior occurred during each interval. This technique is useful if the behavior occurs at a steady rate.

2. *Time sample recording.* This approach ''results in a measure of the number of times the behavior was observed to occur at pre-specified sampling points in time, (e.g., at the end of every 10-second period, or at the end of every 15-minute period)'' (p.8). The school psychologist can observe several pupils at the time session by selecting different observation cycles for each one. The major disadvantage of this method is the smaller sample of behavior during the observation time and the likelihood that a specific behavior will not occur during the observation period.

3. *Event recording.* This approach ''results in a measure of the precise number of occurrences of the behavior during the entire observation session, (e.g., Chris spelled 26 words correctly in 20 minutes)'' (p.9). This approach is recommended for behaviors that occur often, seldom, or briefly, which are situations when interval and time sampling are less accurate.

4. *Duration recording.* This approach "results in a measure of the precise length of time each behavior continued (e.g., Tracey colored for 23 minutes)" (p.9). This is a more difficult approach since the observer must record both the time when the behavior began and when it ceased. It is recommended when the preceding three methods are not possible.

5. *Latency recording.* This approach "results in a measure of the precise length of time between a specified classroom event and the onset or completion of the defined behavior, (e.g., the teacher asks Jim to stand up, and 16 seconds later Jim stands)" (p.10). Since this method is also difficult to measure, it is recommended when the first three are not possible.

In their book, Alessi and Kaye included procedures for determining the reliability and validity for these five approaches to recording, a necessary part in the process of instrument development or selection.

There may be times when the school psychologist wishes to obtain a general overview through informal observation by noting activities, the setting, or other aspects of the classroom in order to get a feel for the atmosphere and/or the referral problem (Mowder, 1983). Such observations may be particularly useful if the teacher or parent seems to have difficulty in pinpointing the problem. Through informal and more casual observation, the school psychologist may be in a better position to assist them in formulating their concerns more specifically.

School psychologists interested in pursuing a more intensive child study observational approach are referred to Irwin and Bushnell (1980) and Vasta (1982).

Although there are limitations, particularly related to its time-consuming aspects, in the use of observation, it is a valuable component in the assessment process and can provide additional information that will complement the more formal procedures (Alessi, 1980; Keller, 1980).

Consultation

Smith (1980) viewed the major problem with assessment, both formal and informal, as the failure to use the information obtained. Consultation is considered an indirect service that may yield greater benefits than direct services to a particular child, particularly when the problem area is rooted in the ecological setting and when the caseload of the school psychologist becomes unmanageable (Tombari & Davis, 1979). Consultation provides a mechanism for making more effective use of assessment information in work with parents, teachers, and administrators, especially information on organizational problems.

Through consultation, school psychologists can often be more effective in working with teachers to facilitate their understanding of children and to help them find a solution to the children's problems (Tombari & Davis, 1979). In a 7-year study of a school consultation program, Ritter (1981) found that teachers did increase their abilities to cope with children's problems when participating in a program of information sharing with a consultant who also acted as a supportive agent. Consultation can provide valuable input in the evaluation of learning and intervention outcomes (Phye, 1979) and in meeting the mental health needs of students (Clarizio, 1979).

Bergan (1977) described the three roles in the consultation process:

1. *The consultant role.* The consultant is responsible for establishing the stages in the consultation process and making psychological information available to the consultee.

2. *The consultee role.* The consultee has four roles: to provide a description of the problem to the consultant; to evaluate whether plans proposed by the consultant have the potential of success with the child; to be of direct service to the child and collect data when appropriate; and to supervise others, such as parents and classroom aides who may have responsibility for working with the child.

3. *The client role.* The major role for the child is to change in the direction of the goal which has been established during the consultation.

The general goals of the consultation are to effect change in the client, the consultee, or the organizational structure (Bergan, 1977). This latter goal is increasingly recommended for school psychologists as an indirect but more efficient means of working with behavior problems of individual children because of its impact on the total setting (Bergan, 1977; Birney, 1981; Conoley, 1980; Merrell & Jerrell, 1981).

Although consultation has many advantages as an indirect service in the role of the school psychologist, it is time-consuming and requires that the school psychologist possess flexibility and empathy to be successful (Fine, Grantham & Meyers, 1981).

SUMMARY

Criticisms of standardized tests and pressures to view the child's problems as emanating from forces outside rather than inside the child are leading to an increasing interest in employing the ecological approach in assessment. This approach, adapted from biology, views the child as an organism functioning within a particular setting or ecology and interacting with the various parts of that setting. The ecological approach is particularly appropriate in school psychology because many problems of children who are referred are not due to variables within the child but rather are related to the setting in which the child is expected to function.

The ecological approach calls for less formal standardized instruments. Three such non-test-based procedures were described in this chapter: interviews, observation, and consultation. Interviews with parents, teachers, the child, and relevant others in the setting should be an ongoing activity during the entire process of assessment. Observations serve to complement the more formal standardized procedures as well as validate their results. Finally, consultation with parents, teachers, the child, and administrators is a valuable means of attempting to effect change in the setting.

REFERENCES

Alessi, G. J. (1980). Behavioral observation for the school psychologist: Responsive-discrepancy model. *The School Psychology Review, 9*(1) 31-45.

Alessi, G. J., & Kaye, J. H. (1983). *Behavioral assessment for school psychologists.* Kent OH: National Association of School Psychologists.

Barker, R. G. (1965). Explorations in ecological psychology. *American Psychologist, 20,* 1-14.

Barker, R. G. (1968). *Ecological psychology: Concepts and methods for studying the environment of human behavior.* Stanford CA: Stanford University Press.

Berdine, W. H., & Cegelka, P. T. (1980). *Teaching the trainable retarded.* Columbus OH: Charles E. Merrill.

Bergan, J. R. (1977). *Behavioral consultation.* Columbus OH: Charles E. Merrill.

Bigge, J. L. (1976). *Teaching individuals with physical and multiple disabilities.* Columbus OH: Charles E. Merrill.

Birney, D. (1981). Consulting with administrators: The consultee centered approach. In J. C. Conoley (Ed.), *Consultation in schools* (pp. 103-56). New York: Academic Press.

Bradfield, R. H. & Criner, J. (1975). *Classroom interaction analysis.* San Raphael CA: Academic Therapy.

Bradley, R., & Caldwell, B. (1976). Early home environment and changes in mental test performance in children from 6 to 36 months. *Developmental Psychology, 12,* 93-97.

Bradley, R., & Caldwell, B. (1977). Home observation for measurement of the environment: A validation study of screening efficiency. *American Journal of Mental Deficiency, 81,* 417-420.

Carlson, C. I., Scott, M., & Eklund, S. J. (1980). Ecological theory and method for behavioral assessment. *The School Psychology Review, 9*(1), 75-82.

Clarizio, H. F. (1979). School psychologists and the mental health needs of students. In G. D. Phye & D. J. Reschly (Eds.), *School psychology: Perspectives and issues* (pp. 309-341). New York: Academic Press.

Conoley, J. C. (1980). Organizational assessment. *The School Psychology Review, 9*(1), 83-89.

Dillon, J. T. (1981). Defects of questioning as an interview technique. In J. L. Carroll (Ed.), *Contemporary school psychology: Selected readings from Psychology in the Schools* (2nd ed.) (pp. 73-78). Brandon VT: Clinical Psychology Publishing Co.

Feagans, L. (1972). Ecological theory as a model for constructing a theory of emotional disturbance. In W. C. Rhodes & M. I. Tracy (Eds.), *A study of child variance, Vol. 1: Conceptual models.* (pp. 323-389). Ann Arbor: University of Michigan.

Fine, M. J., Grantham, V. L., & Meyers, J. (1981). In J. L. Carroll (Ed.), *Contemporary school psychology: Selected readings from Psychology in the Schools* (2nd ed.) (pp. 127-133). Brandon VT: Clinical Psychology Publishing Co.

Good, T. L., & Brophy, J. E. (1978). *Looking in classrooms.* New York: Harper & Row.

Gump, P. V., Schoggen, P., & Redl, F. (1963). The behavior of the same child in different milieus. In R. G. Barker (Ed.), *The stream of behavior: Exploration of its structure and content* (pp. 169-202). New York: Meredith.

Henderson, R. W., Bergan, J. R., & Hurt, M. Jr. (1972). Development and validation of the Henderson Environmental Learning Process Scale. *Journal of Social Psychology, 88,* 185-196.

Hobbs, N. (1966). Helping disturbed children: Psychological and ecological strategies. *American Psychologist, 21,* 1105-1115.

Irwin, D. M., & Bushnell, M. M. (1980). *Observational strategies for child study.* New York: Holt, Rinehart, & Winston.

Jones, R., Reid, J., & Patterson, G. (1975). Naturalistic observation in clinical assessment. In P. McReynolds (Ed.), *Advances in psychological assessment* (Vol. 3) (pp. 42-95). San Francisco: Jossey-Bass.

Keller, H. R. (1980). Issues in the use of observational assessment. *The School Psychology Review, 9*(1) 21-30.

Laten, S., & Katz, G. A. (1975). *A theoretical model for assessment of adolescents: The ecological/behavioral approach.* Madison WI: Madison Public Schools.

Long, N. J., Morse, W. C., & Newman, R. G. (1980). *Conflict in the classroom: The education of emotionally disturbed children.* Belmont CA: Wadsworth.

Lynch, W. W. (1977). Guidelines to the use of classroom observation instruments by school psychologists. *School Psychology Monograph, 3*(1), 1-22.

Merrell, J. M., & Jerrell, S. L. (1981). Organizational consultation in school systems. In J. C. Conoley (Ed.), *Consultation in schools* (pp. 103-156). New York: Academic Press.

Moos, R. H. (1974). *Evaluating treatment environments: A social ecological approach.* New York: Wiley Interscience.

Moos, R.H. (1975). Assessment and impact of social climate. In P. McReynolds (Ed.), *Advances in psychological assessment* (Vol. 3) (pp. 8-41). San Francisco: Jossey-Bass.

Moos, R. H. (1979). *Evaluating educational environments.* San Francisco: Jossey-Bass.

Mowder, B. A. (1983). Assessment and intervention in school psychological services. In G. W. Hynd (Ed.), *The school psychologist: An introduction* (pp. 145-167). Syracuse NY: Syracuse University Press.

Murray, H. (1938). *Explorations in personality.* New York: Oxford University Press.

Nagle, R. J. (1983). Psychological assessment: Cognitive domain. In G. W. Hynd (Ed.), *The School psychologist: An introduction* (pp. 169-194). Syracuse NY: Syracuse University Press.

Phye, G. D. (1979). School psychologists as consultants in the evaluation of learning and intervention outcomes. In G. D. Phye & D. J. Reschly (Eds.), *School Psychology: Perspectives and issues* (pp. 257-280). New York: Academic Press.

Prieto, A. G., & Rutherford, R. B., Jr. (1977). An ecological assessment technique for behaviorally disordered and learning disabled children. *Journal of Behavior Disorders, 2,* 169-175.

Rhodes, W. C. (1967). The disturbing child: A problem of ecological management. *Exceptional Children, 33*(7), 449-455.

Rhodes, W. C., & Tracy, M. I. (Eds.). (1972). *A study of child variance, Vol. 1: Conceptual models.* Ann Arbor: University of Michigan.

Ritter, D. R. (1981). Effects of a school consultation program upon referral patterns of teachers. In J. L. Carroll (Ed.), *Contemporary school psychology: Selected readings from Psychology in the Schools* (2nd ed.) (pp. 141-145). Brandon VT: Clinical Psychology Publishing Co.

Sitko, M. C., Fink, A. H., & Gillespie, P. H. (1977). Utilizing suprematic observation for decision making in school psychology. *School Psychology Monograph, 2*(1), 23-44.

Smith, C. R. (1980). Assessment alternatives: Non-standardized procedures. *The School Psychology Review, 9*(1), 46-57.

Sprafkin, R. P. (1980). The assessment of social skills: An overview. *The School Psychology Review, 9*(1), 14-20.

Tidwell, R. (1981). Informal assessment to modify the role and image of the school psychologist. In J. L. Carroll (Ed.), *Contemporary school psychology: Selected readings from Psychology in the Schools* (2nd ed.) (pp. 42-47). Brandon VT: Clinical Psychology Publishing Co.

Tombari, M., & Davis, R. A. (1979). *Behavioral consultation.* In G. D. Phye & D. J. Reschly (Eds.), *School psychology: Perspectives and issues* (pp. 281-307). New York: Academic Press.

Tucker, J. A. (n.d.). *Non-test-based assessment.* Minneapolis MN: The National School Psychology Inservice Training Network.

Vasta, R. (1982). *Strategies and techniques of child study.* New York: Academic Press.

Wallace, G., & Larsen, S. C. (1978). *Educational assessment of learning problems: Testing for teaching.* Rockleigh NJ: Allyn & Bacon.

Wilson, C. C. (1980). Behavioral assessment: Questionnaires. *The School Psychology Review, 9*(1), 58-66.

ADDITIONAL RESOURCES

Almy, M., & Genishi, C. (1979). *Ways of studying children.* New York: Teachers College Press.

Conoley, J. C. (Ed.). (1981). *Consultation in schools.* New York: Academic Press.

Emmer, E., & Millett, G. (1970). *Improving teaching through experimentation: A laboratory approach.* Englewood Cliffs NJ: Prentice-Hall.

Greenberg, H. (1969). *Teaching with feeling.* New York: Macmillan.

Hunter, C.P. (1977). Classroom observation instruments and teacher inservice training by school psychologists. *School Psychology Monograph, 3*(2), 23-54.

Lahey, M., & Kazdin, A.E. (Eds.) (1982). *Advances in clinical child psychology.* (Vol. 5) New York: Plenum Press.

Swanson, H. L., & Watson, B. L. (1982). *Educational and psychological assessment of exceptional children: Theories, strategies, and applications.* St. Louis: C. V. Mosby.

PART II

AREAS OF EXCEPTIONALITY

The chapters in Part II provide content concerning characteristics and educational needs of exceptional pupils which is especially valuable to the school psychologist who has no background in special education. Each chapter presents an overview of a categorical area with emphasis on material that is most relevant for the assessment process. References and additional resources are included at the end of each chapter. We recommend that school psychologists add to their libraries any of the currently available texts for introductory courses in special education. A list of some recent books is included at the end of this section. These texts will serve as a convenient resource for additional information, especially on educational modifications and procedures that may be necessary for each type of exceptional child.

We have adopted a categorical approach because federal and most state rules and regulations require that exceptional children be "labeled" in order to be eligible for special education programs and services. The school psychologist should become thoroughly familiar with the labels, definitions, criteria for determining eligibility, and specific assessment procedures required in current federal, state, and local district rules and regulations governing the delivery of special education programs and services on the local level.

Federal guidelines may be obtained from the U. S. Government Printing Office. State rules and regulations vary; school psychologists should obtain a current copy from their state department of education.

All states are required to submit to the U. S. Department of Education a state plan for the delivery of special education programs and services if they intend to qualify for federal funds under Public Law 94-142. This document, also available from the state department of education, may give the school psychologist details concerning the special education program in that state. In addition, some local and intermediate or regional school districts have their own plans and regulations. School psychologists should be familiar with all such documents.

We are aware of the issues and dangers inherent in the labeling process (see Bartel & Guskin, 1980; Goffman, 1963; Hobbs, 1975). We caution school psychologists, therefore, to look at each child as an individual and to recommend the most appropriate educational program or service to meet the child's educational needs.

P.L. 94-142 requires that a continuum of placement options be available so that each handicapped child may be placed in the environment that is least restrictive. School psychologists should know the services available in the school district as well as options for placement outside the school district. As noted in Chapter 1, the lack of a full continuum, especially for low incidence handicapping conditions, often presents a dilemma to the school psychologist in recommending an appropriate placement. Reynolds and Birch (1982) provided in Chapter 2 of their book a good description of the continuum for those school psychologists not familiar with the organizational structure of the special education service delivery system. For a summary of advantages and disadvantages of the various options, the reader is referred to Rusalem and Rusalem (1980).

Part II begins with a chapter on gifted children, even though children are neither included under those provisions of P.L. 94-142 nor under most state mandatory special education legislation. The subsequent three chapters are devoted to the high incidence categorical areas with some overlapping behavioral characteristics: mental retardation, learning disabilities, and emotional disturbances. The next three chapters are devoted to low incidence categorical areas: physical handicaps and the sensory impairments of vision and hearing, the areas where school psychologists usually feel least knowledgeable (Gerken, 1979). The final chapter discusses briefly the role of the school psychologist in working with the speech and language pathologist on communication problems.

Assessment instruments recommended in the chapters in this part are listed in Appendix H together with addresses of publishers.

REFERENCES

Bartel, N. R., & Guskin, S. L. (1980). A handicap as a social phenomenon. In W. M. Cruickshank, (Ed.), *Psychology of exceptional children and youth* (pp. 45-73). Englewood Cliffs NJ: Prentice-Hall.

Gerken, K. (1979). Assessment of high risk preschoolers and children and adolescents with low incident handicapping conditions. In G. Phye & D. Reschly (Eds.), *School psychology: Perspectives and issues* (pp. 157-190). New York: Academic Press.

Goffman, E. (1963). *Stigma.* Englewood Cliffs NJ: Prentice-Hall.

Hobbs, N. (Ed.). (1975). *Issues in the classification of children.* San Francisco: Jossey-Bass.

Reynolds, M. C., & Birch, J. W. (1982). *Teaching exceptional children in all America's schools.* (Chap. 2). Reston VA: The Council for Exceptional Children.

Rusalem, H., & Rusalem, H. (1980). Psychological aspects of special education environments. In W. M. Cruickshank (Ed.), *Psychology of exceptional children and youth* (pp. 136-70). Englewood Cliffs NJ: Prentice-Hall.

SELECTED INTRODUCTORY TEXTS IN SPECIAL EDUCATION

Blackhurst, A. E., & Berdine, W. J. (1981). *An introduction to special education.* Boston: Little, Brown.

Blake, K. A. (1981). *Educating exceptional pupils.* Reading MA: Addison-Wesley.

Cartwright, G. P., Cartwright, C. A., & Ward, M. E. (1981). *Educating special learners.* Belmont CA: Wadsworth.

Gearheart, B. R. (1980). *Special education for the '80s.* St. Louis: C. V. Mosby.

Hallahan, D. P., & Kaufman, J. M. (1982). *Exceptional Children: Introduction to special education.* Englewood Cliffs NJ: Prentice-Hall.

Haring, N. G. (1978). *Behavior of exceptional children: An introduction to special education.* Columbus: Charles E. Merrill.

Heward, W. L, & Orlansky, M. D. (1980). *Exceptional children.* Columbus: Charles E. Merrill.

Kirk, S. A., & Gallagher, J. J. (1983). *Educating exceptional children* (4th ed.). Boston: Houghton Mifflin.

Meyen, E. L. (1982). *Exceptional children and youth.* Denver: Love Publishing Co.

Reynolds, M. C., & Birch, J. W. (1982). *Teaching exceptional children in all America's schools.* Reston VA: The Council for Exceptional Children.

Ysseldyke, J. E., & Algozzine, B. (1984). *Introduction to special education.* Boston: Houghton Mifflin.

CHAPTER 4

The Gifted and Talented

Amy Swan

Gifted and talented students differ from the others discussed in this book in that they have talents or abilities that are above the average or norm, and specific provisions for them stir heated controversy regarding whether or not they need special attention from educators. The need for special classes and programs is seldom an issue in a discussion of handicapped children; however, special programs for gifted students are at issue, and, in fact, the very existence of a gifted and talented segment of the population is in dispute (Durr, 1964).

The philosophical disagreements concerning giftedness, coupled with the absence of federally mandated policy on the education of gifted and talented children places educators in an awkward situation. In addition to requests from teachers and parents to assess and make recommendations regarding the giftedness of individual children, school psychologists are often called upon to recommend, design, and help implement educational programs for them at the local level with neither restrictions nor guidance from legislation nor precedent. Clearly, the professional who wishes to plan programs for gifted and talented students and to budget limited funds for that purpose has a great many questions to consider and numerous problems to solve.

The purpose of this chapter is to shed some light on persistent questions regarding the definition of the population, their characteristics, needs, identification, and programming.

DEFINITION OF THE ISSUES AND THE POPULATION

Summary of Issues

The controversy concerning gifted and talented children appears to have a variety of sources, not the least of which is our national ideology of equality. The "all men are created equal" notion upon which our democracy is built is not compatible with the idea that some persons are more intellectually able or creative than others. Instead, the tacit assumption is that, when given the opportunity, *all* persons are capable of a high level of accomplishment. This ideology is reflected in public programs designed to extend equal opportunities to all the disadvantaged segments of the population. Given such deeply embedded notions about human potential, to assert that gifted and talented children exist and, further, that they should receive special attention in schools, is at odds with these ideals and elicits criticism as being elitist and undemocratic.

In addition, many consider that gifted and talented children have already received more than their share of opportunities and that any help should go to those who need it most. Perhaps the very term *gifted*, which implies something that is passively received without necessarily being earned, perpetuates this view of giftedness as an unfair advantage to be neutralized rather than nurtured (Vail, 1979).

The concept of giftedness is also difficult to define and operationalize. The criterion often used is an IQ score. This fact in itself arouses another round of protests based upon criticism of IQ tests. The arguments surrounding intelligence testing are intimately bound with the equality ideologies already mentioned, as well as with concerns about their role in racial and sex discrimination. Thus, as a result of current practice, the issue of gifted and talented education carries with it the baggage of the IQ controversy.

Definition of the Population

There are a great many definitions of the terms *gifted* and *talented* and little agreement among educators as to which are correct. Some insist that the two terms refer to different groups, but their definitions do little to clarify alleged differences. *The Dictionary of Behavioral Science* (Wolman, 1973), for example, holds that gifted individuals have a high degree of intellectual ability or special talent and that talented individuals show an innate ability in a particular area. Some others have even further subdivided the gifted into equally vague categories such as "extremely gifted," "first-order gifted," and "second-order gifted" (Good, 1973). In many cases, however, the terms *gifted* and *talented* are used interchangeably to refer to a wide variety of special abilities in any combination.

Historically, those identified as gifted were those who attained a particular IQ score. The IQ score cutoff used varies among researchers, but it is usually two standard deviations or more above the mean (typically 130 or higher). This procedure has been severely criticized for failing to identify individuals with talents in nonacademic areas and thus contributing to a restricted definition of giftedness (see Gallagher, 1975; Vail, 1979). In 1972 the United States Commissioner of Education defined gifted to include:

> Those identified by professionally qualified persons who, by virtue of outstanding abilities, are capable of high performance. These are children who require differentiated educational programs and/or services beyond those normally provided by the regular school program in order to realize their contributions to self and society.
>
> Children capable of high performance include those with demonstrated achievement and/or potential ability in any of the following areas, singly or in combination:
>
> 1. General intellectual ability
> 2. Specific academic aptitude
> 3. Creative or productive thinking
> 4. Leadership ability
> 5. Visual and performing arts
> (Marland, 1972, p.10)

Prior to Public Law 95-561 (the Education Amendments of 1978), psychomotor ability was included in the definition and, as of 1978, 24 states continued to use the definition that included psychomotor ability (Karnes & Collins, 1978).

This widely accepted definition has several notable features. First, the definition itself asserts the need for special programming for gifted children, assuming that the goal of education is to develop individual capabilities to the fullest extent. Second, individuals can be identified as gifted in the traditional way, through observation of their exceptional performance, or by uncovering a *potential* for achievement. The latter group, although more difficult to identify, may actually need assistance more than those with manifested achievement. Finally, the definition offers a useful breakdown of five areas of ability that can aid in establishing broadly based identification procedures. The categories go well beyond the traditional notions of giftedness (categories 1 and 2 only), making it a more comprehensive definition. This definition will serve as the basis for the remainder of this chapter.

Characteristics of Gifted and Talented Individuals

Gifted and talented populations are not homogenous groups. Some generalizations, however, can be made about the characteristics of individuals in each of the five categories listed in the Marland definition. Recall that a gifted child is not expected to exhibit *all* of the following traits and may have potential in only one category. In addition, large individual differences are found among gifted children.

General Intellectual Ability

Children who fit this category learn rapidly, easily, and efficiently. They display great curiosity about a wide variety of subjects and often make collections of items that are advanced or unusual for their age. They have a good memory, a long attention span for things of interest, a capacity for self-direction, and a large vocabulary.

Evidence of exceptionality is seen early in life since children of this group usually walk and talk early. They often show an interest in words and frequently are able to read before entering school. They enjoy reading and often choose books written for older readers.

The thought processes of children with exceptional general intellectual ability are qualitatively different from those of average children. They make early passage through the Piagetian stages of cognitive development, and they have superior reasoning ability.

Specific Academic Aptitude

This classification has a variety of subcategories identified by the specific academic discipline in which the child shows ability or promise. Scientific ability and writing talent are described here although others, such as mathematical ability, exist.

Along with a number of the characteristics cited in the previous section (reading ability, intellectual curiosity, long attention span), children with scientific ability show a specific interest in scientific topics. They read a great deal of scientific material and may be the classroom experts on a particular topic. They tend to spend much time working on special experiments of their own design and are persistent in seeking the reasons for and cause of events. They will often do more than an assignment calls for and are able to rise above failures met in experiments and projects.

Children who show exceptional writing ability are able to develop a story from its beginning to an interesting conclusion. Whether told orally or written, the ideas and details are well organized within the story, and interesting descriptive words are chosen. These children are able to give a refreshing twist, even to an old idea.

Creative or Productive Thinking Ability

Creative (productive, divergent) thinking takes a variety of forms. The fluent individual is able to produce a great number of ideas at a moment's notice. Flexibility in creative thought refers to the production of a wide variety of ideas. The original thinker produces novel and unique ideas and associative creativity in the ability to combine old or unrelated ideas in new ways. Of course, these forms of creative ability are not mutually exclusive, and they are present in different proportions in creative children.

Children of this category tend to be less inhibited, less conventional, and less conforming than their peers. Their autonomy and assertiveness may combine to make them appear to be behavior problems in an environment where nonconformity is not tolerated. The creative child tends to have a high energy level, good aesthetic judgments, and the ability to be constructively critical.

Leadership Ability

Children with exceptional leadership ability are liked and respected by peers, are charismatic, and enter into activities with contagious enthusiasm. They are often elected to offices and asked for ideas and suggestions. They are also frequently called upon by peers to make decisions for the group or settle disputes. As natural leaders, they are able to judge the abilities of others and enlist their talents to reach group goals. They manage groups well and are influential among their peers. Their talent may be either helpful to the classroom teacher (or other authority figure) or disruptive; they can lead peers to desirable as well as undesirable goals and can be a threat to the teacher's leadership with other pupils.

Ability in Visual and Performing Arts

Three subcategories appear in this classification, although dancing ability may be a viable addition to consider.

Children with exceptional dramatic ability are often good storytellers who readily shift from one role to another, use different voices, and communicate with gestures and facial expressions. They get a great deal of satisfaction from dramatizing and often make up original plays. They are able to mimic people and animals and enjoy evoking emotional responses from listeners.

Musical ability, like dramatic ability, is fairly easy to recognize in children. Musically talented children enjoy musical activities and have good sensitivity to rhythm. They have a keen sense of pitch and are very aware of music. They often play one or more instruments and/or sing well, and they may write original music.

Artistic children enjoy doing art work in their spare time and readily experiment with different media and subjects. They use art to express feelings, and they do original work. Besides producing art, they are interested in the work of others and find beauty in unexpected places.

From these descriptions it becomes apparent that there is some degree of overlap among categories, but the wide variety of abilities among gifted children should be noticed. Descriptions of personality traits have been largely omitted here because they vary widely. Specific issues of adjustment are discussed in a later section.

Need for Special Services for Gifted Children

While it is obvious that many gifted individuals develop into productive adults without special attention from educators, it is difficult to estimate the number of gifted students whose talent goes unrecognized and underdeveloped. Studies suggest that 15 to 25% of students with IQ scores above 120 are not performing up to their ability (Thomas & Crescimbeni, 1966), and some even drop out of school. Further, an estimated 75% of gifted and talented persons do not reach the level of educational attainment they should (Reynolds & Birch, 1982). This underachievement translates into an inestimable loss to society in terms of scientific discoveries, inventions, and works of art that fail to be produced. Promoting excellence among the gifted is beneficial to society as a whole.

Another rationale for providing services to identify and nurture giftedness is found in the realization that many underachieving gifted individuals are members of minority groups (Kirk & Gallagher, 1983). Perhaps, contrary to popular argument, the failure to promote education for the gifted perpetuates elitism by subtly discriminating against minorities who may need more help in realizing their potential.

Identification and special services for those among the handicapped population who also are gifted is a neglected area that should not be overlooked. In their efforts to meet educational needs related to an emotional disturbance, learning disability, sensory or physical impairment, special educators often neglect to include educational needs in the area of giftedness in their planning. A highly gifted or talented child with a handicapping condition can often create a greater challenge for an appropriate education because of the giftedness than because of the handicapping condition. Identification procedures and services for gifted children should also include those who are handicapped so that these children can achieve their potential to a greater extent.

Recognition of the need for nurturing gifted girls has been one result of the women's movement (Kirk & Gallagher, 1983). Gifted girls tend to be overlooked in identification procedures; to be discouraged from pursuing certain careers, especially in mathematics and science; and to become socialized into traditional societal roles.

Special services, especially broadly based identification procedures, are needed so that groups mentioned here will not be prohibited from attaining their maximum potential.

IDENTIFICATION OF GIFTED AND TALENTED CHILDREN

As the definition of giftedness has expanded beyond the child's obtaining an IQ score of 130/140 or more, so must the identification process expand. Obviously, an IQ score will be of little help in attempting to identify a musically talented child, a child with leadership ability, or a creative individual, since most IQ tests were not designed for those purposes.

Procedures for screening should be sufficiently broad that underachieving, minority, and handicapped gifted students will not be excluded. Identification procedures also need to be varied in order to locate the full spectrum of gifted children, not just those with general intellectual ability. (See the section on Practical Considerations later in this chapter.)

Need for Early Identification

Gifted children are in greatest need of guidance when they first begin school. Continuous identification programs, however, are needed throughout the school years for a variety of reasons. First, in our mobile society, students move in and out of districts regularly, making a one-time screening inadequate. Second, no process is perfect; continuous identification can help to find individuals who were overlooked in earlier rounds of identification or who were identified earlier as having potential that later was not realized. Third, some aspects of exceptionality may appear in the later grades, when there may be more opportunity to demonstrate specialized abilities or when general academic advancement becomes more pronounced.

Overlooked Groups

Some groups, such as culturally different children, underachievers, preschoolers, and handicapped children, may be more difficult to identify. The use of multiple measures with these groups is especially helpful.

Culturally different children may not be as verbally proficient as their peers; therefore, measures that do not concentrate on verbal fluency should be employed. One approach to identification is to focus on those characteristics that are valued by a particular minority group (Bernal, 1981). This method demands that various cultures be studied thoroughly to develop culture-specific definitions of giftedness. Such an approach might be practical in a setting with a large minority population.

Because preschool children develop at such a rapid rate cognitively, physically, and emotionally and with individual variations, gifted individuals in this population are often overlooked or may be overidentified. To aid in their identification, parents can be provided with lists of characteristics to look for in their children including some of the following traits: keen sense of humor, high degree of inquisitiveness, good memory, interest in books, high tolerance for frustration, and/or good imagination (Nolte, 1976). Lists of preschool traits that are arranged around the five categories described earlier may be especially helpful.

Handicapped and underachieving children are also often overlooked. The special education classrooms should not be excluded from a screening program for giftedness. Learning disabilities, mental impairment, emotional disturbance, and sensory impairments do not preclude the presence of giftedness in these children. Teachers need to be especially sensitive to the presence of creativity, leadership activity, and artistic ability in these children.

Guidelines for Identification

Since the characteristics of gifted children are so diverse, the assessment should encompass not only the cognitive realm but also the social, aesthetic, and creative dimensions. However, the actual selection of assessment instruments and procedures is frequently determined by the type of program available or being planned within the school district. Since the diversity of characteristics makes the provision of services to meet the heterogeneous needs of all gifted and talented children difficult, school districts usually conduct programs for selected segments of the population. The following guidelines for the selection of assessment instruments and identification procedures are organized around the five categories listed in the Marland (1972) definition.

General Intellectual Ability

The routine testing program of most school districts includes group tests of intelligence. Children who attain a score two standard deviations above the mean on such tests should be assessed further by individual tests of intelligence. For this purpose, the Stanford Binet and Wechsler series are usually appropriate.

The weakness of relying on group intelligence test results for identification purposes lies in the possibility that the groups described in the preceding section will be overlooked. Thus, teacher nomination should be employed to supplement the results of group tests. Children so nominated should also be given individual tests of intelligence. It should be noted that interpretation of test results should be done in light of the weaknesses of such measures in their use with mentally retarded children, as discussed in Chapter 5.

Achievement test results should also be considered, although some children who score high on tests of intelligence may be underachievers for a variety of reasons.

Specific Academic Aptitude

Children with outstanding abilities in a subject matter area such as mathematics or science may be identified first by teacher nomination. Individual tests of intelligence and achievement should then be administered. Peer nominations may also be a useful identification procedure.

Some children with outstanding abilities in specific subject areas may be overlooked because they pursue their interests outside of school. Thus, routine student and parent interviews and interest surveys should be employed to supplement information about the child's interests as evidenced by school activities.

Creative or Productive Thinking

Highly creative children may first come to the attention of teachers because they are behavior problems or they evidence behavior that tends not to conform to the norms of the class. Individual tests of intelligence should be administered to such children as well as tests of divergent thinking. Instruments appropriate for this purpose include the Torrance Tests of Creative Thinking (Verbal and Figural) and the Creativity Assessment Packet.

Because the divergent thinking and actions of highly creative children may be disruptive in the classroom setting and objectionable to some teachers, school psychologists need to work with teachers to help them attain a greater understanding of these children's needs and to assist them in modifying the school curriculum so as to channel gifted children's interests in constructive ways.

Leadership Ability

Children with outstanding skills in leadership are usually identified by their teachers and/or peers. Nomination by teachers through ratings of traits and by peers through sociograms and social acceptance scales are usually appropriate. The challenge to the school is in channeling the leadership skills in positive and constructive directions.

Visual and Performing Arts

School districts with well developed programs in art, music, and dramatics will often find that students with such talents select these activities voluntarily. School districts where such programs are not well developed may need to rely on teacher nominations through observation; peer nominations through questionnaires that include such items as "Who is best in -----?"; or parent nominations through interviews about the child's interests and activities outside of school.

Creative abilities in writing should not be overlooked. Sensitive teachers of English composition are often helpful in identifying pupils with such talents as well as in nurturing their abilities.

PROGRAMMING FOR GIFTED AND TALENTED STUDENTS

Options for the Gifted and Talented

Program options for gifted students are necessary because giftedness is multifaceted. A program that offers only a single alternative will necessarily be underserving the full range of gifted children. The three broad categories of options include grouping, acceleration, and enrichment. In order to meet the diverse needs of gifted pupils, school programs should include appropriate elements of all three options.

Grouping involves classifying students on one or more criteria and bringing them together for instruction. It can be implemented at all levels, as in the nongraded school, thus providing for the special needs of all students through one method. In a more traditional setting, a full- or part-time special class or a resource room arrangement can be implemented. An itinerant or consultant teacher model may also be appropriate for some districts. Obviously, these options are more useful for children with general intellectual ability, specific academic aptitude, and artistic ability. The special class or special school option is the one most likely to arouse controversy, so any system considering such a program would be well advised to research the pros and cons thoroughly prior to initiating such a program (Gallagher, 1975).

Acceleration refers to the process of advancing through the usual pattern of subject matter at a faster than usual rate. The easiest time to implement this option is at the preschool level, by allowing entrance to kindergarten at age 4 for gifted children. Grade skipping is also a possibility. Although educators need to be alert to the possibility of social adjustment problems and skill gaps, several studies have shown that existence of these problems has been greatly exaggerated (Thomas & Crescimbeni, 1966). Acceleration may also take place at the high school level with early graduation. Some students elect to take college classes part-time during their high school years. This option has special appeal for students with specific academic aptitude or artistic ability, and it can be implemented fairly easily on an individual basis. The argument that acceleration is not good for social adjustment is not supported by research (Gallagher, 1975).

Enrichment is frequently mentioned as a means of handling the special needs of gifted children in the regular classroom, but too often it becomes busy work. Enrichment activities should allow gifted children to reach a deeper understanding of the topic under study. The options for enrichment are as limitless as the potentials of the children; activities can take the form of independent study, special learning kits, team teaching, small group instruction, lectures and demonstrations, instructional TV, and computer-assisted instruction. Sharing special projects with other students is also beneficial in providing motivation for gifted students and enriching the education of children of average ability. Although enrichment would seem to be a solution for the educational programming dilemma, Gallagher (1975) has listed three major difficulties: the range of abilities in the classroom, the teacher's lack of knowledge in content areas, and the teacher's lack of knowledge of special methods. Implementing an effective enrichment program requires careful planning on the part of the teachers and administrators involved.

It is important to note that these programming alternatives do not always require homogenous grouping. Much can be accomplished in the regular classroom with individualized instruction for all children in the classroom. Some gifted children are currently well served in regular classrooms with after-school activities available for enrichment and with a curriculum individualized to meet their needs and challenge their superior abilities.

Other options for programming include summer school classes; special community programs such as those conducted by art museums; foreign exchange programs; private tutoring or instruction for special skills in activities such as music, art, dance, gymnastics, or use of computers; field trips; and participation in artistic and academic competitions at the local, state, national, and international levels. A word of caution: Although gifted students are probably the most able to take advantage of enrichment activities, these opportunities should not be consistently denied to students of average ability. They, too, can develop enthusiasm for learning by departing from routine and studying something of particular interest.

Because the learning of academically gifted students tends to be qualitatively different from that of their peers, it is not always necessary for them to go through the entire sequence of activities in the regular curriculum. To adjust for their differences, students should routinely be allowed to demonstrate their competencies and be released from further unnecessary and duplicative requirements.

Other Features of a Program

A comprehensive program requires inservice training for the teachers who are dealing with gifted children in their classrooms. Teachers need to be provided with the resources to recognize individual needs of gifted and talented children and to plan meaningful enrichment programs for them. In particular, teachers need to be sensitized to the needs and characteristics of creative children, who are so often misunderstood and squelched in schools. School psychologists can be helpful in interpreting the special needs of gifted and talented students to teachers and in participating in planning and conducting inservice training programs.

As with any special school program, the program for gifted children should be evaluated periodically. This evaluation should assess the program's goal attainment, measure terminal outcomes, and set new goals. Research on student and community attitudes toward the program would also be appropriate.

To help alleviate some of these difficulties, the school psychologist can often give direct help to gifted and talented children who are having school and personal adjustment problems, provided this kind of service meets with the approval of school administrators and parents. Indirect assistance can be given through consultation with teachers, work on curriculum committees, and work with parent groups, all of which are activities that may lead to modifications in the school curriculum to make it a greater challenge.

Gifted children may sometimes have trouble developing good work habits. This may stem from the fact that they often do not need to exert much energy to complete the assignments they are given. As a result, they may have difficulty in sustaining effort and have problems when set on their own to do independent study or when they enter a more demanding and competitive situation, such as college.

Some of these exceptional students may come into personality conflicts with teachers. Occasionally a teacher feels threatened by the superior abilities of a gifted child and will use sarcasm, ridicule, or disinterest to squelch the child. Gifted children may also be mislabeled as behavior problems or lazy students by adults who do not recognize their abilities. The consultation skills of the school psychologist may provide help to teachers (or others) having such difficulties.

Regardless of these potential problems, gifted children show remarkable resiliency. In fact, relatively few of them have significant problems in social and emotional adjustment. The stereotype of the eccentric bookworm does not fit the reality of the gifted individual (Gallagher, 1975).

The Family of the Gifted Child

As a preschooler, a gifted child can be difficult. The ceaseless energy and exploration can leave caregivers exhausted and confused. Later on, some parents need help to see their gifted child as an individual rather than as, for example, "a math whiz" (Vail, 1979).

Achieving a balance of attention and care in any family is difficult, but the problem is even more acute for the famlies of gifted children. The natural rivalry among siblings may become an arena for the display of talents, but, if the gifted child always wins, problems develop.

Parents of gifted children must handle these problems, and they must often face them alone. Parents of average children often have little sympathy to waste on the problems of raising a gifted child (Vail, 1979). Thus, parent groups are a valuable component of a program where parents can find mutual support for the challenges they meet in raising an exceptional child.

PRACTICAL CONSIDERATIONS IN PROGRAMMING

School districts initiating programs for gifted and talented children face several questions. First, a decision must be made regarding the subgroup(s) to be served, because this will determine the size and nature of the program. Perhaps it is best to begin with the five areas in the Marland definition and identify what school resources are currently available to meet the needs of each subgroup. For example, if there is already a well developed music program available, the musically talented group may not need to be added to the working definition.

Next, estimates should be made of how many students qualify for the subgroup(s) currently underserved and for whom programs should be planned. Unfortunately, the available resources often dictate the scope of the program rather than the demonstrated need. Thus, a decision must be made to employ some mechanism for deciding on the priority group(s) targeted for programming. The mechanism should result in selection of a group of children sufficiently homogenous to allow for an educationally sound program. For example, some schools resort to an IQ cutoff score. This procedure permits easy estimation of program size and is a quick identification method; however, as noted in an earlier chapter, there are numerous weaknesses in relying on the results of any standardized test of intelligence as a single measure for labeling and grouping children.

In these days of tight budgets, securing adequate resources may be a major problem. Lack of funding should not preclude a program (acceleration, for example, is inexpensive), but it does severely limit the scope of intervention. Related to this lack of funding is the problem of space. As budgets are cut and schools are closed and consolidated, space for special classes and projects is difficult to find. A successful program for gifted and talented children requires qualified teachers. Not everyone can teach gifted children successfully. There are few states with certification requirements for teachers of the gifted and talented, and few university programs that offer a full sequence of course work in this area. Qualified teachers for programs for the gifted may be difficult to find. Finally, as discussed earlier, negative community reaction may present another problem. Understanding the reasons for the reaction and anticipating it will help, but sensitive public relations work may need to be done to counteract existing negative attitudes. Again, parent organizations can be especially helpful in this regard.

SUMMARY

Although they are not included under the provisions of Public Law 94-142, programs for gifted and talented children should be considered in any planning by school districts for meeting individual needs. Gifted and talented children tend to be overlooked if they are members of a minority group, are handicapped, are underachievers, or are girls. Any identification procedure should ensure that these groups are not overlooked. Assessment procedures and educational programming should include the broad subcategories of giftedness and talent: general intellectual ability, specific academic aptitude, creative or productive thinking, leadership ability, and ability in visual and performing arts. Educational programs should be planned carefully and should include appropriate elements of specialized instruction, acceleration, and enrichment. In initiating a program, school personnel should be particularly sensitive to community attitudes toward such specialized services.

REFERENCES

Bernal, E. M. (1981). *Methods of identifying gifted minority students* (ERIC/TM Report 72). ED 204 418. 33 pp. Princeton NJ: ERIC Clearinghouse on Tests and Measurements.

Durr, W. K (1964). *The gifted student.* New York: Oxford University Press.

Gallagher, J. (1975). *Teaching the gifted child* (2nd ed.). Boston: Allyn & Bacon.

Good, C. V. (Ed.). (1973). *Dictionary of education* (3rd ed.). New York: McGraw Hill.

Karnes, F. A., & Collins, E. C. (1978). State definitions of the gifted and talented: A report and analysis. *Journal for the Education of the Gifted, 1,* 44-62.

Kirk, S. A. & Gallagher, J. J. (1983). *Educating exceptional children* (4th ed). Boston: Houghton Mifflin.

Marland, S. (Ed.). (1972). *Education of the gifted and talented.* (Report to the Congress of the United States by the U. S. Commissioner of Education.) Washington DC: U. S. Government Printing Office.

Nolte, J. (1976). *Nearly . . . everything you've always wanted to know about the gifted and talented.* Greenfield WI: Council for the Gifted and Talented.

Reynolds, M. C., & Birch, J. W. (1982). *Teaching exceptional children in all America's schools.* Reston VA: The Council for Exceptional Children.

Thomas, G. I., & Crescimbeni, J. (1966). *Guiding the gifted child.* New York: Random House.

Vail, P.L. (1979). *The world of the gifted child.* New York: Walker & Co.

Wolman, B. B. (Ed.). (1973). *Dictionary of behavioral science.* New York: Van Nostrand Reinhold.

ADDITIONAL RESOURCES

French, J. L. (1975). The gifted. In M. V. Wisland, *Psychoeducational diagnosis of exceptional children* (pp. 306-328). Springfield IL: Charles C Thomas.

Getzels, J., & Jackson, P. (1962). *Creativity and intelligence.* New York: John Wiley.

Gowman, J. C., & Torrance, E. P. (Eds.). (1971). *Educating the ablest.* New York: Peacock Printing.

Guilford, J. P. (1968). *Intelligence, creativity, and their educational implications.* San Diego: Knapp.

Karnes, F. A., & Collins, E. C. (1980). *Handbook of instructional resources and references for teaching the gifted.* Boston: Allyn & Bacon.

Laycock, F. (1979). *Gifted children.* Glenview IL: Scott, Foresman.

Newland, T. E. (1976). *The gifted in socioeducational perspective.* Englewood Cliffs NJ: Prentice-Hall.

Tannebaum, A. J. (1983). *Gifted children: Psychological and educational perspectives.* New York: Macmillan.

Terman, L. M. (1925). *Mental and physical traits of a thousand gifted children.* Stanford CA: Stanford University Press.

Terman, L. M. & Oden, M. (1947). *Genetic studies of genius, Vol. 4, The gifted child grows up.* Stanford CA: Stanford University Press.

Terman, L. M. & Oden, M. (1959). *The gifted group at mid-life.* Stanford CA: Stanford University Press.

Torrance, E. P. (1970). *Creative learning and teaching.* New York: Dodd, Mead.

Torrance, E. P. (1970). *Encouraging creativity in the classroom.* Dubuque IA: William C. Brown.

Torrance, E. P. (1980). Psychology of gifted children and youth. In W. M. Cruickshank, *Psychology of exceptional children and youth* (4th ed.) (pp. 409-496). Englewood Cliff: Prentice-Hall.

CHAPTER 5

Mental Retardation

John Ardizzone
Geraldine T. Scholl

Mental retardation is one of the high incidence categorical areas in special education, accounting for about 2 to 3% of the school population. The term encompasses a wide range of ability levels, which makes generalizations about the nature and needs of any one individual difficult.

Misdiagnosis is a serious problem in this categorical area. Socioeconomic and cultural factors may restrict the experiential background of many children and thus influence results of tests administered to them, because standardized tests are usually normed on a typical middle-class sample. Problems and issues of using such tests with certain populations are discussed in Chapter 1. Other impairments, such as hearing loss, autism, and severe emotional disturbances, cause children with these conditions to perform on tests as though they had a lower level of intellectual functioning; thus they appear to be mentally retarded. Finally, the need for a differential diagnosis of children with educable mental retardation, emotional disturbance, or learning disabilities for purposes of financial reimbursement to local districts frequently presents a challenge to the school psychologist. Children with these three conditions share some similar behavioral characteristics.

For these reasons it is important for the school psychologist to have a basic understanding of what mental retardation is and how it may impinge on an individual's behavior and development.

This chapter presents an overview of the condition, including definition, terminology, and etiological factors; characteristics of the levels of retardation and their impact on growth and development; and implications of these for the process of assessment.

OVERVIEW

Definition

The most widely accepted definition of mental retardation is that adopted by the American Association on Mental Deficiency (AAMD).

> Mental retardation refers to significantly subaverage general intelligence functioning resulting in or associated with concurrent impairments in adaptive behavior and manifested during the developmental period.
>
> Significantly subaverage is defined as an IQ score of 70 or below on standardized measures of intelligence . . . .
>
> General intellectual functioning is operationally defined as the results obtained by assessment with one or more of the individually administered standardized general intelligence tests developed for the purpose.
>
> Impairments in adaptive behavior are defined as significant limitations in an individual's effectiveness in meeting the standards of maturation, learning, personal independence, and/or social responsibility that are expected for his or her age level and cultural group, as determined by clinical assessment and, usually, standardized scales.
>
> Developmental period is defined as the period of time between conception and the 18th birthday. Developmental deficits may be manifested by slow, arrested, or incomplete development resulting from brain damage, degenerative processes in the central nervous system, or regression from previously normal states due to psycho-social factors. (Grossman, 1983, p. 11)

Thus for a diagnosis of mental retardation two aspects must be present: a measured level of intellectual functioning as indicated by an IQ of 70 or below and an impairment in adaptive behavior.

Aside from the usual considerations concerning validity and reliability for assessment instruments used with any one child, the emphasis on a specific IQ for the determination of "significantly subaverage general intellectual functioning" raises questions about the influence of cultural factors on test performance (Heller, Holtzman, & Messick, 1982). Several proposals to modify the cultural aspects included in the 1973 definition (Grossman, 1973) are still relevant. Dunn (1973) proposed that norms according to ethnic or racial subgroups be used for ascertaining the level of intellectual functioning. This use of multiple subgroup norms, however, would become complicated when applied to the school setting, where children are expected to perform according to total group norms or an average that is derived primarily from samples drawn from the middle class. The conclusion of normal intellectual functioning from an assessment using subgroup norms may lead the teacher to have higher expectations of cognitive functioning on school tasks. Thus the use of subgroup norms may result in a distinct disadvantage to the child when applied to an educational situation. Some children may even be deprived of specialized programs and services that they need in order to succeed in school (MacMillan, 1982).

Mercer (1973) made extensive studies of placement practices in California and found a greater tendency to label and to place in special classes children from other ethnic and racial groups. She proposed the use of her System of Multicultural Pluralistic Assessment (SOMPA) as a method of determining how the child's present level of functioning takes into account previous opportunities for learning. She viewed the need for considering mental retardation from the perspective of a social system. MacMillan (1982) recommended that the social system model, such as she proposed, be used first in the assessment process and that it be supplemented with procedures from a clinical model.

The relationship of sociocultural variables to a child's performance on formal assessment measures of intellectual functioning as well as on cognitive tasks in the school setting should not be overlooked. However, in making a determination of the impact of these variables, the school psychologist should employ informal assessment measures to supplement results of the formal instruments and arrive at a clinical judgment based on a variety of observations.

The assessment of "impairments in adaptive behavior" likewise presents a challenge. Variations in behavior may be related to age, a particular situation, and cultural background. Instruments for assessing this aspect are generally recent in origin. Some of these available instruments are discussed in a later section of this chapter.

Terminology

Various descriptive terms are applied to the different subgroups of mental retardation. Table 5-1 summarizes some of the more commonly used descriptions.

The heterogeneity of the population is evident from a study of this table, which also illustrates the difficulty of applying the same label of "mental retardation" to such a wide range of functioning. Characteristics and needs of each subgroup are discussed in a later section.

TABLE 5-1

Levels of Severity in Mental Retardation

AAMD (Grossman, 1983)		Educational Expectations (Chinn, Drew, & Logan, et al, 1979)		Piagetian stages of cognitive development (MacMillan, 1982)
Levels	*IQ*	*Description*	*IQ*	*Stages*
Mild	50-55 to app. 70	Educable	50-75	Concrete operations
Moderate	35-40 to 50-55	Trainable	20-49	Preoperational
Severe	20-25 to 35-40	Custodial	below 20	Sensorimotor
Profound	Below 20 or 25			

Etiological Factors in Mental Retardation

Knowledge and understanding of the etiology of mental retardation in a particular child will often help the school psychologist interpret the results of an assessment and formulate an appropriate educational plan in a particular setting. Such information is also important for any work with parents that the school psychologist may undertake.

Grossman (1983) described the mentally retarded population as being divided into two groups that sometimes overlap. Clinical types "generally demonstrate some central nervous system pathology, usually have IQs in the moderate or below range, have associated handicaps" or stigmata, and can often be diagnosed from birth or early childhood (p. 12). The second group "appear to be neurologically intact, have no readily detectable physical signs or clinical laboratory evidence related to retardation, function in the mildly retarded range of intelligence, and are heavily concentrated in the lowest socioeconomic segments of society" (p. 13). For the purposes of this chapter, etiological factors will be summarized according to these two broad groupings.

Biologic Origin

Nine out of ten cases of mental retardation attributed to biological factors are prenatal in origin and are evident at birth (Grossman, 1983). Prenatal and perinatal factors include infectious diseases, genetic factors, prematurity and low birth weight, and other biomedical factors.

Infectious Diseases. Prenatal infections, particularly rubella during the first trimester, syphilis, herpes simplex II, and toxoplasmosis, may cause a number of impairments in addition to mental deficiency to the fetus (Moore & Moore, 1977). These include visual and hearing losses, physical problems such as congenital heart conditions and respiratory deficits, and microcephaly.

Genetic Factors. A number of conditions associated with mental retardation involve genetic factors. The reader is referred to Robinson and Robinson (1976), Moore and Moore (1977), and MacMillan (1982) for a discussion of the mechanism of genetic inheritance and for descriptions of other genetic syndromes. Three of the more prevalent ones will be noted here.

Down's syndrome is the most common chromosomal cause of mental retardation and accounts for approximately 10% of those included in the moderate to severe level of mental retardation (Robinson & Robinson, 1976). Children with Down's syndrome are characterized by a combination of one or more of the following: lateral upward slope of the eyes, small nose, drooping mouth, fissured and protruding tongue, a flattened head, short and stubby fingers, and a general stocky nature. They frequently have other physical problems, most commonly a defect in the development of the heart. Their development during the first year of life is sometimes not noticeably abnormal, but by age 3 or 4, their development begins to level off, and by the time they reach adulthood most of them fall into the moderately retarded range, with a few in the severely and a few in the mildly retarded ranges (Robinson & Robinson, 1976).

Turner's syndrome is a chromosomal aberration in which there is a single X sex chromosome. The child is always female. The condition is characterized by retardation in growth and sexual development, so that the child does not always develop secondary sex characteristics during puberty. Some physical anomalies, such as cardiac malformations, may also be present. Mental retardation is not always a characteristic of this condition, but a number of children do fall in the mild mental retardation range because they usually have some cognitive deficits, especially in space-form perception (Chinn, Drew, & Logan, 1979).

Phenylketonuria (PKU) is an inherited enzyme deficiency that can cause mental retardation if it is not treated. Children with PKU are unable to metabolize phenylalanine, a substance found in most proteins, with the result that progressive brain damage occurs. If untreated, infants show delayed development both physically and mentally; some have variable pigmentation in the skin and hair; and their urine gives off a musty odor due to phenylpyruvic acid (Sarason, 1969;

Schultz, 1983b). As screening programs for newborns and early dietary intervention for PKU have increased, the number of children with retarded mental development from PKU has decreased in recent years (MacMillan, 1982).

Many genetic abnormalities, including Down's syndrome, are detectable during pregnancy by amniocentesis. In this medical procedure amniotic fluid is drawn from the intrauterine amniotic sac and the cell structure is examined microscopically for genetic abnormalities. On learning the probability that their child may have some type of genetic abnormality, parents can begin to discuss with their medical doctor and social worker the implications of the birth of a handicapped child. They may also wish to discuss with their religious advisor the moral, religious, and ethical questions concerning a decision to choose or not choose abortion. With guidance from a social worker or a preschool special education counselor, parents who do not choose abortion can begin the difficult process of coping with the emotional aspects of adjusting to having a child with a handicapping condition. Parents who do choose abortion may need continued support from a social worker to deal with any guilt feelings that may arise later concerning their decision. They may also wish to consult with their medical doctor concerning potential problems with future pregnancies.

Prematurity. Low birth weight infants, that is, those under 2,500 grams or 5½ pounds, are considered at risk whether they are premature or full term. Such infants are more likely to have cerebral palsy or other neurological damage and have a greater probability of dying during the perinatal period (Neisworth & Smith, 1978).

Other Medical Factors. Pregnancy, particularly the first trimester, is a vulnerable period when the fetus is at the mercy of the environment (Chinn, et al., 1979). Robinson and Robinson (1976) listed a number of hazards to the developing fetus that may result in mental retardation by causing damage to the central nervous system: malnutrition in the mother, which can result in premature birth and low birth weight; maternal smoking; use of alcohol; and other forms of substance abuse during pregnancy. In recent years there has been increasing concern with the high incidence of fetal alcohol syndrome (FAS), which seems to be associated with chronic alcoholism and binge drinking during pregnancy (Grossman, 1983; Neisworth & Smith, 1978). Children with FAS are usually small at birth and exhibit behavior problems and physical abnormalities in addition to mental retardation (Schultz, 1983a).

There are several abnormal maternal-fetal interactions that may be hazardous to the developing fetus. Rh factor incompatibility is commonly known as a factor that may cause damage to the central nervous system. When the mother's Rh factor is negative and that of the fetus is positive, the mother's body develops antibodies that destroy the blood cells of the fetus. Fortunately medical science is sufficiently advanced that many of the problems accompanying the incompatible blood factors can now be prevented (Moore & Moore, 1977).

Conditions related to diabetes in the mother increase the risks for both mother and infant. These include hypertension, increased possibility of infections, and increased likelihood of miscarriage and perinatal death (MacMillan, 1982).

Although the process of giving birth proceeds normally for most women, in some cases there are potential hazards (Robinson & Robinson, 1976). Improper positioning of the fetus, as in a breach birth, increases the danger of anoxia, which may result in brain damage. Lack of oxygen to the brain of the fetus may also result from a twisted umbilical cord (Neisworth & Smith, 1978).

Postnatal Factors.. Mental retardation may also result from factors that occur after birth, some of which are related to hazards in the environment. Children who ingest paint containing lead may acquire lead poisoning, which has been associated with brain damage. Other substances that may be causative factors include mercury, radiation, nitrates, and pesticides (Moore & Moore, 1977).

Some infectious diseases, such as Reyes syndrome, meningitis, and encephalitis, may also result in damage to the central nervous system. Trauma as a result of child abuse and automobile accidents are increasingly common causes of severe head injury, which can result in neurological damage and mental impairment (Moore & Moore, 1977).

Many of these causative factors could be eliminated from the environment, thereby decreasing the incidence of mental retardation, but prevention will take the concerted effort of a society committed to a clean, safe, and healthful environment for all citizens.

The many and varied causes of mental retardation discussed in this section point to the necessity of obtaining a complete case history of the child's early development, with special attention to the pregnancy of the mother and events surrounding the birth. (See Appendix D for a sample form). Information critical to understanding the etiology of the child's mental retardation can be helpful in working with the parents and in planning a school program that will minimize the child's deficiencies and maximize his or her potential.

Social and Environmental Factors

Most of the etiological factors included in the preceding sections have a known relationship to mental retardation. However, for most individuals who are classified as mentally retarded, particularly those

with mild retardation, discrete causal factors are often not readily identifiable (Grossman, 1983). Robinson and Robinson (1976) described
three clusters of characteristics that may be considered underlying
causes of mental retardation related in some degree to environmental
factors but that have no strong supporting research evidence:
psychosocial disadvantage, emotional disturbance, and brain damage.

Psychosocial Disadvantage. A diagnosis of psychosocial disadvantage
is presumptive, relying on an absence of neurological symptoms.
Children are not ordinarily identified until they reach school age and,
when identified as mentally retarded, they tend to be placed in classes
or programs for educable mentally retarded students. Environmental
factors, particularly those associated with a life of poverty, are often
present: overcrowded living conditions, poor nutrition, lack of access
to good health care, and overall decreased ability of the family to cope
with these circumstances. Families tend to be disorganized; the home
setting is often overstimulating in the visual and auditory modalities;
and there is a lack of exposure to school-type materials such as books
and magazines that provide intellectual stimulation for the child.
Children from such homes are at a distinct disadvantage, because they
must learn to function in the middle-class environment of the school
and at the same time cope with the reality of poverty within their home
environment (Neisworth & Smith, 1978).

Caution must be exercised in assessing such children, because they
may be labeled too quickly and then never lose their label while they
are in school. On the other hand, without the label, many do not receive
the services they need to succeed in school. Moore and Moore (1977)
recommended complete multidisciplinary evaluations including
measures of social competence so that a sound base for educational,
psychological, and medical intervention can be built.

In their discussion of psychosocial factors, Robinson and Robinson
(1976) concluded that "improving the life situation of the poor may
be the single most important step toward preventing mental handicaps" (p. 178).

Emotional disturbance. Severely emotionally disturbed children, particularly those with early infantile autism, are often misdiagnosed as
mentally retarded because of poor performance on individual tests of
intelligence and deficits in adaptive behavior. Characteristics and needs
of these children are discussed in Chapter 7; autism is discussed in
Chapter 8. Similarly, children with learning disabilities are often
misdiagnosed as mentally retarded because of their poor performance
on standardized tests of achievement as well as intelligence and their
frequent reading problems.

Much has been written about the need for arriving at a differential diagnosis of mental retardation or learning disabilities or emotional disturbance. Sometimes such a differentiation is necessary in order to arrive at a prognosis or prediction of outcomes for treatment procedures or to refer the child for placement in the most appropriate setting for his or her needs. There is considerable disagreement about whether such a differential diagnosis is necessary or even possible. Robinson and Robinson (1976) suggested that the focus of assessment should be placed on discovering how the condition came about and what can be done to help the child rather than to attempt identification of which is primary.

Brain Damage. Robinson & Robinson (1976) concluded that many moderately retarded and almost all severely and profoundly retarded children show signs of severe brain damage. Characteristics such as hyperactivity and perceptual problems that are found in brain-damaged children of normal intelligence, who are frequently labeled as learning disabled, may also be found among the retarded population. The brain damage, however, tends to be more diffuse in the severely and profoundly mentally retarded population than in those who have normal or near normal intelligence.

Considering the complex nature of mental retardation and its heterogeneous etiological factors, it is unfortunate that the same label is applied to individuals whose functioning spans such a wide spectrum. In the performance of their role in assessment and participation in educational planning, school psychologists will frequently encounter problems in attempting to explain "educable" or "mild" mental retardation to parents and teachers, many of whom may view that term as a permanent and educationally hopeless condition. School psychologists need to know the characteristics, educational needs, and major differences found in the various groups identified as "mild," "moderate," "severe," and "profound," and they must be able to interpret this information to parents and teachers in a meaningful way. The following section summarizes some of this information.

CHARACTERISTICS AND NEEDS

To arrive at a decision regarding diagnosis and placement, it is necessary for the school psychologist to know the characteristics and needs of individuals with varying levels of mental retardation in order to form a realistic view of their potential level of functioning. This discussion is divided into four sections according to the levels of severity shown in Table 5-1: mild, moderate, severe, and profound.

Mild Mental Retardation

The first group, mildly retarded individuals, includes about 89% of the retarded population, which is approximately 2 to 3% of the school-age population (Gearheart & Litton, 1979). Many in this category do not look significantly different from their normal peers and frequently appear less retarded when they leave school and pursue activities that do not call attention to their restricted intellectual abilities. Many of them show evidence of the sociocultural factors described in the preceding section (Shonkoff, 1982). Academic achievement will probably not exceed fifth or sixth grade level; they can grasp basic abstractions, concrete learning relationships, and simplified concepts.

Usually children with mild mental retardation are not identified until they reach school age. In the early elementary grades, these children can frequently remain in the regular classroom with individualized instruction and the aid of a resource room or consultant teacher. In the later elementary and secondary school grades, a special class placement may be more appropriate as the gap between their academic achievement and that of their normal peers widens. Behavior problems may appear because of the frustration arising from their inability to compete with their peers, their poor social skills, and their general immaturity in comparison with normal peers.

The school program should emphasize academic skills as tools to enhance social competence, personal adequacy, and future occupational skills. In junior high or middle school, the program emphasis should be on prevocational skills and the essential and practical academic content necessary for independent living. High school should emphasize vocational training with work/study programs, and academic classes should stress practical life skills. Guidance for personal and job-related problems and preparation for living independently should also include training in activities for recreation, leisure time, and social skills.

As adults, those with mild mental retardation can succeed in semiskilled jobs, can become self-supporting individuals, and in general can lead independent lives (Payne, Polloway, Smith, & Payne, 1981).

For more details concerning educational programs see Cegelka and Prehm (1982) and Payne, Polloway, Smith, and Payne (1981).

Moderate Mental Retardation

Moderately retarded individuals constitute about 0.3% in the general population and 10% of the retarded population (Gearheart & Litton, 1979). In physical appearance, they look "different." As noted in a previous section, a large number of Down's syndrome children are included in this grouping. Multiple impairments including seizures, cerebral palsy, hearing and visual losses, and other physical problems are commonly found. Their speech is usually understandable but is very concrete and linguistically simple.

Educational programming concentrates on teaching self-help and social skills. Academic areas focus on elementary number concepts, such as making change and basic operations of addition and subtraction, and language arts concentrating on oral communication and reading familiar signs for their own safety. The academic program should focus on functional academic skills that are useful for personal living as adults.

Some moderately retarded adults may be able to hold unskilled jobs, but most will work in sheltered settings (Gearheart & Litton, 1979). With minimal supervision, most are capable of homemaking skills and manual activities around the home. Their understanding of the value of money is often limited. Their low level of social awareness makes it difficult for them to make or keep close friends.

For more detailed information on educational aspects see Berdine and Cegelka (1980), Cegelka and Prehm (1982), and Gearheart and Litton (1979).

Severe Mental Retardation

The severely and profoundly retarded together comprise about 3% of the retarded population and about 0.1% of the total population (Gearheart & Litton, 1979). Historically, persons included in both groups were kept at home, or more often institutionalized, with little opportunity for learning. Prior to Public Law 94-142, they were excluded from public education programs.

Since most have sustained central nervous system damage, it is difficult to generalize about their characteristics. They require an interdisciplinary approach for the treatment of their accompanying emotional, physical, sensory, and behavioral handicaps.

Those classified as severely retarded usually have limited ability to respond to even the most pronounced auditory, visual, physical, or social stimuli. They have a greatly slowed developmental rate, so that progress is difficult to assess except over a long period of time. They have poor communication skills even in nonverbal communication. Their personal and social skills are at a very low level, and many are unable to feed and dress themselves or to control bladder and bowel function.

Generally they can be helped to learn to communicate, if not by oral then by manual methods. They have limited capacity for independence in self-care. They are unable to learn even low-level functional academic skills. However, in a controlled environment, with supervision, some may be able to contribute minimally to their self-support through repetitive manual tasks performed either at home or in a sheltered setting.

Programming for this group tends to take place in residential settings, in segregated special schools, or at home. Curriculum development is approached through normal developmental patterns of infants and young children up to the first 72 months. Providing some form of communication is a primary intervention goal. In assessing progress, it is necessary to look for small, incremental skills and fragments of skills to find strengths on which to build.

Cegelka and Prehm (1982) have offered more specific details regarding characteristics and educational programming for this group.

Profound Mental Retardation

The profoundly retarded are best characterized by the extensive damage they suffer in all bodily systems. They tend to have complex combinations of sensory and motor impairments with a high incidence of vision and hearing problems, cerebral palsy, physical malformations, and severe neurological damage. Children in this group are usually identifiable at birth or shortly thereafter by physical abnormalities and very low scores on the Apgar scale, which rates on a scale of 1 to 10 the heart rate, respiration, color, muscle tone, and response to stimulation within the first 5 minutes after birth (Blackman, 1983). Many require life-sustaining processes for some period after birth. Their fragile health conditions often lead to frequent illnesses and sometimes an early death. Some display minimal response levels and few reflexes. In some cases only respiration and digestion are intact (Cleland, 1979).

Therapy is often required to aid them in learning to suck, swallow, and chew, which are essential skills that must be acquired before any attempts at developing oral communication can be initiated. Many lack even the ability to make eye contact. Locomotion is usually very restricted, and most are confined to a wheelchair. They lack the capacity to learn by imitation, but eventually many learn to respond through behavior modification techniques. Cegelka and Prehm (1982) have suggested that, with optimal educational programming, many in this group are capable of acquiring a higher level of skill, especially in the area of self-help, than has previously been considered possible. Future efforts should focus on improving the quality of life for this group.

As adults, those with profound retardation may be able to obey simple commands, to vocalize some simple greeting, and to feed themselves partially.

There are many controversies concerning the expenditure of public funds for educational programs for this group and to some extent for the severely retarded. Some of the issues and questions that have been raised include the following.

1. Is it reasonable to spend large amounts of money on the necessary human resources, facilities, and equipment required for the education of profoundly retarded individuals when the ultimate outcome is so limited?
2. Should the life of a severely handicapped neonate be maintained if life-sustaining equipment is required?
3. At what point should the level of functioning be considered so low that educational services need not be provided?
4. Do programs operated for these children constitute "education"?

Whatever the answers to these questions, educational programs are a current reality. In implementing appropriate educational programs some basic considerations are necessary. First, early identification is a necessary part of the program, and work with parents should be initiated as soon as the child is identified. Second, teachers and other professional personnel must be prepared who will be satisfied with working on very elementary tasks and subtasks and who will derive satisfaction through seeing very slow progress (Cleland, 1979). Third, educational programs based on currently available research findings should "take on a behavioral approach, be individually prescribed, be directed toward functional skills, be systematically applied, and provide transdisciplinary services" (Cegelka & Prehm, 1982, p. 342).

ASSESSMENT CONSIDERATIONS

Because of the heterogeneity of the population, assessment implications vary for the different levels. This section is divided into three parts based on the levels described in the previous section.

Mild Mental Retardation

The intelligence testing movement grew out of efforts to diagnose and plan educational programs for retarded children. It is interesting, therefore, that the current controversy over intelligence testing relates more to this categorical group than to any other in special education. As related in Chapter 1, the major issues revolve about the effects of labeling and the use of instruments standardized on a white middle-class population with children who, because of ethnic, racial, or socioeconomic differences, lack the background of experiences that would enable them to meet the norms. The controversy relates primarily to the mildly or educable mentally retarded level, where numbers of school-age children from minority groups are disproportionately classified and placed in special education programs (Bickel, 1982; Mac-Millan, 1982). These children are usually not identified until school age when, for the first time, many of them meet and are expected to conform to middle-class norms and culture.

In assessing children in the mild or educable mentally retarded group, school psychologists should draw on a variety of instruments, selecting from each those items and subtests that are most appropriate to answer the referral questions. This requires that they know the advantages and disadvantages of each standardized test, rating scale, or technique for informal assessment for specific children.

Several of the standardized tests of intelligence familiar to most school psychologists may be useful provided they are aware of the limitations and issues discussed in Chapter 1. The Wechsler series provides both verbal and nonverbal measures of intellectual functioning. A selective use of subtests may provide the most appropriate battery for specific children. The Stanford Binet usually provides a reliable assessment of lower functioning children. Again, the selective use of items may increase its utility for some children. Although the Arthur Adaption of the Leiter International Performance Scale has numerous weaknesses in reliability, validity, and standardization, it can provide qualitative information on those children who seem to have difficulty responding verbally. The recently published Kaufman Assessment Battery for Children (K-ABC) includes scales for measuring simultaneous and sequential mental processing abilities and a scale for measuring achievement, thereby including intelligence and achievement scales in one instrument.

Standardized measures of achievement may also help school psychologists in assessing the child's current level of functioning in school subject areas as well as helping them to determine whether there is the severe discrepancy between achievement and level of intelligence that may be indicative of learning disabilities.

In addition to measures of mental or cognitive abilities, measures of adaptive behavior are necessary so that developmental lags may be identified. The American Association on Mental Deficiency Adaptive Behavior Scale (AAMD ABS) devised by Nihira, Foster, Shellhaas, and Leland (1969) is highly recommended for this purpose (MacMillan, 1982). This scale has been standardized on institutionalized and public school populations (Lambert, Windmiller, Tharinger, & Cole, 1981). Grossman (1983) included in an appendix (pp. 203-208) illustrations of the highest level of adaptive behavior functions by chronological age and level of mental retardation, which should be useful for school psychologists in assessing adaptive behavior and in identifying specific areas for educational planning.

There are several other instruments that focus on adaptive and social skills behavior. The Vineland Adaptive Behavior Scale assesses self-help, self-direction, locomotion, occupation, communication, and socialization. The Cain-Levine Social Competency Scale includes scales for self-help, initiative, social skills, and communication.

With children suspected of being mildly mentally retarded, school psychologists must determine whether there is a difference between potential and actual level of functioning so that they might give some suggestions on how the child can be expected to function in the classroom and what can be done to assist the child in making maximum use of abilities.

Moderate Mental Retardation

Children classified in the trainable, severe, or profound categories are more likely to be identified prior to school entrance. Sometimes initial assessment may be done by a clinical, school, developmental, or pediatric psychologist in a medical or clinical setting. The school psychologist will be expected to reevaluate on a periodic basis as indicated in federal, state, or local district guidelines and may be involved in working with the teaching staff on program planning.

To assess children who fall in the moderate or trainable level of mental retardation, a variety of assessment procedures must be used. Because of limited language and speech development, nonverbal tests or nonverbal portions of standardized tests must usually be employed. Subtests of the Wechsler and the Stanford Binet can be useful. The Raven Progressive Matrices is a nonverbal measure that is likely to be useful when it is used in conjunction with other measures of intelligence.

For children with limited ability to communicate, informal assessment, particularly through home and classroom observation, may be the most valuable source of information. For lower functioning groups, developmental rating scales and adaptive rating scales, especially the AAMD ABS, may be particularly useful. Assessment by a speech and language therapist is essential to determine current level of functioning and plan remedial instruction. (See Chapter 11.)

In choosing any instrument, scale, or informal assessment technique, the school psychologist must know the advantages and disadvantages of each of them and select the most appropriate one to answer the referral question and to assist in planning an appropriate educational program. Planning must be done in conjunction with members of other disciplines, because lower functioning children require a multidisciplinary approach for their education and training.

Severe/Profound Mental Retardation

The problems of assessing children who fall within the severe/profound range are similar to and more intensive than those mentioned for the moderate level. In the absence of speech and language, developmental scales must be used. Some that may be helpful include the Gesell Developmental Schedules, the Cattell Infant Intelligence Scale, and the Bayley Scales of Infant Development.

Observation of self-help, social skills, family and peer relations, and general adaptive behavior both in the home and at school are likewise helpful in formulating recommendations for school programs. In working with this group of children, it is essential that the school psychologist function as a member of an interdisciplinary team.

SUMMARY

The wide range of abilities found within the population of children classified as mentally retarded makes it difficult to generalize about either their nature and needs or guidelines for assessment.

For the educable group, school psychologists must be aware of the controversies surrounding labeling and the use of standardized instruments for assessment. Many children at this level of functioning are not considered retarded in settings other than the school and will, as adults, have the potential for making an adequate adjustment as self-supporting, independent citizens. The assessment process should take into account their potential as adults. For the three lower functioning levels there is less optimism for future independent living. Assessment and recommendations for educational programming should focus on maximizing their self-help skills and potentials for functioning as independently as possible within sheltered settings.

REFERENCES

Berdine, W. H., & Cegelka, P. T. (1980). *Teaching the trainable retarded.* Columbus: Charles E. Merrill.

Bickel, W. E. (1982). Classifying mentally retarded students: A review of placement practices in special education. In K. A. Heller, W. H. Holtzman, & S. Messick (Eds.), *Placing children in special education: A strategy for equity.* (pp. 182-229). Washington DC: National Academy Press.

Blackman, J. A. (1983). Perinatal injury. In J. A. Blackman (Ed.), *Medical aspects of developmental disabilities in children birth to three* (pp. 187-195). Iowa City IA: University Hospital School, The University of Iowa.

Cegelka, P. T., & Prehm, H. J. (1982). *Mental retardation: From categories to people.* Columbus: Charles E. Merrill.

Chinn, P. C., Drew, C. J., & Logan, D. R. (1979). *Mental retardation: A life cycle approach.* St. Louis: C. V. Mosby.

Cleland, C. C. (1979). *The profoundly mentally retarded.* Englewood Cliffs NJ: Prentice-Hall.

Dunn, L. M. (1973). *Exceptional children in the schools* (2nd ed.). New York: Holt.

Gearheart, B. R., & Litton, F. W. (1979). *The trainable retarded: A foundations approach.* (2nd ed.). St. Louis: C. V. Mosby.

Grossman, H. J. (Ed.). (1973) *Manual on terminology and classification in mental retardation* (1973 revision). Washington DC: American Association on Mental Deficiency.

Grossman, H. J. (Ed.). (1983). *Classification in mental retardation.* Washington DC: American Association on Mental Deficiency.

Heller, K. A., Holtzman, W. H., & Messick, S. (Eds.). (1982). *Placing children in special education: A strategy for equity.* Washington DC: National Academy Press.

Lambert, N., Windmiller, M., Tharinger, D., & Cole, L. (1981). *AAMD adaptive behavior scale,* (School ed.). Washington DC: American Association on Mental Deficiency.

MacMillan, D. L. (1982). *Mental retardation in school and society.* Boston: Little, Brown.

Mercer, J. R. (1973). *Labeling the mentally retarded.* Berkeley: University of California Press.

Moore, B. C., and Moore, S. M. (1977). *Mental retardation: Causes and prevention.* Columbus: Charles E. Merrill.

Neisworth, J. T., & Smith, R. M. (1978). *Retardation: Issues, assessment and intervention.* New York: McGraw-Hill.

Nihira, K., Foster, R., Shellhaas, M., & Leland, H. (1969). *AAMD Adaptive Behavior Scale.* Washington DC: American Association on Mental Deficiency.

Payne, J. S., Polloway, E. A., Smith, J. E., Jr., & Payne, R. E. (1981). *Strategies for teaching the mentally retarded* (2nd ed.). Columbus: Charles E. Merrill.

Robinson, N. M., & Robinson, H. B. (1976). *The mentally retarded child: A psychological approach* (2nd ed.). New York: McGraw-Hill.

Sarason, S. B., & Doris, J. (1969). *Psychological problems in mental deficiency.* New York: Harper & Row.

Schultz, F. R. (1983a). Fetal alcohol syndrome. In J. A. Blackman (Ed.), *Medical aspects of developmental disabilities in children birth to three* (pp. 109-110). Iowa City: University Hospital School, The University of Iowa.

Schultz, F. R. (1983b). Phenylketonuria and other metabolic diseases. In J. A. Blackman (Ed.), *Medical aspects of developmental disabilities in children birth to three.* (pp. 197-201). Iowa City: University Hospital School, The University of Iowa.

Shonkoff J. (1982). Biological and social factors contributing to mild mental retardation. In K. A. Heller, W. H. Holtzman, & S. Messick, (Eds.), *Placing children in special education: A strategy for equity* (pp. 133-181). Washington DC: National Academy Press.

ADDITIONAL RESOURCES

Birch, J. W. (n.d.). *Mainstreaming: Educable mentally retarded children in regular classes*. Reston VA: The Council for Exceptional Children.

Brown, L. K. (1980). Psychology and mental retardation. In W. M. Cruickshank (Ed.), *Psychology of exceptional children and youth* (4th ed.) (pp. 435-468). Englewood Cliffs NJ: Prentice-Hall.

Farran, D. C., Haskins, R., & Gallagher, J. J. (1980). Poverty and mental retardation: A search for explanations. *Ecology of exceptional children*. San Francisco: Jossey-Bass.

Hutt, M. L., & Gibby, R. G. (1976). *The mentally retarded child: Development, education and treatment*. Boston: Allyn & Bacon.

Jordan, T. E. (1976). *The mentally retarded* (4th ed.). Columbus: Charles E. Merrill.

Mercer, C. D., & Snell, M. E. (1977). *Learning theory research in mental retardation: Implications for teaching*. Columbus: Charles E. Merrill.

Mueller, M. W. (1974). Mental retardation. In M. V. Wisland (Ed.), *Psychoeducational diagnosis of exceptional children* (pp. 102-158). Springfield IL: Charles C Thomas.

Neisworth, J. T., & Smith, R. M. (1978). *Retardation: Issues, assessment and intervention*. New York: McGraw-Hill.

Sellin, D. F. (1979). *Mental retardation: Nature, needs and advocacy*. Boston: Allyn & Bacon.

Snell, M. E., (Ed.). (1983). *Systematic instruction of the moderately and severely handicapped* (2nd ed.). Columbus: Charles E. Merrill.

CHAPTER 6

Learning Disabilities

Eileen Mollen

Learning disabilities is probably the most controversial categorical area in special education today. There is little agreement among professionals in the field concerning definition, etiology, assessment procedures, or remediation. Yet this label accounts for more children being served in special education than any other categorical group. During the 1982-1983 school year, 1,745,865 children, or 3.83% of the total school population, were receiving special education and related services under Public Law 94-142, the Education for All Handicapped Children Act of 1975, and Public Law 89-313 as incorporated in Chapter 1 of the Education Consolidation and Improvement Act of 1981, under the category of "learning disabled" (Kirk & Chalfant, 1984). In a few states, children so labeled account for half or more of all those being served. It is little wonder, then, that increasing concern is appearing in the literature about the large numbers of children in school who are identified as having learning disabilities (see Epps, Ysseldyke, & Algozzine, 1983; Shepard, Smith, & Vojr, 1983; Smith, 1982).

The school psychologist is most often the primary professional concerned with assessment and interpretation of results, coordinating various observations and reports, and determining appropriate recommendations for placement and intervention for children suspected of being learning disabled. In addition, the school psychologist plays a large role in legal and instructional decisions, consults with school personnel and parents, and counsels the learning disabled child with regard to difficulties. Thus, current and applied information on these topics is critical to enable the school psychologist to work effectively with parents, learning disabled children, and professionals on the inter-disciplinary team.

School psychologists are often faced with youngsters who, despite apparently normal intellectual capacity, fail to learn under the prevailing instructional conditions. They hear such phrases as "If he would just apply himself, he could do the work"; "I can't get her to pay attention—she never follows instructions"; or "It's so frustrating. I spend so much time with him. He seems to be trying so hard, but I can't seem to get through to him." How does the school psychologist begin to address these concerns?

The plight of the learning disabled child is complex and puzzling. There are countless myths and theories regarding the field of learning disabilities, and the problems that these children face are far from clearly understood. Much controversy surrounds existing theoretical explanations. However, there is some knowledge and understanding of the characteristics, assessment, and interventions of learning problems that should not be overlooked while theories are being presented, tested, and disputed. School psychologists have a responsibility to sort through the literature and read critically.

For those who feel the need for a stronger background in learning disabilities, a two-part approach is suggested. First, reading two or three basic texts and examining recent journals will provide current theoretical perspectives, legal and educational issues, characteristics of learning disorders, and information about assessment and interventions. The question of how to define learning disabilities is so controversial that reading on the topic can become confusing, with the child getting "lost." For that reason, it is recommended that the school psychologist spend time observing and working with learning disabled children in classrooms, talking with their teachers, and engaging in active hypothesis-testing. An important part of the evaluation of learning disabilities is a knowledge of the levels of academic performance expectations for these children in the classroom.

It is critical for the school psychologist to have a good grasp of normal cognitive development and expected behavior patterns of school-age children in order to determine what could signal a problem. Consider, for example, a child who has persistent difficulty with directionality, reverses letters and words, demonstrates poor motor coordination, or has some articulation problems with "r's" and "l's." A 6-year-old with one or more of these characteristics may simply need a little "maturing time," and thus the symptom would not be cause for alarm, whereas these same characteristics in a 10-year-old might be "red flags" for learning problems; and further evaluation may be warranted.

This chapter will provide an overview of the current definitional issues, characteristics of learning disabled children, assessment techniques, and other areas of concern for these children.

DEFINITIONS

The definitions of learning disabilities vary greatly. Within federal guidelines, each state adopts its own definition and in some instances local school districts determine their own. Section 121a.5 of Public Law 94-142 defines learning disabilities as follows:

> Specific learning disability means a disorder in one or more of the basic psychological processes involved in understanding or in using language, spoken or written, which may manifest itself in an imperfect ability to listen, think, speak, read, write, spell, or to do mathematical calculations. The term includes such conditions as perceptual handicaps, brain injury, minimal brain dysfunction, dyslexia, and developmental aphasia. The term does not include children who have learning problems which are primarily the result of visual, hearing, or motor handicaps, or mental retardation, of emotional disturbance, or of environmental, cultural, or economic disadvantage. (DHEW, 1977a).

The following criteria are designated in Section 121a.541 of P.L. 94-142 for determining the existence of a specific learning disability:

> The child does not achieve commensurate with his or her age and ability levels in one or more of the areas [listed below] when provided with learning experiences appropriate for the child's age and ability levels; and the team (specified in the law) finds that a child has a severe discrepancy between achievement and the intellectual ability in one or more of the following areas: (i) oral expression; (ii) listening comprehension; (iii) written expression; (iv) basic reading skill; (v) reading comprehension; (vi) mathematical calculations; or (vii) mathematical reasoning. (DHEW, 1977b)

Recently, objections to this definition have been raised on the grounds that it does not allow for consensus among professionals. The objections were based on what professionals and parents believed were inadequate inclusion and exclusion clauses, resulting in confusion regarding eligibility criteria (cf. Myers & Hammill, 1982). In response to this general criticism, the National Joint Council for Learning Disabilities presented a new definition:

> Learning disability is a generic term that refers to a heterogeneous group of disorders manifested by significant difficulties in the acquisition and use of listening, speaking, reading, writing, reasoning, or mathematical abilities. These disorders are intrinsic to the individual and presumed to be due to central nervous system dysfunction. Even though a learn-

ing disability may occur concomitantly with other handicapping conditions (e.g., sensory impairment, mental retardation, social and emotional disturbance) or environmental influences (e.g., cultural differences, insufficient/inappropriate instruction, psychogenic factors), it is not the direct result of those conditions or influences. (Hammill, Leigh, McNutt, & Larsen, 1981, pp. 339-340.)

Learning disabilities are considered by some professionals to be due to central nervous system (CNS) dysfunction, which may be caused by genetic or biochemical factors (usually present at birth) or trauma. However, the exact etiological agent of the learning disability can rarely be identified, and the state of the art in pediatric neurology is not sufficiently sophisticated to pinpoint specific areas of damage in the brain that could account for the learning disorder. In the vast majority of cases, evidence of CNS dysfunction is deduced from one or more soft neurological signs that are inconclusive and add little information of value to the process of assessment or to the determination of an appropriate placement and development of an educational plan to remediate the learning problem. For educational purposes, this information is not critical; etiology does not generally dictate the mode of intervention in the classroom unless a specific biochemical cause is involved. Instead, educational intervention addresses the behavioral manifestations of the learning problem. (See Kirk & Chalfant, 1984.)

Many children currently labeled as learning disabled experience school failure and achievement deficits that can be attributed to factors other than neurological or biochemical factors. Poor instruction, lack of motivation, inconsistent school attendance, family problems, and emotional difficulties frequently contribute to poor school performance. Test scores alone do not reveal the cause of an achievement deficit. School psychologists need to probe for all possible explanations for school failure before the label of learning disabled is applied.

Given the growing concerns over the alarmingly high number of children who are classified as learning disabled, care must be taken for appropriate special education classification. While the currently used definitions for learning disabilities are not ideal, clearly delineated inclusion criteria must be followed before a learning disabilities classification is made for any child. Two recent studies have identified some of the problems in this area. Using 14 operational definitions from the professional literature grouped into the categories of ability-achievement discrepancy, grade placement-achievement discrepancy, and scatter, Epps, Ysseldyke, and Algozzine (1983) found that the application of different definitions of learning disabilities did produce differences that were significant in the numbers of children identified. Further, the three categories of definitions did not distinguish consistently between children identified as learning disabled and those not learning disabled. A study by Shepard, Smith, and Vojr (1983), designed to describe the characteristics of children who had been classified as learning disabled by school personnel, found that over half of the children identified were classified using criteria that were not consistent with federal regulations and professional literature. A large number of children who are failing in school due to causes other than those outlined in the federal guidelines are being labeled "learning disabled." School psychologists need to be aware of the growing concerns about definitions and misclassification resulting in over-inclusion of children in the learning disabilities category.

CHARACTERISTICS OF LEARNING DISABLED CHILDREN

As the definitions outline, the learning disabled child may experience impairment in one or more areas of cognitive functioning. These can be organized into five global areas: spoken language (including listening and speaking), written language, reading, arithmetic, and reasoning.

Spoken Language

Disorders of spoken language involve either delay or deviation from the expected pattern of language development; they include a wide range of communication disorders. There is increasing evidence that language dysfunction is a prevalent and debilitating area of learning disabilities. Consider how important communication is to everyday functioning. The child who is unable to process language is extremely handicapped in school and at home. Language dysfunction can be characterized by disorders of formulation as well as understanding of language. The child with auditory processing problems hears, but does not integrate or interpret what is heard so that it is useful or meaningful. Symptoms can range from difficulty in following directions to inability to organize the retelling of a story. Language disorders can be very specific or global, and they should be explored thoroughly. A language specialist is a valuable member of the assessment team for the child with language disorders. The reader is referred to Johnson and Myklebust (1967) for a description of the broad range of spoken language dysfunctions and their remediation.

Written Language

Written language requires the integration of a number of complex abilities: encoding, oral language, visual perception, motor control, organization of ideas, memory, and discrimination. Johnson and

Myklebust (1967) described three categories of written language disorders. Poor visual-motor integration can result in the inability to copy letters, words, or numbers. Deficits in visual memory can result in the inability to revisualize words or letters, although the individual may be able to read and copy. The child with a deficiency in formulation and syntax can copy and revisualize words, but has difficulty with organization of thoughts into meaningful written communication. This child typically speaks in a more meaningful way than he or she writes.

Reading

Reading disability is characterized by the failure to learn to read under normal teaching conditions. Dyslexia, or reading disability, can result from impairment in the visual or auditory modes, and remediation is typically implemented to circumvent the area of dysfunction and to make use of the mode that is most effective for the child (Vellutino, 1980). Because conventional teaching techniques usually have not been effective for these children, a specific reading curriculum designed to meet the needs of the individual must be implemented. Lerner (1981) has provided an overview of reading disability and described both the reading techniques typically used in classrooms and special remedial approaches to teaching reading.

Modification of the child's daily reading program may range from minor support by the classroom teacher to alternative methods of reading instruction. Commonly used approaches to teaching reading (e.g., phonics, linguistics, language-experience approach, individualized reading, linguistics, and the initial teaching alphabet) can be effectively modified to enable many learning disabled children to read. Some of the alternative approaches that have proved successful for many children and adults with reading disabilities include the Gillingham method (Orton, 1966), a highly structured phonics approach; the Fernald technique (Fernald, 1943), a multisensory approach; and Glass Analysis (Glass, 1973), a method of decoding letter clusters within words.

Mathematics

Children who have difficulty with spatial concepts or quantitative thinking may have a specific learning disability in the area of mathematics. Mathematics is a symbolic language involving arithmetic calculation and numerical reasoning. Impairment may occur in either of these areas of mathematics. Dysfunction in any one of a number of skill areas can contribute to poor mathematical functioning. Children with impaired spatial relationships or difficulty with visual perception, symbolic representation, or memory are at risk for difficulty in achievement in this area. While arithmetic may be the only area of disability for some children, the problems of symbolic reasoning and/or memory experienced by many learning disabled children sometimes result in an impairment in mathematical functioning. See Lerner (1981) for a discussion of these disorders and remediation techniques.

Reasoning

Although there has been little definitive research on disorders of reasoning, the behaviors that are characteristic of many learning disabled children warrant the inclusion of this "catch-all" category. A list of behaviors that suggest processing disorders is provided here to outline some of the areas of concern.

1. Concrete behavior characterized by a dependence upon immediate experience as opposed to abstract behavior that transcends any given immediate experience and results in the formation of conceptual categories.
2. Poorly differentiated, unstable, and inconsistent generalizations.
3. Little differentiation of part-whole relationships.
4. Either passive-apathetic (curious about nothing) or hyperactive, driven, impulsive (curious about everything) behavior.
5. Poor short-term or long-term retention.
6. Either a marked lack in persistence or compulsive perseveration.
7. Field dependence as opposed to field independence.
8. Internally controlled versus externally controlled behavior.
9. Rigidity; resistance to change.
   (Myers & Hammill, 1982, pp. 39-40)

In addition, speed of processing is another area of concern to those who work with learning disabled children. A child who is extremely slow in processing information may have academic difficulty. It appears that this is an area which may interfere with school performance for some learning disabled children.

Correlates of Learning Disabilities

Parents and teachers are often concerned about additional characteristics that are frequently observed in learning disabled children. Perceptual and motor dysfunction, hyperactivity, and attention deficits are commonly associated with learning disabilities. However, it must be noted that, although these are often correlates of learning disabilities and can serve as diagnostic indicators, they are not causes of the learning dysfunctions that children experience (Myers & Hammill, 1982).

Professionals in the field of learning disabilities now acknowledge that remediation of perceptual disorders and motor performance alone will not alleviate the learning problem (Kirk & Chalfant, 1984). If a child is dyslexic, then remediation should be geared directly to the reading problem. For the child who is hyperactive, behavioral interventions, and in some cases medication, may reduce the child's activity level and increase the attention span, but the underlying learning problem remains. However, the child may become more accessible to instruction, and remediation attempts will usually be more effective when the hyperactivity and distractibility are controlled.

ASSESSMENT

One of the most important areas of concern in respect to learning disabled children is that of assessment (McLoughlin & Lewis, 1981). For the child with academic achievement problems, the quality of the school experience may depend on the sensitivity, thoroughness, and classroom applicability of the assessment process. Psychoeducational diagnosis facilitates educational and behavioral programming for the learning disabled child.

Test Selection

Test selection involves a number of factors. The school psychologist must consider the purpose of the instrument in relation to the needs of the child. The tests should be chosen to answer the specific questions that have been raised about the learning characteristics of the individual child.

Prior to the use of any test, the school psychologist must establish whether or not the validity and reliability coefficients of the selected measure are strong (Salvia & Ysseldyke, 1981). If the data suggest that the test is not valid or that the reliability is poor or unknown, then regardless of face validity the test should be used cautiously and with these limitations clearly in mind. It is also important to identify the population on which the instrument was standardized. If the norming group is significantly different from the individual to be tested, the results may not be valid for that particular child. Again, if such an instrument is used, interpretation of the results should be made very carefully in light of the standardization limitations.

Discriminating test selection is necessary to clarify the atypical learning characteristics of the learning disabled child. Salvia and Ysseldyke (1981) have provided a comprehensive review of test theory and application for special education with an in-depth discussion of the test considerations mentioned here.

Documenting Ability Achievement Discrepancies

School psychologists should employ a number of individually administered assessment measures to pinpoint problem areas for the learning disabled child and to recommend appropriate educational interventions (Sattler, 1982). These measures frequently include standardized aptitude and achievement tests. The administration of both a measure of intellectual ability and a measure of achievement documents the existence of a severe discrepancy between expected developmental level and actual performance in certain areas of cognitive functioning as required in the federal guidelines.

In an attempt to arrive at a procedure for calculating the discrepancy between achievement and intellectual ability, numerous alternatives are suggested in the literature. The use of each alternative with any one child would undoubtedly result in variations in identifying or not identifying the child as learning disabled. Epps, et al. (1983) used 14 operational definitions selected from the literature for their study of how the application of different definitions was related to numbers of pupils identified. The definitions were divided into three groupings: ability-achievement discrepancy, which included the 1976 federal formula, three variations of the 1977 federal definition using increasing discrepancy differences, and two formulae proposed in the literature: grade placement-achievement discrepancy, which included four increasingly lower limits of the pupil's standard scores on academic achievement measures without taking into consideration results of tests of intellectual ability; and four forms of scatter in performance on the WISC-R Verbal-Performance Scale. Their conclusion was that "learning disabilities is an ill-defined disorder with too little consistency among definitions to allow for reliable prediction of LD classification" (p. 350) (See Kaufman, 1979).

Shepard (1983) viewed the problem of how discrepancy is typically assessed as being more serious than which formula to use. In her studies of learning disabled children in Colorado, she found that many professionals, both school psychologists and teachers of pupils with learning disabilities, had limited knowledge of what constitutes technically adequate tests and frequently selected inadequate tests even when more valid instruments were available. In addition, they had limited knowledge of the range of statistically normal variations in the typical classroom.

In light of current controversies about procedures to be employed for identification, school psychologists are advised to be selective about instruments to be employed in the assessment process; to be knowledgeable about what definitions and policies are mandated or recommended in their respective state and local districts for determining the label of learning disabled and to be aware of limitations in these definitions; and to know what constitutes the range of normality in the typical classroom. In reality, the main concern should be to determine what a particular child needs and what is available in the school system to meet those needs.

School psychologists should be aware that most achievement tests rely heavily on reading ability and speed of performance, one or both of which may be the child's problem area. This may mask or accentuate the discrepancy between aptitude and achievement, since the task demands are often similar to those on the performance indicators.

Informal Assessment

The school psychologist should also assess the child's performance in academics informally. This may be accomplished through interviews with the teacher(s) about the curricular expectations for that particular classroom; examination of the child's written work in comparison with the expectations for that classroom, group of pupils, and teacher; and observation of the child's academic functioning. Informal assessment, particularly through classroom observation, provides important information concerning how a child functions within the classroom setting as contrasted with the one-to-one interaction during an assessment. The school psychologist should observe how the child follows directions, the quality and quantity of on-task behavior, circumstances surrounding distractibility, particular behaviors that are outside the classroom norm, the child's learning style, and social interactions both with adults and peers. Classroom observations also provide the school psychologist with a realistic framework within which to make recommendations that are consistent with the curriculum and expectations of the school. Since the child must function within the approved curriculum of the school, the school psychologist can be of greatest assistance to the teacher if he or she knows the curriculum and can make a curriculum-based assessment of the child's problems (see Chapter 3).

Other Diagnostic Tests

Because many learning disability problems are related to deficiencies in academic areas, diagnostic tests in reading and arithmetic may shed additional light on specific problems (Swanson & Watson, 1982). The school psychologist may also want to include measures of perceptual-motor function, personality and emotional adjustment measures, language function tests, or other tests designed to address specific areas of cognitive functioning that may be problematic for the child.

Each instrument selected for the assessment process should be designed to measure some specific area(s) of cognitive functioning. School psychologists should familiarize themselves with the purpose of each test and how it measures the designated performance area(s). It must be determined whether the test is heavily dependent upon verbal response, whether success requires integration of auditory and/or visual information, or whether the test is a power or speed test. School psychologists must determine whether the child fails to perform well on some of these tests because of lack of ability, or because the manner of presentation (or task demand) taps an area of the child's weakness that is indicative of a disability. Knowledge about the format of each test will allow the school psychologist to pinpoint the child's strengths and weaknesses with greater precision and confidence.

If the child has a language problem, the school psychologist may need to consult with the school's speech and language pathologist about appropriate assessment instruments for this area or refer the child to this specialist for more intensive assessment (see Chapter 11).

Trial Teaching

A useful method for determining how a child learns is to try to teach the child something. (Cruickshank, Morse & Johns, 1980). Trial teaching is an informal assessment technique that allows the examiner to monitor and, if necessary, modify the task in order to optimize learning (see Chapter 2). In this way, the psychologist can not only identify modes of presentation that appear not to work for a particular child, but also can begin to make suggestions for curriculum implementation based on modifications that are effective.

Interpreting and Reporting Test Results

The information gained from standardized and informal measures represents only part of the evaluation process for the learning disabled child. It is also necessary to integrate this knowledge about the child's learning characteristics into the individual curriculum plan. Specifically, it is the responsibility of the school psychologist to interpret the results of testing to the child's parents and teachers in such a way that reasonable curriculum adjustments can be established.

A frequent complaint among personnel who either have chosen to work with learning disabled children or have been assigned a child with learning disabilities is that test reports have no applied merit and are frequently filled with jargon, making them difficult to interpret by those working directly with the child. It is not sufficient to identify a learning disabled child; appropriate intervention techniques must also be recommended.

These intervention techniques are not necessarily the sole responsibility of the school psychologist. Ongoing dialogue with teachers and parents regarding the child's learning characteristics and what has worked (or failed to work) for the child in the past will prove invaluable for educational planning.

Equally important to this dialogue among professionals and parents is the sharing of observations about the child's functioning in various settings. These observations should include not only what the child produces but how the child approaches a task. Following are some sample questions to guide the observation of learner characteristics:

1. Does the child approach tasks in an impulsive manner?
2. Does the child's work seem logical and sequential, or is the approach to tasks disorganized and inefficient?
3. Does the child often need instructions or information repeated or rephrased?
4. Is the child easily distracted or able to focus on the task despite extraneous noise and visual input?
5. Does the child appear to process information or produce work much more slowly than would be expected?
6. Does the child exhibit evidence of frustration, lack of motivation, or anxiety when faced with difficult tasks?
7. Does the child appear to have intact sensory modalities?
8. Does one sensory modality appear to process information more or less efficiently than any other?
9. Does the child seem easily confused or lost?
10. Does the child appear to exhibit excessive activity compared with others of similar age?

OTHER AREAS OF CONCERN IN ASSESSMENT

Sensory Impairment

One step in the assessment process that is often overlooked, but that is critical to diagnostic outcome, is the evaluation of a child's hearing and vision. Deficits in sensory functioning can interfere with the learning process. The hearing and vision screening tests routinely administered in schools are not sensitive to all the factors that may contribute to learning problems. The existence of a sensory impairment should be ruled out at the beginning of the evaluation process. It is important not to overlook so obvious an explanation for learning problems. It is unnecessary, as well as unethical, to subject a child to extensive psychological testing when the explanation for those problems is a hearing loss or a visual problem such a far-sightedness.

The child may exhibit specific behaviors that signal the possibility of a sensory impairment, indicating the need for a thorough evaluation by a vision specialist or an audiologist. Children who have difficulty learning may favor one ear for listening, frequently ask for repetition of verbal messages, speak with poor articulation (indicating that they do not hear the sounds they must reproduce), or appear to ignore questions or statements directed to them. (See Chapter 9.) Similarly, children with visual problems may favor one eye or squint, appear to use poor visual-motor integration, and/or rub their eyes or blink frequently. (See Chapter 10.)

Occasionally a child who is referred for learning problems is found to perform poorly on tasks that require visual-motor integration. This poorly understood dysfunction is frequently considered to be a neurological impairment, but it can also result from inefficient use of the eyes or a mechanical dysfunction of vision, sometimes one that is correctable by glasses or by eye exercises up to certain ages.

The existence of a sensory impairment does not rule out other factors that contribute to learning problems. The complex nature of learning disabilities requires exploration of any areas of dysfunction that seem related to the child's learning problems.

Behavioral and Emotional Problems

Children with learning problems often experience considerable feelings of failure, frustration, and embarrassment as a result of their lack of achievement. The inability to perform tasks that appear effortless for others can be devastating to the emotional growth of these children. In addition to (or possibly as a result of) their cognitive processing difficulties, many learning disabled children exhibit poor social interaction skills and misperceive social situations.

As task demands and academic performance expectations increase with each year of schooling, a child's learning disabilities become increasingly handicapping. Adolescence is a particularly difficult period for the learning disabled student. The consequences of the disabilities are more apparent, schoolwork is a struggle, and relationships may be strained during this time when youngsters are so sensitive about conformity and success. (Cruickshank, et al., 1980).

Behavior problems and poor self-concept are common reactions to ongoing frustrations and confusion. An emotional overlay often accompanies learning disorders, and it is often impossible to identify which problem occurred first. As a result, intervention becomes complex. Educational planning must address the whole child, including both academic and emotional needs.

Some children employ coping mechanisms or strategies to compensate for their learning difficulties. These techniques can range from appropriate (e.g., asking for clarification) to inappropriate (e.g., acting-out behavior to avoid a difficult task) and from skillful to ineffective use of strategies to achieve success. Through observation, the school psychologist and teacher can determine which strategy (or strategies) the child may already employ and whether or not they are effective and efficient. See Chapter 7 for additional information regarding emotional problems.

SUMMARY

The heterogeneous nature of the learning disabled population requires that each child's assessment be individually designed and implemented. Careful selection of test materials is required to answer the referral question about the learner. Assessment is the process by which the school psychologist uses observation, interaction with teachers, standardized testing, and informal assessment measures to describe learner characteristics, not only for identification of learning disabilities but also for appropriate academic planning. Critical to this process is talking with affected children about their own learning problems, how they compensate, what works for them, and what is frustrating for them. School psychologists draw on their own experiences and knowledge of assessment and learning disabilities to determine the best educational program for each child.

The role of the school psychologist goes beyond the assessment of learning disabilities. Responsibility includes information-sharing and problem-solving with other education personnel, sharing information with parents, counseling children with learning problems, and coordinating services for each youngster.

REFERENCES

Cruickshank, W. M., Morse, W. C., & Johns, J. K. (1980). *Learning disabilities: The struggle from adolescence toward adulthood.* Syracuse: Syracuse University Press.

DHEW. (1977a, August 23). Education of handicapped children. Part II. *Federal Register.*

DHEW. (1977b, December 29). Assistance to states for education of handicapped children: Procedures for evaluating specific learning disabilities. Part III. *Federal Register.*

Epps, S., Ysseldyke, J. E., & Algozzine, B. (1983). Impact of different definitions of learning disabilities on the number of students identified. *Journal of Psychoeducational Assessement, 1,* 341-352.

Fernald, G. (1943). *Remedial techniques in basic school subjects.* New York: McGraw-Hill.

Glass, G. (1973). *Teaching decoding as separate from reading.* Garden City NY: Adelphi University Press.

Hammill, D. D., Leigh, J., McNutt, G., & Larsen, S. (1981). A new definition of learning disabilities. *The Learning Disability Quarterly, 4,* 339-340.

Johnson, D. J., and Mykelbust, H. R. (1967). *Learning disabilities: Educational principles and practices.* New York: Grune & Stratton.

Kaufman, A. S. (1979). *Intelligent testing with the WISC-R.* New York: Wiley.

Kirk, S. A., & Chalfant, J. C. (1984). *Academic and developmental learning disabilities.* Denver: Love Publishing Co.

Lerner, J. (1981). *Learning disabilities: Theories, diagnosis, and teaching strategies.* Boston: Houghton Mifflin.

McLoughlin, J. A., & Lewis, R. B. (1981). *Assessing special students.* Columbus: Charles E. Merrill.

Myers, P., & Hammill, D. D. (1982). *Learning disabilities: Basic concepts, assessment practices, and intervention strategies.* Austin TX: Pro-Ed.

Orton, J. (1966). The Orton-Gillingham approach. In J. Money (Ed.), *The disabled reader* (pp. 119-146). Baltimore: Houghton Mifflin.

Salvia, J. & Ysseldyke, J.E. (1981). *Assessment in special and remedial education* (2nd ed.). Boston: Houghton Mifflin.

Sattler, J. M. (1982). *Assessment of children's intelligence and special abilities.* Boston: Allyn & Bacon.

Shepard, L. (1983, Fall). The role of measurement in educational policy: Lessons from the identification of learning disabilities. *Educational Measurement Issues and Practices, 2,* 4-8.

Shepard, L. A., Smith, M. L., & Vojr, C. P. (1983). Characteristics of pupils identified as learning disabled. *American Educational Research Journal, 20,* 309-331.

Smith, M. L. (1982). *How educators decide who is learning disabled: Challenge to psychology and public policy in the schools.* Springfield IL: Charles C Thomas.

Swanson, H. L., & Watson, B. L. (1982). *Educational and psychological assessment of exceptional children: Theories, strategies, and applications.* St. Louis: C. V. Mosby.

Vellutino, F.R. (1980). *Dyslexia: Theory and research.* Cambridge: The MIT Press.

ADDITIONAL RESOURCES

Bryan, T. H., & Bryan, J. H. (1978). *Understanding learning disabilities.* Palo Alto: Mayfield.

Cruickshank, W. M., & Paul, J. I. (1980). The psychological characteristics of children with learning disabilities. In W. M. Cruickshank (Ed.), *Psychology of exceptional children and youth* (4th ed.) (pp. 497-541). Englewood Cliffs NJ: Prentice-Hall.

Gerber, A. & Bryen, D. N. (1981). *Language and learning disabilities.* Baltimore: University Park Press.

Goodman, L., & Mann, L. (1976). *Learning disabilities in the secondary schools: Issues and practices.* New York: Grune & Stratton.

Horvath, M. J., Kass, C. E., & Ferrell, W. E. (1980). An example of the use of fuzzy set concepts in modeling learning disability. *American Educational Research Journal, 17,* 309-324.

Pennington, B. (1982). Assessment of learning disabilities in preschool children. In G. Ulrey & S. J. Rogers, (Eds.), *Psychological assessment of handicapped infants and young children* (pp. 135-141). New York: Thieme-Stratton.

Smith, C. R. (1983). *Learning disabilities: The interaction of learner, task, and setting.* Boston: Little, Brown.

Ysseldyke, J. E., Algozzine, B., Richey, L., & Garden, J. (1982). Declaring students eligible for learning disability services: Why bother with the data? *Learning Disability Quarterly, 5,* 37-44.

Zigmond, N., Vallecorsa, A., & Silverman, R. (1983). *Assessment for instructional planning in special education.* Englewood Cliffs NJ: Prentice-Hall.

CHAPTER 7

The Emotionally Disturbed

Robin L. Brown

According to the National Enrollment Statistics 1982–1983 from the U.S. Department of Education, pupils labeled as *Emotionally Disturbed* accounted for about one-fifth of those receiving special education and related services under Public Law 94-142, the Education for All Handicapped Children Act of 1975, and Public Law 89-313, as incorporated in Chapter 1 of the Education Consolidation and Improvement Act of 1984. Although fewer in number than pupils with learning disabilities and mental impairments, the pupils discussed in this chapter share some common characteristics with these two groups that complicate the task for the school psychologists who must make a differential diagnosis in order to obtain services for them.

One major problem lies in the label to be used for these pupils. There is great variability in terminology among the states. Of the 50 states, 16 use *seriously emotionally disturbed* or *emotionally disturbed*, and an additional 10 substitute the terms *handicapped* or *impaired* for *disturbed;* 13 states use *behavior,* usually in combination with *disorder,* and 5 use *social,* usually in combination with *emotional* (NASDSE, 1983). In the absence of a uniform term, this chapter will use the terms *emotionally disturbed* and *emotionally impaired* interchangeably. School psychologists should become familiar with the terms used in their particular states.

Another major problem is the lack of consensus regarding elements in an effective program for these pupils. Following an extensive review of the literature, Grosenick and Huntze (1983) concluded that "the literature is not reflective of well-conceptualized programs" but is "stronger in reflecting programming strategies" (p. 20). This issue may be related to the problems of terminology.

Finally, this categorical area shares with the areas of learning disabilities and mental retardation, issues regarding definition. This is discussed in the following section.

The purpose of this chapter is to acquaint the school psychologist with the nature and needs of the emotionally disturbed child. The aim is not to present a definitive or exhaustive review of the wide array of issues, but rather to focus on those that have implications for the assessment process.

The chapter is divided into three major sections. The first section is an overview of definitions and classification systems, the second section discusses special considerations in the assessment process, and the final section reviews some issues related to programming.

OVERVIEW

Definitions

Emotional disturbance is one of the more difficult categories in special education to define. Although there have been many attempts, as yet there is no "official" or widely accepted definition (Reeve and Kauffman, 1978). One reason for this lack of agreement is that there are numerous unresolved problem areas:

1. The lack of instruments that measure personality, adjustment, or other such constructs precisely or that are sufficiently reliable to provide a valid basis for defining emotional disturbances.

2. The wide variety of conceptual models that exist within psychology and education, each of which views and defines emotional disturbance somewhat differently.

3. The inclusion of both excesses and deficits, unlike other categories in which the child needs special services because of either falling below average (e.g., visually impaired) or above average (e.g., gifted) on some quantitative dimension, and the existence of behaviors that cover a wide range of nearly infinite variety and combinations.

4. The expectations of appropriate behavior that vary among different social and cultural groups and from setting to setting, making it difficult to judge whether or not a child's behavior is disturbed.

5. The often transient nature of behavior problems and the manifestation of the same behaviors by "normal" children at some time during their development.

6. The wide variety of social agencies that deal with emotional disturbances, each one using a specific prescribed definition to determine eligibility for their service and thereby making it difficult to establish a definition that is useful to all (e.g., courts, clinics, schools, families).

Despite these problems a number of definitions are in current use by professionals, often reflecting a particular theoretical orientation or serving a particular purpose. For example, one definition from the psychodynamic orientation is:

Impairment of emotional growth during some stage of development with the resultant distrust toward self and others and hostility generated from anxiety. (Moustakas, 1953, p. 19)

Another definition from the behavioral perspective is:

Disorders that consist of inadequate or inappropriate behavior which is learned and can therefore be changed through application of learning procedures. (Dupont, 1969, p. 6)

The ecological orientation offers yet another definition:

Behavioral disorders are defined as a variety of excessive, chronic behaviors which violate the perceiver's expectations of appropriateness and which the perceiver wishes to see stopped. (Graubard, 1973, p. 246)

Some definitions offer descriptions of behaviors or characteristics of emotionally disturbed children. For instance, Bower (1969) offered a definition that emphasizes behaviors seen in the classroom. He characterized the emotionally disturbed child as one who exhibits one or more of the following five characteristics to a marked extent over a period of time:

1. An inability to learn which cannot be explained by intellectual, sensory, neuropsychological, or general health factors.
2. An inability to build or maintain satisfactory interpersonal relationships with peers and teachers.
3. Inappropriate or immature types of behaviors or feelings under normal conditions.
4. A general pervasive mood of unhappiness or depression.
5. A tendency to develop physical symptoms, pains, or fears associated with personal or school problems. (p. 22–23)

This definition became the prototype for the definition included in P.L. 94-142.

Ross (1974) provided a definition that emphasizes behaviors in relation to social norms and adult judgments of the frequency and the intensity of these behaviors:

> A psychological disorder is present when a child emits behavior that deviates from a discretionary and relative social norm and that occurs with a frequency and intensity that authoritative adults in the child's environment judge, under the circumstances, to be either too high or too low. (p. 14)

The definitions offered by Bower, Graubard, and Ross have many strong points; however, each has a significant weakness that without correction renders the definition of little use in educational programming. Bower's definition provides clear, to-the-point descriptions of behaviors relevant to education, but it does not include any reference to social norms. Thus, Bower has failed to recognize the variety of acceptable behaviors among social and cultural groups. Ross and Graubard have not included any mention of the child's own perception of his or her behavior. Graubard has also neglected problems resulting from a lack of appropriate behaviors or deficiencies, mentioning only excessive behaviors.

Defining emotional impairment is thus not a simple matter. Many who work with children question the necessity of placing so much emphasis on establishing a definition. They are often heard to say (as is evident from the definitions mentioned here) that it is obvious which children are disturbed and the problem of definition is only a semantic one. However, this statement is tantamount to saying that the emotionally disturbed child is one who is so labeled by adults who have authority. As Kauffman (1977) pointed out, this leaves the answer to the question of what is emotional impairment open to chance: who is considering the questions and that individual's tolerance for behavioral differences. Since definitions are used to identify those children about whom we are concerned, they are too important to be left to such subjective judgments.

Definitions of emotional impairment reflect the way in which the problem is conceptualized—the orientation one has toward its nature and origin. This in turn influences what types of interventions will be considered. Definitions also specify the population to be served and influence the determination of who receives the interventions.

Legislative, administrative, and funding decisions and the training and employment of personnel are all guided by the definitions in use (Kauffman, 1977). Therefore, the issue of defining emotional impairment is an important one.

Classification Systems

Classification systems have been developed in an attempt to overcome one of the major problems in establishing a broad definition of emotional impairment—the wide variety of behaviors and levels of severity found among the affected children. These systems are based on the notion that similarities exist despite the variety of characteristics among emotionally disturbed children. These similarities are used as a basis for classification of emotionally disturbed children into subgroups. Classification is a common practice, the rationale for its use being that by placing a child into a subgroup, statements can be made about the nature of the child's difficulties and needs that are useful to professionals. Placement in a particular subgroup allows prediction of the child's response to various interventions and aids in treatment planning.

Various systems of classification have been developed for emotionally impaired children, but most are psychiatrically oriented and have little relevance for education. An approach to classification that has been identified as useful in educational settings is the *factor analytic* or *dimensional* approach (Hobbs, 1975). This approach involves identifying behavioral groups consisting of highly intercorrelated behaviors.

Categories of Behavior Traits

One such dimensional system was developed by Quay (1979). Quay's system is useful because most of the characteristics are described in behavioral terms and can therefore be useful in assessment. Quay identified four clusters or categories of behavior traits: conduct disorder, personality disorder, immaturity cluster, and socialized delinquency.

Conduct Disorder. The conduct disorder group is comprised of children who are generally described as aggressive and who exhibit behaviors seen as disturbing. Frequently found characteristics describing conduct disorders are:

fighting, assaultiveness	irresponsibility
disobedience, defiance	bossiness, bullying
destructiveness	boisterousness, noisiness
temper tantrums	attention-seeking
impertinence	verbal abusiveness
disruptiveness	untrustworthiness, lying, stealing

Personality Disorder. Children in the personality disorder group are withdrawn and socially isolated. Characteristics frequently found in these children are those associated with feelings of inferiority:

anxiety	crying, infrequent smiling
shyness	reticence, secretiveness
social withdrawal	lack of self-confidence
self-consciousness	unhappiness, chronic sadness
hypersensitivity, being easily hurt	

Immaturity. The third cluster, immaturity, includes children who have a poorly developed behavioral repertoire and difficulty coping with environmental demands. Behaviors commonly seen among these children are:

short attention span	passivity, lack of initiative
poor concentration	boredom, disinterest
daydreaming	preference for younger playmates
clumsiness	sluggishness, drowsiness
preoccupation	lack of perserverance, failure to finish things
messiness, sloppiness	

Socialized Delinquency. Socialized delinquency is related to juvenile delinquency, and it includes children whose behavior has been developed in response to environmental circumstances rather than to personal distress. Often in the context of the social structure in which they are found, these behaviors are not clearly maladaptive. Characteristics frequently found to be associated with this cluster are:

having "bad" companions	truancy from school
engaging in cooperative stealing	staying out late at night
loyalty to delinquent groups	running away from home
membership in a gang	defiance of authority

Although each group has a number of behaviors commonly associated with it, not all of them are present in any one emotionally impaired child. Usually a combination of three or four from a category are present. There are also situations in which a child may exhibit behaviors from more than one of these categories. Quay's system appears to be valid and it is useful to school psychologists in identifying emotional impairment and organizing problem behaviors in a meaningful way (Quay, 1972). However, this system is descriptive, it does not provide a basis for psychological or educational intervention (Kauffman, 1977).

Morse's Subcategories of Emotional Impairment

The classification system developed by Morse (1979) postulates four subcategories of emotional impairment: reactive disorders, neurotic disorders, inadequate socialization, and psychotic disorders.

Reactive Disorders. Reactive disorders are those involving a conflict between the child and the environment; that is, the conflict is mostly external and precipitating conditions can be identified. With the occurrence of a stressful event or situation, the child's social support system breaks down and the child becomes unable to cope adequately with the situation. These children become depressed, regress, suffer losses of self-esteem, and often act out or strike out in frustration. Although these children often are unable to do their school work, the precipitating condition is usually not related to school, but rather is in the general life situation. Reactive behavior problems are temporary and not a pattern of behavior; thus the prognosis is highly favorable. With intervention, the behavior can be prevented from becoming an established pattern.

Neurotic Disorders. Neurotic disorders are those involving a conflict between the child's impulses and controls. The conflict is an internal one brought about by a clash between the child's needs and desires and what he or she has been taught is right or wrong. The child often experiences a great deal of guilt and anxiety over these needs and desires, which results in very low self-esteem. In addition, there are often problems concerning such feelings as acceptance-rejection, love, fear, anger, despair, and hope. It is common for such children to blame themselves for conditions beyond their control (e.g., parental divorce). Although these children know what behavior is appropriate, they lack the skills to carry it out. Often they continue to test situations and people. Common patterns of behavior among this group are acting out in ways that are destructive to persons and property; self-defeating actions; depression, sometimes to the extent of doing bodily harm to themselves; psychosomatic symptoms; and passive-aggressive acts.

Lowered school achievement and poor social relationships are also frequently present.

Inadequate Socialization. Those children who are inadequately socialized are a social management problem in school primarily because of their aggressive and/or destructive behavior. This group of children is involved in conflicts with authority and social requirements. The means they have developed to deal with these conflicts have become inflexible. While the children with reactive disorders or neurotic disorders suffer anguish over their conflicts, these children, because they lack an appropriate set of internalized values, do not. When anxiety is present, it is often related to the possibility of apprehension and punishment rather than guilt. Typically such children lack empathy or any recognition of other's rights and feelings, and they tend to be self-serving in their behavior. The type of behavior seen in such children varies with the severity of the impairment.

Children with milder inadequate socialization disorders are those whose social development is arrested at a primitive level. Typically they are unkempt, impulsive, and immature; they accomplish very little school work, and they often produce hostile, rejecting responses from others. These children have generally been neglected by their parents, which has resulted in a lack of love, care, or attention, and lack of exposure to reasonable, age-appropriate social-behavioral expectations. In the more severely disturbed children there is much more impulsivity as well as violence, aggression, and defiance. They often are truant, steal, and travel in gangs. Frequently they crave excitement, and in seeking it they engage in random aggression and assault upon others. Basically, these children lack identification with an appropriate adult model, and in extreme cases they have no capacity to form meaningful interpersonal relationships. Unlike the behavior problems observed with reactive and neurotic disorders, those seen with inadequate socialization disorder have much persistence and depth and require more intense interventions.

Psychotic Disorders. Children in the psychotic group are the most seriously impaired. They are not always able to differentiate their fantasies from actual events, and thus may distort or misperceive reality. Often they do not know who they are or where they are and do not relate to people appropriately. In addition, they have many communication difficulties and fail to learn as other children do. Two subgroups exist within the psychotic group. One includes those children who demonstrate severe disability in infancy. These children lack appropriate language, are unable to relate to people or objects in an appropriate way, and often exhibit idiosyncratic and at times bizarre motor behaviors. The behavior of these children varies from passivity and withdrawal to hyperactivity and destructiveness. The second subgroup includes those children who, after apparently normal development, begin to lose contact with reality. Identity of self becomes unclear, age-appropriate coping skills greatly diminish, and social development is arrested or regresses. Withdrawal into fantasy, paranoid reactions, phobias, hallucinations, and/or delusions often occur. Both subgroups present a severe and comprehensive disability requiring intensive broad-based interventions.

As Morse (1979) has pointed out, the descriptions of the groups are abstractions of how children actually behave. Rarely are pure cases found; each child develops an individualistic profile of deficits and assets. Morse's system, like Quay's; can help the school psychologist to identify emotional impairments and to gain an understanding of the various patterns of maladjustment underlying the symptoms. Although rather subjective and lacking in reliability data, Morse's system appears to be somewhat more useful than Quay's; it goes beyond description to prescription. Still, despite its greater possibility for usefulness, Morse's system fails to bridge the gap from identification to treatment. Neither Quay's nor Morse's classification system provides a means of conceptualizing emotional impairment that is educationally relevant.

Hewett and Taylor (1980) attempted to create a classification system that would translate descriptions of emotional impairment into educationally relevant concepts. Their system, which employs a functional-descriptive approach, is based on Hewett's (1968) developmental sequence of basic competencies needed for learning. He identified six levels of learning competence: attention, response, order, exploratory, social, and mastery. The emotionally impaired child is one who has failed to acquire one or more of these levels of learning competence (Hewett & Taylor, 1980). Hewett and Taylor compiled the various descriptions of behavior problems contained in the many classification systems of emotional impairment and found that the majority of these behaviors could be represented as negative variants of the six levels of learning competency (Table 7-1). These negative variants could result from either too much or too little of the appropriate behavior. For example, a child who has not acquired competence in attention may not attend to the task either because of distractibility (too little attention) or because of narrow, fixated attention on specific stimuli (too much attention). Essentially, this system changes the issue from "What do we call the child?" to "What does the child need in order to be a more effective student?" This "needs to learn" or educational framework makes it possible to see more clearly how the child can be helped. Interventions would be directed at helping the child acquire the learning competencies that are lacking.

TABLE 7-1

Common Characteristics of Disturbed Children Viewed as Negative Variants of Learning Competencies

Basic competencies needed for learning	Characteristics resulting from differing amounts of the appropriate behavior				
	Far too little	Too little	Optimal	Too much	Far too much
Attention	Disturbances in sensory perception	Excessive daydreaming Poor memory Short attention span In own world	Proper attention	Selective attention	Fixation on certain stimuli
Response (motor)	Immobilization	Sluggishness Passivity Drowsiness Clumsiness Depression	Proper motor response	Hyperactivity Restlessness	Self-stimulation
Response (verbal)	Failure to develop speech	Does not use language to communicate	Proper verbal response	Extremely talkative	Uses profanity Verbally abusive
Order	Self-injurious Lawlessness Destructiveness	Disruptiveness Attention seeking Irresponsibility Disobedience	Orderliness	Overly conforming	Resistance to change Compulsive
Exploratory	Bizarre or stereotyped behavior Bizarre interests	Anxiety Preoccupation Does not know how to have fun Shyness	Proper exploratory behavior	Plunges into activities	Impulsive Moves from activity to activity

TABLE 7-1 (Continued)

Common Characteristics of Disturbed Children Viewed as Negative Variants of Learning Competencies

Basic competencies needed for learning	Characteristics resulting from differing amounts of the appropriate behavior				
	Far too little	Too little	Optimal	Too much	Far too much
Social	Preoccupied with inanimate objects Extreme isolation Inability to relate	Social withdrawal Alienates others Aloofness Prefers younger peers Bossiness Secretiveness Fighting Temper tantrums	Proper social behavior	Hypersensitive Jealousy Overly dependent	Inability to function alone
Mastery	Blunted, uneven or fragmented intellectual development	Lacks self-care skills Lacks basic school skills Laziness	Mastery	Preoccupation with academics	Overintellectual-ization

Note. Table adapted from Hewett & Taylor, 1980, p. 100.

Hewett and Taylor (1980) have also developed a plan called the *ABC's of the IPE*, which breaks each of the six levels of learning competencies into three stages: A—skill areas, B—subcomponents of the skills, and C—short-term objectives. These are spelled out quite specifically and are accompanied by activities and tasks for increasing learning competency.

Although, Hewett and Taylor's system is not perfect, it makes a significant contribution toward solving the definition and classification dilemma. Unlike other available systems, this one does what classifications are supposed to do—it groups children by similar characteristics which then guide selection of intervention strategies. Another strength of this system is that it minimizes the effects of labeling by taking emotional impairment out of the realm of "deviancy"; it changes the focus from defect within the child to lack of skills, which can be learned. This system further takes into account the diverse behaviors among children with emotional difficulties. Hewett and Taylor's system is one that can be of much use to the school psychologist in the areas of assessment and intervention. Since there is no particular investment in etiology, this system is compatible with many theoretical orientations and programs.

Although to date no definition or classification system is fully adequate, those described here can be useful to school psychologists in working with children as long as they remain alert to the deficits and drawbacks of the system used and to the possible misuses of labeling. Assignment of children to the various categories must be done carefully and only after a thorough assessment and diagnosis have been made.

SPECIAL CONSIDERATIONS IN THE ASSESSMENT PROCESS

In Chapter 2, the five steps in the assessment process were described. For the emotionally impaired child, the selection of techniques for assessing emotional problems (step two) is perhaps more controversial than for any other category. Because no agreement exists on the definition or theoretical basis of emotional impairment, there is no consensus on the type of information that is most relevant. As a result, the orientation of the individual school psychologist becomes critical in determining priorities for data collection. There is a risk that the particular orientation of a school psychologist may act as a screening device causing the exclusion of data that do not fit with his or her position.

In order to avoid this bias, Morse, in an unpublished paper prepared for the Hawaii Special Education Department in 1975, recommended that the assessment be designed to give equal attention to understanding the child and the environment. Morse suggested several areas that should be included in such an assessment: cognitive ability, achievement, affective development, self-esteem, interpersonal relationships, neurological integration, developmental factors, behaviors in various situations, and environmental factors. This information can be obtained through a variety of techniques. In deciding which to use, the school psychologist should consider the advantages and disadvantages of each and the range of information that can be obtained by combining different methods.

To aid school psychologists in the selection of assessment instruments, the next section provides a brief review of those commonly used. (See Appendix H "Assessment Resources," for addresses of publishing companies and information on the availability of these instruments.)

Intelligence Tests

Assessment of the child's intellectual and cognitive problem-solving abilities is an important aspect of differential diagnosis. It is essential to distinguish those having emotional difficulties as a result of mental retardation or learning disabilities from those whose emotional difficulties are causing academic problems. Individual intelligence tests are most often used for this purpose. The potential for gaining insight into the child's personality from such tests should not be overlooked. An intelligence test should be selected as much for the qualitative features it offers as for the quantitative. The best test is one that will provide many opportunities for clinical observations. Intelligence tests that are commonly used include:

Wechsler Intelligence Scales—WPPSI, WISC-R, WAIS-R
Stanford Binet
Leiter International Performance Scale
Columbia Mental Maturity Scale
Ravens Progressive Matrices
Peabody Picture Vocabulary Test, Revised
Pictorial Test of Intelligence
McCarthy Scales of Children's Abilities

With experience the school psychologist will discover those tests that work better in eliciting optimal performance and in providing qualitative data with certain types of children. For example, children who are referred with high distractibility and short attention span seem to respond better to the Stanford Binet than to the Wechsler Scales. The Binet may hold the child's attention longer because of the variety of tasks presented, whereas the Wechsler requires many items of the same nature to be presented in sequence.

Younger children who have a history of not cooperating on evaluations or academic tasks seem to respond best to the Leiter. Its novel stimuli, colors, and game-like approach seem to attract and even fascinate the most "difficult" child. The Leiter, the Peabody, The Pictorial Test of Intelligence, and the Columbia are very useful in working with children who have speech and language difficulties. The McCarthy is useful for children whose academic achievement has been low and for whom the WISC-R may prove frustrating. In addition to its wider age range, the McCarthy provides multiple opportunities for clinical observation.

Achievement Tests

Achievement tests are useful in instances in which the child is having difficulty in a particular subject. They can aid in discovering whether the problem is due to a learning disability or is more general in nature. Tests of educational achievement that are widely used include:

Peabody Individual Achievement Test
Wide Range Achievement Test
Durrell Analysis of Reading Difficulty
Woodcock Reading Tests
Gray Oral Reading
Gates-McKellop Reading Diagnostic Tests
Key Math Diagnostic Test
Stanford Diagnostic Arithmetic Test

Projective Tests

Projective tests provide an opportunity to observe children as they express themselves in an individualistic manner. These tests, because they are less structured, allow for a wide range of reactions from a child and can be a rich source of information about how the child approaches a task (Dyer, 1974). Projective tests are purported to reveal unconscious feelings and conflicts of a child and thereby provide information about important and enduring personality characteristics that would otherwise be inaccessible. However, there is no clear evidence that children reveal feelings of which they are unaware on tests (O'Leary & Johnson, 1979). The results of studies that have examined the relationship between responses on projective tests and overt behavior are also conflicting (O'Leary & Johnson, 1979). Therefore, it is doubtful whether projective tests are of use in predicting behavior or have validity in terms of explaining existing behavior.

The most widely used projective tests are the Rorschach Inkblot Test and the Thematic Apperception Test (TAT). Studies on the usefulness of these two tests in the differential diagnosis of emotional impairment reveal that their validity is questionable (Magnussen, 1979; O'Leary & Johnson, 1979). Thus, with a few exceptions, scores from the TAT and Rorschach do not have sufficient validity to be used to diagnose a child as emotionally impaired. The exceptions to this are the need achievement indexes from the TAT (O'Leary & Johnson, 1979) and the developmental level scores from the Rorschach (Goldfried, Stricker, & Weiner, 1971). Despite the lack of validity for results of these tests, they can provide the school psychologist with impressions of a child's dominant moods, frustrations, conflicts, and modes of perception. These impressions can be used to generate hypotheses about the child; however, the hypotheses must be validated by direct observation of the child or by parent or teacher reports.

Some projective techniques may be very useful despite their uncertain validity. The Draw-a-Person and Family Drawing can be helpful in eliciting information from children that they might otherwise be reluctant to disclose. It is not that children's unconscious thoughts are revealed; it is that these methods make the issues less personal, and thus less threatening, allowing children to talk about them more comfortably. The Rorschach can provide information about children's approaches to the world and to problem solving—how well they can tolerate ambiguity, how they integrate various parts and aspects into a whole, and whether the product makes sense. Children's TAT stories provide useful information about whether they understand cause and effect and the concept of consequences, whether they are able to think things through to a logical conclusion, to what extent they are able to resolve dilemmas present in the stories, and how appropriate the resolutions are. It is possible, however, to obtain this information from simpler, less time-consuming methods such as classroom observation and trial teaching.

The decision to use projective tests in the assessment of emotionally impaired children must be made with great care. The utility of the method must be weighed against its costs. Utility will vary depending on the nature of the referral problem, what information is needed, and what decisions need to be made. The predictive validity, time, and training and experience of the examiner should always be considered in making this decision. If the decision is made to use projective tests, the following have been found useful:

Rorschach	Rohde Sentence Completion
Thematic Apperception Test	Rotter Sentence Completion
Children's Apperception Test	Draw-a-Person
Make a Picture Story	Family Drawings

Rating Scales and Checklists

Both rating scales and checklists have a behavioral focus. These techniques are based on the assumption that children with emotional difficulties differ from other children in the number and intensity of problem behaviors they exhibit. These methods require the rater to examine the behavior of other children and determine the degree to which a particular child differs from others. In general, individuals who interact with the child are asked to assign ratings to the child's behavior on a variety of empirically derived groups of problems. Checklists and rating scales can be completed by the child's teacher, parents, peers, or others involved with the child. Standardized checklists and rating scales are useful in comparing the child's behavior to that of others of the same age, gender, and grade. High reliability and validity have been demonstrated for such instruments when they are completed by parents and/or teachers (O'Leary & Johnson, 1979). These instruments are, of course, crucial to assessment when a behavioral approach to intervention will be used.

Examples of rating scales that have proved useful are:

Behavior Problem Checklist
Walker Problem Behavior Identification Checklist
Devereux Adolescent Behavior Rating Scale
Devereux Child Behavior Rating Scale
Devereux Elementary School Behavior Rating Scale

Each of these rating scales is specific in purpose. The Behavior Problem Checklist, which is relatively simple to complete, lists behaviors in four groups according to Quay's classification system. The Devereux Scales assess behavior symptoms for the individual child or adolescent and for the child functioning in a school setting.

Observational Assessment

This alternative to assessment instruments focuses directly on the child's behavior in a variety of real-life situations. Typically, a particular problem behavior is selected for observation during a given period of time. In addition, the child's other behaviors and behaviors of significant people are observed and recorded. The information collected during observations includes frequency of occurrence, antecedents, consequences, and situations in which the behavior occurs. The goal of such observations is to identify environmental factors that maintain a child's behavior and aspects of the environment that can be manipulated to change the behavior. Behavioral observations require trained observers to ensure reliability. Observations should be planned carefully so they occur across situations and over an extended time period. Frequently the school psychologist's schedule permits only brief observations. Although they are not as reliable or informative, brief observations can nonetheless provide the school psychologist with important information not attainable by other means. Additional suggestions for classroom observation are included in Chapter 3.

Interviews

Interviews can provide valuable information about a child's difficulties. Much information can be gained from interviews with the child's parents. The interview technique in general has been criticized on the basis that the data obtained have little stability and are biased by distortions of the interviewee (Hetherington & Martin, 1979). However, information obtained from parents about a child's current behavior is considered valid (O'Leary & Johnson, 1979). In addition, parental interviews give the psychologist a feeling for the family and the parents' attitudes and behaviors toward the child. Important information such as the child's functioning at home and in the neighborhood, accepted behavior standards at home, and developmental data can be obtained.

It is wise to use a standardized interview procedure; however, it is important to remain flexible. There are many formats for parent interviews available, most of which cover the same basic areas: current life situation in general, family history, health, prenatal and postnatal facts, developmental history, and parental perception of the problem. (See Appendix D for a suggested outline.)

Often neglected in the assessment is an interview with the child. Especially in school settings, contact with the child often consists exclusively of administration of tests. Yet, the child's perception of the situation and the problem and his or her perception of others and self are crucial to intervention. Interviews with children provide information about their developmental level, coping techniques, interpersonal skills, ability to communicate, and attitudes. As with parent interviews, there are numerous formats and outlines available for interviewing children. (See Appendix E for a suggested outline.)

Interviews with children, particularly younger children, can be very difficult due to their limited verbal language skills and frequent reluctance to talk about such issues. The play interview can be used to overcome these difficulties. The child can be given toys such as blocks, clay, darts, paper and pencil, puppets, and dolls. The play interview should include both structured and unstructured activities. The child can be asked to draw specific objects or anything he or she wants. Drawings reveal much about the child's affect, thought processes, and attitudes.

Information can also be obtained from having the child develop a story or scene with puppets or dolls. Games and puzzles that require certain types of abstract thinking or various levels of problem-solving skills can be presented. These activities also provide information about the child's attention span, persistence, and tolerance for frustration. Competitive games such as checkers may also reveal something about the child's self-esteem and manner of relating to authority.

Neurological Observations

Screening for organic causes is an important part of the assessment process. Some of this can be accomplished during the course of the evaluation by observing various aspcts of the child's motor responses and sensory responses. For children primarily presenting conduct problems, it is important to rule out the possibility of an atypical seizure disorder. Questioning parents and child about whether the child experiences strange burning sensations, a foul taste in the mouth, or visual manifestations can aid in determining whether seizures have occurred. "Yes" answers to any of these warrant referral for further investigation.

Observations should be made of the child's level of alertness and any alterations in this level; involuntary twitching, tremors, or unusual posturing of any limb; coordination and gait; eye movements and tracking ability; and any exhibited preferences for sensory modalities. The Bender-Gestalt test, when scored using the Koppitz (1963) developmental system, may be useful in screening for organic causes. Although the test provides a limited sample of perceptual-motor behavior and requires caution when interpreting results, developmental scores on the Bender-Gestalt can reveal possible organicity. Scores on the Bender-Gestalt that are significantly below average and are due to numerous rotations and perseverations are signs that more extensive neurological screening may be warranted.

Interpretation of Results

At the completion of assessment the data collected must be interpreted and integrated to answer the referral questions. As in the selection of assessment techniques, there is no consensus as to how to interpret data. Each theory of emotional disturbance emphasizes a different way of interpretation and results in different views of the child. Dyer (1974) suggested that regardless of one's orientation, it is of greatest utility to approach the data with a particular mind set:

> When the focus of an evaluation is emotional problems, the emphasis is on searching for the particular ways in which the child copes with and defends against hurdles in his/her interpersonal experiences and general development. The child's greatest asset is an ability to organize and integrate his/her resources to react to these hurdles. (p. 275)

Thus, according to Dyer, the focus of assessment should be discovering the nature of the child's coping behaviors and determining whether or not they are effective and efficient. This suggestion appears to be useful and would fit well with any theoretical orientation. To complete the interpretation, the factors affecting the child's development of particular coping behaviors must be identified so that appropriate interventions can be planned.

How can the school psychologist determine these things from the data? A large number of frameworks are available for organizing the data to make this determination possible. Morse, in an unpublished paper prepared for the Hawaii Special Education Department in 1975, proposed one such framework. He suggested organizing the data into five areas: cognitive, affective, biophysical, social, and interpersonal. These then become dimensions of the child's overall functioning so that assets and limitations can be identified. Similarly, these dimensions are used to identify support and stress factors in the child's past and present environment.

Another method of organizing the data was proposed by Cohen (1979). He suggested arranging the data along seven dimensions: the child's level of autonomous functioning; perception of roles and ability to differentiate objects; self-care, self-image, and body image; self-control; quality and content of thought processes; interpersonal skills and relationships; and ethical structure. In each case the age of the child must be considered and the question of whether the child's performance is age-appropriate is asked. This method focuses on the child's movement toward autonomous functioning and socially cooperative behavior. Cohen's method provides a developmental framework within which to consider whether the child's lack of adequate progress in one or more areas indicates emotional difficulties. Although Cohen's framework is useful, it does not include environmental influences. The school psychologist should add this category to avoid biases discussed earlier in this chapter.

Whichever framework for organizing the data is chosen, it is crucial for the examiner to know what to look for in the information obtained. To aid the school psychologist with this task, an outline of questions to keep in mind, areas of concern, and indicators of emotional difficulties are provided in Appendixes B and C.

It is important to note environmental supports and stresses, identify strengths and weaknesses in the child's skills, and compare current functioning and past functioning. In order to help answer the referral questions, the school psychologist should review the information and convergences and divergences across areas and sources of information. Developmental factors and medical factors must be considered when divergences are discovered. Differences in the child's ability levels and skill levels in various situations should be explored for possible explanations. For example, does behavior vary depending on whether the situation is structured or unstructured?

In certifying a child as emotionally impaired for educational purposes, it is often assumed that the child will have academic or other school difficulties. However, the fact that a child has emotional problems does not in itself mean that the child will have academic difficulties. It is not always possible to predict when emotional problems will affect learning. Many severely disturbed children do well academically (Deno, 1978). That there is an interaction between emotional disturbance and learning problems is not challenged here, but there is not sufficient evidence to make cause-and-effect assumptions. In order to acquire academic skills the child must actively participate in the learning process and invest energy in school. Emotional problems can detract from the energy available for school or interfere with the child's participation level and thus result in learning difficulties. Learning disabilities can result in or from emotional problems as well. It is rarely easy to determine which caused which.

There are several factors in emotional problems that may determine whether or not academic problems will develop: the quality of gratification the school provides; the level of accomplishment possible; the degree of protection the classroom environment provides; the child's attitude toward school and learning; sibling relations and the achievement of siblings; and the nature of relationships with the teachers. These factors should be considered in making a diagnosis and in planning treatment. However, learning problems or academic failure should not be the criterion for labeling a child as emotionally impaired.

Special Problems in the Assessment of Emotional Impairment

The actual assessment of children with emotional and/or behavior problems can be difficult and trying to even the most experienced psychologist. There are many aspects of the assessment procedure that parallel situations in which the child has difficulty. Administration of tests, in particular, is often very threatening and may evoke high levels of anxiety. The interaction with an adult authority figure, the school psychologist, can elicit many of the same problems the child has with parents or teachers. As a result of these factors the child may behave in a variety of ways that can render the school psychologist's usual repertoire of approaches to children ineffective. It should be noted that the one-to-one relationship of assessment may create an optimal environment for the emotionally impaired child. In this case the school psychologist will experience less difficulty than teachers and perhaps even have a "model child" in the office. Although these reactions from the child may provide important diagnostic information, they nonetheless must be dealt with in order to obtain the necessary data from the sessions.

Control is a key issue in the assessment process with emotionally impaired children. It is often necessary to give more control to these children than the examiner ordinarily does. A greater degree of flexibility must also be maintained during the assessment process. The psychologist must be prepared to veer from plans, perhaps even administer tests in segments with other activities in between. Management problems can often be avoided by maintaining a balance between structure and control in order to allow the child some freedom and yet still permit a systematic testing procedure. In general, the school psychologist should follow standardized procedures and observe the limits of the child's behavior, but once sufficient data are obtained, the psychologist may wish to discontinue this approach and try innovations. It is important to determine how well the child can perform and what differences occur in performance under less rigorous structure.

Some of the more common problems faced in the assessment of emotionally disturbed children are refusal to talk, hyperactivity, destructiveness, passive resistance, flight from the room, excessive crying, and temper tantrums.

Refusal to Talk

The child who is silent during the early part of the assessment may be extremely anxious. Reassurance, encouragement, and explanations of what will be happening are helpful in reducing the anxiety. The examiner will probably get the best results by gradually increasing the intensity of interactions with the child. Some distance should be maintained at the start of the session, and then gradual attempts to increase the level of closeness should be initiated. This gradual, patient approach usually works, although at times the child may still refuse to talk even then and may remain mute for the major part of the session. It is important to observe the child's nonverbal communications in such instances. Often the child who is verbally unresponsive has much eye contact with the examiner and intently follows the examiner's actions. This could indicate the child's desire to make interpersonal contact.

The psychologist can use cues from the child in order to establish communication. For example, a child who refuses to speak to the examiner may talk indirectly through a pair of toy telephones, by whispering down a tube or into a walkie-talkie, or by using a dictating machine or tape recorder. The examiner can talk to an imaginary third party, making no demands on the child to respond, or can converse with a stuffed animal or puppet. The examiner can also talk to the child through the animal or puppet, which may be less threatening.

With a young child, parallel play can be used. The examiner can begin drawing, building with blocks, or any such activity, and, without directing attention to the child, have materials for the child to play with. The child will usually follow the play. Once the child is engaged in parallel play, interaction can be initiated through the play materials. For example, the examiner can build an extension from a building to connect with the child's or can use an animal figure that wanders into the child's play area and comes in physical and verbal contact with the child's figure.

With older children, tic-tac-toe, checkers, cards, or other such games can provide a mode for making contact. Direct confrontation should be avoided with children who refuse to talk.

Hyperactivity

The hyperactive, destructive, or otherwise actively resistant child can usually be dealt with using similar techniques. The examiner should maintain a steady, firm tone of voice, but express reassurance. Verbal reinforcement and reassurance are important. It may be necessary to break the session into short segments with free play or other breaks in between. Informing the child that after perhaps 10 to 20 minutes of work there will be a play period is often helpful. The child can be given a variety of privileges (e.g., playing with a typewriter, making a ditto and running it off, calling home) contingent on completing certain tasks. For some children excessive activity is due to anxiety, and leaving the door open during the session or allowing a teacher or parent to accompany the child to the session may alleviate this anxiety.

Other Problems

Children who seem to have extreme difficulty attending or remaining seated need to have a controlled environment with a limited amount of stimulation; only the materials being used at the time should be available to the child. The child who becomes destructive or physically aggressive is best dealt with by confrontation as soon as the behavior begins. The examiner should state firmly and unequivocally that the behavior is unacceptable and will not be tolerated. The psychologist should make it very clear to the child that whatever action is necessary will be taken to stop the behavior. If the child continues, gentle restraint may be necessary. The child should be enveloped with the examiner's body if restraint is used, and never grasped in any way that might be painful or result in injury to the child.

In dealing with any such problems, the best approach is to keep in mind that the goal of the assessment is ultimately to benefit the child; that is, it is the child's welfare that is most important, not the assessment itself. At no time should the process take priority over the child. If by continuing, the assessment will become a battle ground or result in an adverse experience for the child, it should be discontinued. The psychologist will then need to rely on observation, teacher reports, parent interviews, and other methods to gather data.

The failure to complete the assessment in the usual manner and the techniques attempted can nevertheless provide additional data about the child's difficulties. The decision to recommend special education programming can be made with this informal information, and more formal assessment of the child can be attempted at a later date. At no time should the fact that the assessment had to be terminated be used against the child. Thus, it is crucial that in working with an emotionally impaired child the school psychologist be aware of his or her own reactions and feelings toward the child. Too often, this point is forgotten, and the school psychologist becomes another one of the child's "successful" defeats of the system and the world at which the child is lashing out.

PROGRAMS FOR EMOTIONALLY DISTURBED CHILDREN

Once determined eligible for classification, the child must be placed in an appropriate program. A general rule for program selection is to choose on the basis of the nature of the individual child's problems and assessment findings, not on the basis of the classification. "It is critical to remember that the severity of the socio-emotional disturbance does not automatically predicate the most adequate form for delivery of special educational service" (Morse, 1975, p. 7, unpublished paper).

Placement Options

Some very disturbed children can function in regular classes, while other, less disturbed children may need a very controlled setting to ameliorate their difficulties. Selection must also be guided by the federal and state mandates, which require that the child be placed in the least restrictive setting in which his or her needs can be met. In addition, the program chosen should be one in which the child can have successful experiences and learn to deal with feelings, pressures, and frustrations. The degree of structure will, in part, depend on the child's level of self-control.

Regular Class Placement

One option is to place the child in a regular classroom with additional individualized support. This support can be a resource class the child attends at specific times on a regular basis; the resource teacher works with the child on academic and emotional issues. The support can be provided through the helping teacher (Morse, 1976), who provides consultation, liaison services, and crisis intervention to the child, teacher, peers, and parents. The focus is on blending affective-cognitive interventions through relationships. To be successful, all school personnel must cooperate among themselves and with outside services.

Special Class Placement with Mainstreaming

The child whose problems require a more structured approach can be placed in a special class and mainstreamed for certain activities. Morse (1979) has suggested that the following questions be considered when mainstreaming is being planned:

1. Can the teacher provide the child the necessary tolerance with consistency?
2. Can the teacher accept and deal with individualizing the program to fit the child's capabilities?
3. Will the teacher be able to communicate with the child regarding problem areas?
4. Is the mainstream peer culture a hospitable one that will not exacerbate the child's problems?
5. Is there immediate, nonpunitive backup when the teacher needs it?

Successful mainstreaming requires availability of additional school-related services (e.g., therapy from the school social worker or school psychologist) and community resources (e.g., big brother/sister, tutors, recreation groups, parent involvement).

Self-Contained Classes

Some emotionally disturbed children need a more protected and specialized environment than the regular classroom can offer. These children may be placed in a self-contained classroom where they remain with the same teacher for the entire day. This class includes other emotionally impaired children and typically is quite small. A program of special education is provided that is specifically geared toward children who are emotionally impaired; the program may range from a strict behavior modification approach to a dynamic, humanistic one, and often is eclectic. The teacher should be specially trained to work with children who have behavior problems and emotional difficulties. Because the class is small, the individual needs of the children can be met. The self-contained classroom offers children the stability of one teacher and a few peers and can provide them with a primary group experience in which relationships are emphasized—one of the most important aspects of any program for emotionally impaired students (Morse, 1979).

Residential Programs

There are some emotionally impaired children who need to be in an environment that is totally controlled. Residential programs are indicated when the family is unable to provide the support needed for other programs or is detrimental to the child's treatment program. A residential situation is the only way in which 24-hour multidisciplinary efforts can be provided. For the older child a halfway house and/or a sheltered workshop may be alternatives to the residential treatment centers.

Arguments Against Segregation

The programs described vary in the degree to which they segregate the child. In most instances, total segregation is not the best alternative. Totally segregated programs are based on the assumption that the child's behaviors can be changed more rapidly in such a setting, thus facilitating the child's return to a regular class. Those in favor of such programs have cited in support of their position evidence from studies in which children showed improvements (O'Leary & Johnson, 1979). However, O'Leary and Johnson have also pointed out that these studies failed to compare the changes reported to changes in children placed in less segregated programs. In light of conflicting research findings, no definitive conclusions can be made about the relative benefits from these programs.

Deno (1978) found that segregation of emotionally impaired children often results in their behavior getting worse rather than better. Furthermore, improvements that occur in segregated programs do not always carry over to the "regular" environment. The children develop the ability to cope more adequately in a special setting with limited demands, but that does not necessarily prepare them for the increased ambiguity of the nonsegregated world (Deno, 1978).

Benefits of Mainstreaming

To avoid this problem, "treatment in situ" or *mainstreaming,* as it has recently become known, is recommended. Mainstreaming not only ensures that improvements the child makes will carry over to the natural environment but also provides an opportunity to observe the child's ability to deal successfully with this environment and assess the interventions and progress made. In addition, mainstreaming averts the self-devaluation that sometimes occurs in children in segregated classes. When the emotionally impaired child is kept in the natural environment, significant others in the child's life are encouraged to make changes and thereby become part of the solution (Deno, 1978).

Making Placement Decisions

Placement of any child should be based on the potential of that placement for providing the child with what is needed. The value of a program does not stem from what type of class it is, but from what is done for and with the child in that setting. Whether or not mainstreaming should be part of the child's program depends on what interventions are needed. For example, it must be determined whether it would be better to relocate the child temporarily in order to intensify interventions, or whether less intensive intervention and a more gradual transition would be better. The school psychologist should also determine what resources are necessary to provide the optimal amount of structure and supervision and where these can best be found. Placement must be decided on an individual basis; there is no one program that will be effective with all emotionally impaired children.

Providing Additional Support

At times educational programming alone is not enough to meet the needs of the child. In these cases some form of additional support is necessary. This additional support is usually some type of counseling or psychotherapy, but it can also be in the form of using other community resources. In some situations the school psychologist will be the direct provider of this service and in others will be indirectly involved. In either case the role is important. As direct service provider the school psychologist can act as the child's therapist, engage in guidance counseling with the child's parents, and provide consultation to the child's teacher(s). Indirect services include advocacy and liaison between community resources and the school.

Whether the school psychologist is consulting with school personnel or others, a major emphasis should be helping those involved with the child understand that there is no quick solution to emotional problems. In this role, the school psychologist acts to dispel myths by developing awareness and understanding of emotional problems and by changing negative attitudes of those involved with the child. The school psychologist, as consultant, can help others develop skills to work with emotionally impaired children. For instance, the school psychologist can train teachers in the use of the Life Space Interview (Redl, 1959), systematic management, and behavioral techniques, and in the analysis of child behavior and learning tasks.

Although it is rarely done within the school system, work with parents can maximize the potential benefits of a special education program. Often parents are resistant to having their child placed in a special program because of the negative connotations attached to the label. Parents can become defensive and uncooperative, thus making the child's adjustment difficult. The school psychologist can reduce potential problems with parents and facilitate better school-home relations through conferences with the parents or acting as a liaison between parent and school. In working with parents of emotionally impaired children, the school psychologist should attempt to dispel their feelings of guilt and hopelessness. This entails honestly describing what the problem is, helping parents see that the child's behavior needs to be brought under control, and establishing optimistic expectations for improvement (Arnold, 1978). The school psychologist as liaison can help the parents understand the special education certification process and the school's special education program and goals, and be available to parents when they have questions or problems regarding the child's school progress or program.

SUMMARY

Issues concerning definition are critical in this categorical area. Who gets labeled as emotionally disturbed depends in large measure on external variables related to the ecological setting of the child or the particular set of circumstances that call attention to the child's deviant behavior. Classification systems, although imperfect, may be helpful to school psychologists in identifying children with emotional impairments. Careful selection of appropriate instruments for assessment should be made in order to make a differential diagnosis and avoid a misdiagnosis of educable mental retardation or learning disabilities. The assessment procedure may present a challenge to the school psychologist because of the child's behavior; the psychologist may need to rely more on informal than formal assessment measures. In order to be successful remedial programs should include attention to the child's family and other school and community variables.

REFERENCES

Arnold, L. E. (1978). *Helping parents help their children.* New York: Brunner Mazel.

Bower, E. (1969). *Early identification of the emotionally handicapped.* Springfield IL: Charles C Thomas.

Cohen, R. (Ed.). (1979). Assessment. In J. D. Noshpitz (Ed.), *Basic handbook of child psychiatry, Volume 1. Development* (pp. 485-551). New York: Basic Books.

Deno, E. (1978). *Educational children with emotional, learning and behavioral problems.* Minneapolis: Leadership Training Institute, University of Minnesota.

Dupont, H. (Ed.). (1969). *Educating emotionally disturbed children: Readings.* New York: Holt, Rinehart & Winston.

Dyer, C. O. (1974). Socially and emotionally handicapped. In M. Wisland (Ed.), *Psychoeducational diagnosis of exceptional children* (pp. 233-305). Springfield IL: Charles C Thomas.

Goldfried, M. R., Stricker, G., & Weiner, I. B. (1971). *Rorschach handbook of clinical and research applications.* Englewood Cliffs NJ: Prentice-Hall.

Graubard, P. S. (1973). Children with behavioral difficulties. In L. M. Dunn (Ed.), *Exceptional children in the schools* (2nd ed.) (pp. 245-295). New York: Holt, Rinehart & Winston.

Grosenick, J. K., & Huntze, S. L. (1983). *National needs analysis leadership training project: More questions than answers: Review and analysis of programs for behaviorally disordered children and youth.* Columbia MO: University of Missouri-Columbia Department of Special Education.

Hetherington, E. M., & Martin, B. (1979). Family interaction. In H. Quay & J. Werry (Eds.), *Psychopathological disorders of childhood* (2nd ed.) (pp. 247-302). New York: John Wiley.

Hewett, F. M. (1968). *The emotionally disturbed child in the classroom* (2nd ed.). Boston: Allyn & Bacon.

Hewett, F. M., & Taylor, F. (1980). *The emotionally disturbed child in the classroom* (3rd ed.). Boston: Allyn & Bacon.

Hobbs, N. (Ed.). (1975). *Issues in the classification of children* (Vol. I). San Francisco: Jossey-Bass.

Kauffman, J. M. (1977). *Characteristics of children's behavior disorders.* Columbus OH: Charles E. Merrill.

Koppitz, E. M. (1963). *The Bender Gestalt Test for Young Children.* New York: Grune & Stratton.

Magnussen, M. G. (1979). Psychometric and projective techniques. In J. D. Noshpitz (Ed.), *Basic handbook of child psychiatry, Volume I. Development* (pp. 553-568). New York: Basic Books.

Morse, W. C. (1976). The helping teacher/crisis teacher concept. *Focus on Exceptional Children,* 8(4), 1-12.

Morse, W. C. (1979). *Humanistic teaching for exceptional children: An introduction to special education.* Syracuse NY: Syracuse University Press.

Moustakas, C. E. (1953). *Children in play therapy.* New York: McGraw Hill.

National Association of State Directors of Special Education (NASDSE). (1983, November 25). *Liaison Bulletin,* 10(2), p. 4.

O'Leary, K. D., & Johnson, S. B. (1979). Psychological assessment. In H. Quay & J. Werry (Eds.), *Psychopathological disorders of childhood* (2nd ed.) (pp. 210-246). New York: Wiley.

Quay, H. (1972). Patterns of aggression, withdrawal and immaturity. In H. Quay & J. Werry (Eds.), *Psychopathological disorders of childhood* (pp. 1-29). New York: John Wiley.

Quay, H. (1979). Classification. In H. Quay & J. Werry (Eds.), *Psychopathological disorders of childhood* (2nd ed.) (pp. 1-42). New York: Wiley.

Redl, F. (1959) Strategy and techniques of the life space interview. *American Journal of Orthopsychiatry,* 29, 1-18.

Reeve, R., & Kauffman, J. M. (1978). The behavior disordered. In N. Haring (Ed.), *Behavior of exceptional children* (2nd ed.) (pp. 123-154). Columbus OH: Charles E. Merrill.

Ross, A. O. (1974.) *Psychological disorders of children.* New York: McGraw Hill.

ADDITIONAL RESOURCES

Deno, E. N. (1978) *Educating children with emotional, learning, and behavior problems.* Minneapolis MN: University of Minnesota, National Support System.

Haring, N. (Ed.). (1978). *Behavior of exceptional children* (2nd ed.) Columbus OH: Charles E. Merrill.

Knoblock, P. (1980). Psychological considerations of emotionally disturbed children. In W. M. Cruickshank, (Ed.), *Psychology of exceptional children and youth* (4th ed.) (pp. 542-574). Englewood Cliffs NJ: Prentice-Hall.

Long, N., Morse, W. C., & Newman, R. (Eds.). (1980). *Conflict in the classroom: The education of emotionally disturbed children* (4th ed.). Belmont CA: Wadsworth.

Morse, W. C., Ardizzone, J., MacDonald, C., & Pasick, P. (1980). *Affective education for special children and youth.* Reston VA: The Council for Exceptional Children.

Paul, J. & Epanchin, B. (Eds.). (1982). *Emotional disturbance in children.* Columbus OH: Charles E. Merrill.

Waterman, J. (1982). Assessment considerations with the emotionally disturbed child. In G. Ulrey, & S. J. Rogers (Eds.), *Psychological assessment of handicapped infants and young children* (pp. 142-148). New York: Thieme-Stratton.

CHAPTER 8

Physical and Multiple Handicaps

Shauna Tindall
Geraldine T. Scholl

Children discussed in this chapter comprise a heterogeneous group. They include those with orthopedic impairments resulting from congenital anomalies, disease, and other causes; those who suffer from health impairments that impinge on their strength, alertness, or vitality; and those who have a combination of impairments. Some of these conditions, while handicapping a child in the performance of certain daily activities, have few educational implications. An example of this is a congenital or acquired absence of a limb. Other conditions such as diabetes or rheumatic fever may not handicap a child educationally but may reduce the child's energy level so that concentration on learning tasks is greatly reduced. Some conditions such as epilepsy do not handicap a child educationally but may have vocational rehabilitation implications that will necessitate careful planning during adolescent years. Finally, some conditions such as cerebral palsy usually do have major educational implications.

This chapter is divided into five sections. The first section presents a description of the various conditions included under the category of physical and other health impairments. It is followed by sections on psychological, educational, and assessment issues. The final section includes a brief discussion of multiple impairments.

DESCRIPTION OF PHYSICAL AND HEALTH IMPAIRMENTS

Since school psychologists are expected to assess for educational diagnosis, placement, and planning purposes, groupings according to educational considerations were adopted for this section. The six groupings of the conditions are: those that may require special education programs and services; those that may require special education programs and services; those that may require some educational modifications, usually in a regular classroom; those that may require restricted physical activities; those that may require emotional support; and those that may require temporary modifications.

Conditions Requiring Special Education Programs and Services

Two conditions are included in this section: cerebral palsy and autism. Although they are quite different, children with each condition will usually require special education programs and services from an interdisciplinary team.

Cerebral Palsy

Cerebral Palsy, as defined by the United Cerebral Palsy Association "is the general term applied to a group of permanently disabling symptoms resulting from damage to the developing brain that may occur before, during or after birth and that results in loss or impairment of control over voluntary muscles" (Goldenson, 1978a, p. 331). Prenatal and perinatal diseases or disturbances (congenital causes) are responsible for about 86% of these cases, while the remainder are acquired through such events as tumors, trauma, or brain hemorrhages. (See Chapter 5 for a discussion of the etiological factors.) Approximately 3 to 6 out of every 1,000 infants are born with cerebral palsy (Calhoun & Hawisher, 1979). Approximately half of the children with cerebral palsy have IQ scores below 70 and are classified as mentally retarded (Cegelka & Prehm, 1982; Robinson & Robinson, 1976). However, it should be noted that this may be an overestimate because the formal and informal assessment instruments that typically are used on a population with multiple impairments may not be appropriate for them (Kirk & Gallagher, 1983).

Cerebral palsy may be classified according to the type of movement disorder: spasticity, athetosis, ataxia, tremor, ridigity, or atonia; or limb involvement: monoplegia, diplegia, paraplegia, or quadriplegia; or severity of the involvement: mild, moderate, or strong (Calhoun & Hawisher, 1979). Associated disorders include speech impairments, visual and auditory losses, seizures, and learning disabilities, as well as emotional disturbances (Goldenson, 1978a). In addition to a medical specialist, assessment for appropriate placement and educational planning must include a variety of other disciplines: physical, occupational, and speech, hearing, and language therapy; audiology; ophthalmology; special education; school social work; and school psychology.

Children with cerebral palsy frequently have multiple impairments and require special education and a variety of supportive services for an appropriate educational program, including physical, occupational, and speech therapies (Healy, 1983). Within-group differences among children with cerebral palsy tend to be great, partly because damage frequently occurs in a different area of the brain for each child and cognitive, motor, and behavioral manifestations can vary. As a result, each child must be viewed as a unique individual.

Autism

In the past autism was classified under the general heading of " emotional disturbance." Although the exact etiology remains elusive and may include multiple causative factors, there is enough research evidence for some professionals to conclude that it is a "physical disease of the brain" (Ritvo, 1976, p. 5). It is included in this section because autistic children are now considered as "other health impaired."

Kirk and Gallagher (1983) presented the following definition of autism from the National Society for Autistic Children:

> Autism is a severely incapacitating life-long developmental disability which usually appears during the first three years of life. It occurs in approximately five out of 10,000 births and is four times more common in boys than in girls. It has been found throughout the world in families of all racial, ethnic, and social backgrounds. (p. 423)

Features of autism include an early onset, probably at birth; disturbances in perception; marked difference in developmental rate; difficulty in relating to others; speech and language disorders; and differences in motility (Ornitz & Ritvo, 1976). Since many of these behavioral characteristics are found in other categories of handicapped children, arriving at a differential diagnosis is often difficult. Autistic children may be misdiagnosed as having delayed language or being hearing impaired because of their language deficiency; or moderately or severely mentally retarded because of their lack of responsiveness to sensory stimuli; or emotionally disturbed because of their inability to relate to others (Schor, 1983a). A differential diagnosis must be made by a multidisciplinary team that includes, in addition to the school psychologist, medical specialists, speech and language specialists, and educators who are knowledgeable about the condition and its characteristics.

Conditions That May Require Special Education Programs and Services

Table 8-1 lists four conditions that may eventually require special education programs and services, partly because of their degenerative characteristics. These conditions are Friedreich's ataxia, muscular dystrophy, spina bifida, and spinal muscle atrophy. Except for spina bifida, where research evidence is not definitive (Howell, 1978a), these conditions are hereditary. Thus family counseling, particularly genetic counseling, is usually recommended. Because of the short life span, the child and family may need support services to cope with the acceptance of a gradually deteriorating condition. Classmates may also need support. Regular class placement should be maintained as long as possible. Eventually the child may need home or hospital instruction because he or she will not be physically able to remain in school. For specific information on conditions in this table, see Bigge (1976); Bleck and Nagel (1983); Calhoun and Hawisher (1979); Goldenson (1978b); and Howell (1978a).

Conditions That May Require Some Educational Modifications

Table 8-2 includes four conditions for which some modifications may be necessary: amputations, arthrogryposis multiplex congenita, traumatic paraplegia and quadriplegia, and poliomyelitis. Usually these modifications are related to the setting, materials used, and techniques for accomplishing motor activities, rather than modifications of teaching strategies, since children with these conditions usually are of normal intelligence.

For a brief period in the early 1960's there were a few cases in this country of congenital absence of limbs due to thalidomide, a sedative used by pregnant women (Calhoun and Hawisher, 1979). The brief appearance of deformities resulting from the use of this drug points to the necessity of restricting intake of all such substances during the critical period of pregnancy.

The rapid decline in the number of children afflicted with poliomyelitis since the advent of the Salk vaccine should demonstrate the effectiveness of such preventive measures. School psychologists should be aware of the need for a school policy on vaccination programs and can be of great assistance in working with parents to over-

TABLE 8-1
Conditions That May Require Special Education Programs and Services

Condition	Definition	Recommended educational placement
Friedreich's ataxia	An inherited disease in which progressive degeneration of peripheral sensory nerves leads to poor balance of the extremities and trunk. Frequent falling or a rolling, lurching gait, shaky or erratic handwriting, and slurred speech are early signs that may appear during the school years. Skeletal deformities are likely to occur as the disease progresses; these, along with the tremor, speech problems, and visual deterioration may interfere with classwork or assessment. A variety of concomitant health disorders may also occur.	Retain in the regular classroom as long as possible; may need strong encouragement to overcome frustration and depression because of weaknesses; some modification in curricular materials and methods may be required as the disease progresses and strength deteriorates. Family may need counseling because of the hereditary nature of the disease. Genetic counseling is important.
Muscular dystrophy	A hereditary disease, with progressive shrinking and degeneration of skeletal or voluntary musculature. Children with poor posture, an awkward or tiptoeing gait, and frequent falling should be referred for medical evaluation. The classic "Gower's sign" of muscular dystrophy is when the child "walks" up his or her legs with his or her hands in order to rise from a sitting position on the floor. Mental impairment manifested by slowness in learning and IQ scores of 80 to 90 exist in about 70% of these children.	May require rest periods due to fatigue, but should be maintained in the regular classroom as long as possible. May eventually need home instruction. Most die in their teens. Counseling with child and family is usually necessary.

TABLE 8-1 (Continued)

Conditions That May Require Special Education Programs and Services

Condition	Definition	Recommended educational placement
Spina bifida Myelomeningocele Meningocele	Congenital open defect in the bony structure of the spinal canal occurring in about 2 to 4 per 1,000 live births, myelomeningoceles predominating. Disabilities include flaccid paralysis of the trunk and legs, bone deformities, loss of sensation, and bladder and bowel paralysis leading to incontinence and kidney infections. Hydrocephalus occurs in 90 to 95% of children with myelomeningocele.	Frequent absence from school and social problems due to incontinence; educational focus on preparation for sedentary occupations. Should be retained in regular classes unless there is mental retardation related to hydrocephalus. Will need counseling and rehabilitation services.
Spinal muscle atrophy	A hereditary disease in which progressive degeneration of spinal cord motor nerves and brain stem leads to weakness and atrophy of muscles very similar to muscular dystrophy. Intelligence is usually in the normal range.	Retain in a regular classroom as long as possible; may need home instruction eventually. Children rarely survive beyond childhood.

TABLE 8-2

Conditions That May Require Some Educational Modifications

Condition	Definition	Modifications
Amputation	Congenital or acquired absence or loss of all or part of the upper and/or lower limb(s). The use of prosthetic arms or legs is usually recommended. Children with upper-limb amputations will use the intact limb as much as possible with the artificial limb as helper. Unilateral arm amputees may remove the prosthesis if it interferes with an activity. Bilateral upper-limb amputees require their prostheses, although they may become adept at using toes and feet for all self-help activities, writing, etc. Lower-limb amputees may walk quite well if only one limb, or only the lower part of both limbs, is missing.	Sports activities, especially swimming, should be encouraged in moderation. Bilateral above-the-knee amputees usually require wheelchairs at least part-time. The range of intelligence is usually normal, and they can usually function well in regular classrooms. Some modifications in materials may be required for upper-limb amputees, at least until they learn dexterity with their prosthetic limbs or learn to use their toes for writing, drawing, and other related activities.
Arthrogryposis multiplex congenita	A congenital, but not hereditary, condition in which the child is born with weak muscles and stiff joints. The child looks like a marionette with such distinctive features as flexed wrists and fingers, curved spine, flexed and externally rotated hips, and thin arms and legs. Associated conditions include congenital heart disease, urinary tract abnormalities, respiratory problems, abdominal hernias, and various facial abnormalities.	Goals of education and rehabilitation are independent walking, self-care, and vocational training. Most have normal intelligence and speech and are functional in a wheelchair. Placement in a regular academic classroom with space for wheelchair. Modifications may be necessary for testing and lessons requiring writing and other hand skills. An electric typewriter may help with developing written communication skills.

TABLE 8-2 (Continued)

Conditions That May Require Some Educational Modifications

Condition	Definition	Modifications
Poliomyelitis	A viral infection of the spinal cord motor cells, resulting in temporary or permanent flaccid paralysis. Incidence is now low because of the Salk vaccine. The IQ range is normal.	A regular academic program is indicated. A child with upper-limb paralysis may require compensatory methods, materials, or equipment. Children with lower-limb paralysis need wheelchairs and building and playground facilities adapted for them.
Traumatic paraplegia and quadriplegia	Permanent paralysis of one or more limbs resulting from injuries usually due to accidents. Quadriplegic children are not likely to attend public schools, but paraplegic children may.	Regular class placement. May need supportive services to deal with frustrations. May have some problems with incontinence. Education should be aimed at independence. Rehabilitation services should be provided to maximize remaining physical potential. Realistic vocational goals may require extensive counseling.

come any objections they may have to immunization programs, whatever the reason for the resistance.

For these four conditions, the greatest need is supportive help from all school personnel for dealing with frustrations that arise from the inability to perform certain motor tasks. This problem may be especially acute in those conditions where loss of motor abilities was sudden and traumatic. Working to develop positive attitudes toward pupils with these impairments should also be a priority for school personnel.

For more information about these conditions, the reader should see Bigge (1976), Bleck and Nagel (1983), Calhoun and Hawisher (1979), and Goldenson (1978b).

Conditions That May Require Restricted Physical Activities

Table 8-3 lists 11 conditions that may require restricted physical activities. Most of these conditions interfere with ambulation and physical activity but not with academic progress, except in those cases where there is prolonged school absence due to periods of hospitalization. In cooperation with the school nurse, the school psychologist may need to interpret a child's physical limitations to other school personnel. Counseling of pupils with these conditions may also be necessary to help them accept the realities of their physical limitations, especially during adolescence. The school psychologist may also be involved in referring children with these conditions to the vocational rehabilitation agency during their secondary school years.

More details regarding these conditions may be found in Blackman (1983), Bleck and Nagel (1983), Goldenson (1978b), and Schor (1983b).

Conditions That May Require Emotional Support

Table 8-4 lists three conditions that may require supportive help from the school psychologist: asthma, sickle cell disease, and juvenile rheumatoid arthritis. Because these are chronic conditions, counseling may be necessary in order for the child to accept the limitations while at the same time preventing the child from taking advantage of the physical condition. Consultation with the teacher may be necessary since the child does not look "sick" and may have periods of normal health and behavior. Counseling with parents of children with sickle cell anemia may be indicated because of the hereditary nature of this condition. For more information about these conditions, see Bigge (1976), Blackman (1983), Bleck and Nagel (1983), Goldenson (1978b) and Gould (1972).

TABLE 8-3

Conditions That May Require Restricted Physical Activities

Condition	Definition	Modifications
Scoliosis	A lateral curvature of the spine, correctable by surgery or a brace, which may interfere with physical activities.	Physical activities may need to be reduced
Legg-Calve-Perthes disease	A degenerative disease of the hip joint, which repairs itself over a period of about 2 years but which may involve school absence and social isolation, braces, or surgery.	Long absences from school may require assistance to catch up. Homebound/hospitalized teaching may be indicated.
Osgood-Schlatter's disease	An inflammation of the knee that will restrict physical activities.	Restricted physical activities.
Osteochondritis dissecans	The breaking of joint cartilage with inflammation in bone and cartilage, most frequently in the knee. In younger children 3 to 6 months' immobilization is sufficient for repair; over 16 years, surgery is necessary.	Physical education must be restricted to spare the joint unnecessary trauma.
Chondromalacia	Softening of cartilage of the kneecap, which may be corrected by special exercises, chemotherapy, or surgery.	School attendance may be interrupted for varying periods of time. Special education programs are helpful.
Torn cartilage	Requires restricted use and active rehabilitation programs to return to full functioning before engaging in active sports.	Restricted physical activities.
Slipped capital femoral epiphysis	A slipping of the growth center at the hip end of the thigh, resulting in leg pain, hip joint stiffness, and sometimes degenerative arthritic changes. Surgery will necessitate prolonged absence from school.	Nonparticipation in active sports for at least a year after surgery.

TABLE 8-3 (Continued)

Conditions That May Require Restricted Physical Activities

Condition	Definition	Modifications
Brittle bone disease Osteogenesis imperfecta	An inherited defect in the bone protein matrix, appearing at birth or developing later in life. Bones may be curved, and thin, translucent-looking skin, excessively mobile joints, and distinctive blue sclera (whites of the eyes) are characteristic. Deafness is common as the child ages, and visual disorders can occur. Intelligence is within the normal range.	Education should aim toward sedentary, intellectually-demanding occupations. Physical education is not permitted these children as their bones break so easily. Children should wear an identification tag or carry a card so that in the event of hospitalization, personnel will not conclude that it is a case of child abuse.
Cystic fibrosis mucoviscidosis	A hereditary disease involving hypersecretion of thickened mucus in the pancreas, lungs, and other organs. The mucus blocks the secretion of enzymes that aid digestion and also the passage of air from the bronchioles in the lungs. This leads to cyst formation and scarring of the pancreas and other organs, and collapse of air sacs in the lungs. Cystic fibrosis is the most common cause of death among genetic disorders and the most common cause of chronic lung disease in Caucasian children (much less for Black, still less for Oriental children). It is estimated that 1 out of every 25 Caucasians carries the recessive gene for cystic fibrosis, and that 1 out of every 1,500 children is born with the disease. Since the average age of death is 14 years, however, these children are not common in public schools. Those who do appear are normally bright, and accommodations will be social rather than academic.	The child should be encouraged to cough (it is not contagious) and allowed to visit the lavatory whenever necessary. If medication is needed during school hours, the child should be provided the opportunity to take it as unobtrusively as possible. Physical exercise within the child's stamina limits should be encouraged, but monitored so that excessive salt loss through sweating does not occur. As much as possible the children should be treated like any other child.

TABLE 8-3 (Continued)

Conditions That May Require Restricted Physical Activities

Condition	Definition	Modifications
Heart disease	May be acquired (from rheumatic fever, for example), but is most often congenital, occurring in about 6 per 1,000 live births. Because of high early mortality rate, the incidence at 10 years of age is closer to 1 per 2,000. Signs include shortness of breath, chest pain, faintness, cyanosis, very rapid heart beat, and unusual fatigue.	In general these children should not participate in competitive athletics. Nonathletic extracurricular activities should be encouraged, and a regular academic program should be followed.
Hemophilia	A hereditary condition in which blood clots slowly or not at all.	Physical activity should be limited to sports such as swimming (*no diving*), golf, calisthenics, and hiking, since strenuous activities or contact sports may cause bleeding into joints. Normal physical and social activities should be allowed as far as possible, and a regular academic program should be maintained.

TABLE 8-4

Conditions That May Require Emotional Support

Condition	Definition	Recommendations
Asthma	A common chronic childhood disease that involves wheezing, coughing, and paroxysmal panting because of allergies or irritations of the bronchi.	The asthmatic child should be treated like all other children in the class, although consideration of allergies should be taken regarding class pets, foods for class parties, and exercise. Mild attacks may be controlled through relaxation without too much attention from the teacher or class. The child should not be permitted to use the disease in order to get his or her own way. Consultation should be provided on routine academic or behavioral problems, since there are no specific learning problems associated with the disease. Intervention may be necessary to prevent emotional problems.
Sickle cell disease	A hereditary form of anemia occurring mainly in Blacks, characterized by sickle-shaped blood cells and an abnormal type of hemoglobin, accompanied by acute abdominal pains, ulceration of the legs, and bone pain. Children with this disease often have life-threatening medical problems and miss a lot of school. Intelligence is in the normal range.	Regular class placement is recommended. Health complaints or lethargy should not be taken lightly.

TABLE 8-4 (Continued)

Conditions That May Require Emotional Support

Condition	Definition	Recommendations
Juvenile rheumatoid arthritis	Painful inflammation of the joints apparently caused by autoimmune attack against normal body materials. The course of the disease lasts about 10 years. The cause is unknown. The disease afflicts between 100,000 and 300,000 children in the U.S. The major problem is the degree to which permanent joint changes occur. Drug therapy, rest, or surgery may be needed.	School personnel must help the child cope with pain, fear, and depression, and must deal with the child's mood changes and slowness of motion. Children taking aspirin may have a high-frequency hearing loss that interferes with speech reception. Some children develop vision problems related to the disease.

Conditions That May Require Temporary Modifications

Table 8-5 lists two conditions, diabetes and epilepsy, that may require special treatment of a temporary nature.

Children with juvenile diabetes mellitus are dependent on insulin. From an early age they are trained to inject their daily doses of insulin, to test their urine, and to control their diet. The critical time when emotional support is usually necessary is during adolescence, when their dietary differences and the need for daily insulin injections may interfere with their adolescent need to be alike and conform to the peer culture. School psychologists may be called upon for counseling these pupils and their families at this time. Referral to a rehabilitation agency may be necessary, because this can be a vocationally handicapping condition.

Epilepsy is often associated with other handicapping conditions, especially mental retardation (Robinson and Robinson, 1976). When there are no other associated conditions, the child should remain in the regular class, since the disorder does not necessarily impair the learning process. Interpretation of the condition is often necessary for the teacher and for other students in the class so that they do not become upset if the child has a seizure during the school day. It should be noted that most children with epilepsy who are in regular classes are under medication that keeps their seizures under control.

For each of these conditions, emotional support for both child and parents may be required from the school psychologist as well as other school personnel, particularly immediately after the initial medical diagnosis is made. Classmates and teachers may need interpretation and help in understanding and coping with the child's attacks or temporary loss of consciousness.

For more information see Blackman (1983), Bleck and Nagel (1983), Ellenberg (1978), Howell (1978b), Robinson and Robinson (1976), and Wolraich (1983).

PSYCHOLOGICAL ISSUES

The interdisciplinary team approach to educating children with physical or health impairments often implies a limited role for the school psychologist. Testing and behavioral observation in the classroom are likely to be the school psychologist's major contributions. Secondarily, or routinely in a school system without other ancillary personnel, the school psychologist may be requested to assist in effecting the mutual adjustment of the child, school peers, and teacher; to provide suggestions regarding alternate educational strategies; and to assist parents in their relationship with the child. The general goal, as in all educa-

TABLE 8-5

Physical and Health Conditions That May Require Temporary or Limited Modifications

Condition	Definition	Recommendations
Juvenile diabetes mellitus	An inherited inability to metabolize food because the body cannot make the hormone known as insulin. Control of the disease requires balance among diet, exercise, and oral or injected insulin. The child acts as his or her own doctor in testing the urine and administering insulin.	Aside from care in choosing snacks and judiciousness in exercise there is no reason for special treatment. School personnel should be aware of the symptoms and emergency treatments of both too much sugar ("incipient ketoacidosis" or diabetic coma) and too little (insulin reaction).
Epilepsy/convulsive disorders	A disorder of the brain characterized by a recurring excessive neuronal discharge. It afflicts 0.5% of the U.S. population, most frequently children under 5 years of age, and males more often than females. Many school-age children who are seizure-prone will be on medication to control their seizures.	School personnel should know how to handle a convulsive generalized tonic-clonic (grand mal) seizure calmly and tactfully, and should not keep the child from participating in regular school activities. The school psychologist may be asked for advice on the social management of these children, especially if a seizure occurs in the classroom. Children referred because of verbal or behavioral tics or staring spells (daydreaming) may need medical evaluation for nonconvulsive absence (petit mal) seizure.

tion, is maximizing the "fit" among the child's strengths, educational tasks, and environmental characteristics so as to provide the best foundation for learning.

Hindrances to Adjustment

Attainment of this goal may be hindered by the general social beliefs and values regarding people with physical limitations that often underlie attitudinal and behavioral problems arising in the child, peers, and the adults who work with the child. The exaggerated stress on physical normality, rather than the ability to perform everyday tasks, as a standard produces devaluation of any person whose appearance is unusual. Further, it is assumed that the person with a physical limitation feels inferior, mourns his or her loss, and is often frustrated, and that special achievements in any area result from "compensation" rather than normal interest. Most damaging of all is the tendency to see a person with one physical limitation as a "disabled person," completely different in all ways from a "normal person" (Bartel & Guskin, 1971). In fact, research in this area has found no clear evidence relating presence or degree of physical limitation to particular personality characteristics or to overall psychological adjustment (Lewandowski & Cruickshank, 1980). Physical disabilities do have profound effects on a person's life, but these vary widely and are related to premorbid personality characteristics rather than to the disability itself (Wright, 1960).

The following discussion aims at clarifying the attitudes and behaviors that are likely to be encountered in dealing with children who have physical or health impairments. Problems and possible interventions are considered in relation to the child, peers, and adults working with the child.

Major Issues in Adjustment

For the school-age child who has a physical limitation, the major issues concern social interactions, motivation to persist in educational and rehabilitation programs, and the adjustment of the child's self-concept to the absence of a body function. Motivating children who are in education and rehabilitation programs is extremely important. Many times therapy involves difficult and painful exercises, and often the child is tempted to stay with dependent adaptations worked out during early or acute phases of the problem. Wright (1960) has suggested a number of questions for professionals to ask themselves regarding this issue:

a. Can the task be recast so that it becomes part of an activity the child likes to do anyway?
b. Is the child's overall experience in the rehabilitation session one of success or failure?
c. Is there a place for extraneous incentives?
d. What else is the child learning?
e. Are background factors (time, place, or social conditions) optimal for learning?
f. What are some of the basic attitudes the child has toward his/her disability and the rehabilitation procedures?
g. Does the motivator feel friendly toward the child and the task? (pp. 330-343)

Careful consideration of these questions will enable the professional working with these children to optimize the fit among child, task, and environment. Successful experiences in the rehabilitation and in the school program will go a long way toward helping the child accept the disability and the adaptations that must be made for it. Since people tend to accept others at the value they place on themselves, the child's self-acceptance will go a long way in promoting acceptance by others and integration into community life as well.

Adjustment to Physical Limitations

If the disability is of recent origin, the child must adjust to a new physical state. For the child whose disabilities are congenital, the school experience may be the first time differences are perceived as undesirable. This realization may initiate a period of shock, denial, and grief; the child may long for the more sheltered setting of home. The ultimate adjustment process involves several kinds of value changes. First, the scope of values is enlarged to include nonphysical characteristics as a basis for judging self-worth. Concomitantly, the physical being is subordinated in importance, and other characteristics such as personality, talents, courage, and intelligence are seen as more valuable. The effect of these changes is the containment of the handicap: The child realizes that a physical limitation need not prevent *all* activities, and begins to align his or her expectations of life-roles more closely with the reality of what can and cannot be done. Finally, there is a shift from comparative values to asset values: from ability relative to others to ability relative to the requirements of living. This then becomes a basis for self-assessment. The abilities and traits the child *has* are seen as assets. Sometimes even the disability itself may be viewed as a source of some valuable traits, and thus is valued (Wright, 1960).

Social Interactions and Adjustment of Self-Esteem

The questions of values and acceptance are also at the root of the child's behavior within the social milieu. The child with a physical limitation has both minority/inferior status and salutory status: Nobody wants to be like the child, but people admire his or her courage and coping. Curiosity and instrusive attempts at helping are the most innocuous of the reactions such children may encounter. Pity, teasing, and taunting are just as common. In some cases the natural coping behaviors may lead to social disapproval; an example is the orthopedically handicapped child's use of creeping or crawling for locomotion. The child's responses to the reactions of others may worsen a disturbed situation, defuse it, or even transform it to a constructive exchange.

A child's reaction to social incidents depends largely on the perception of self and the disability, and this depends on the process of adjustment. Interventions with children who have physical limitations may include counseling—alone or in groups—to help with the adjustment process, to strengthen the child's inner resources and self-esteem, and to "inoculate" against the negative effects of incidents that may occur. Small group discussions among children with varying disabilities and with nonhandicapped peers may include sharing of experiences, discussions of stories or plays involving social situations, roleplaying, and training in social skills. It may also be possible to arrange for real-life experiences with a disabled person who is well adjusted to his or her disability, or in groups of people who have similar, recent disabilities.

Problems with peers include curiosity and discussion of the disability, unwanted help or sympathy, social isolation, ridicule, and taunting. These problems arise from the social values and expectations discussed earlier, from ignorance or misinformation, and from the specific meaning to the perceiver of the disability and successful coping with it. If the child with a disability does not appear to mourn the loss of function, the athlete (or bully) may perceive diminished value to his or her healthy body. The response may be taunting or ridicule in an attempt to establish agreement that the nonhandicapped child is superior. The visibility of a physical impairment facilitates invasion of privacy through staring or questions and insult through comments communicating devaluation of the person. Help may be rejected either because of social anxieties or in a realistic effort to achieve self-reliance. The helper may be acting out of unwanted pity and may not know what kind of help is needed or when.

All too often special needs children experience social isolation outside the classroom. A wheelchair-bound child may be an adequate playmate or friend in class, but on the playground physical games and activities frequently disallow participation by the student with physical limitations. At home, the student may have limited opportunities for casual neighborhood friendships. Other families may hesitate to include the physically limited child in birthday parties or other events because of their own fears or misunderstanding of physical handicaps. These exclusions, though sometimes innocently made, are poignant reminders to the child of the limitations imposed by the handicap or by other people. The school psychologist should be aware of the potential occurrence of this selective isolation. Recess may be particularly anxiety-producing for the child who may need some help in working through this anxiety.

Facilitating Integration

A child returning to school after losing a limb or any other functional ability may elicit a myriad of feelings in others. As adults and peers resolve their feelings of pity, grief, distaste, and fears of their own mortality, the child may be left alone or rejected. The school psychologist may facilitate the reintegration of the child by promoting open communication and discussion of the child's disability within the classroom before and after the child reenters school. The discussion should include emphasis on the abilities and strengths of the child.

Besides informal discussions led by the school psychologist, teacher, principal, or the affected child, there are many affective education programs that may be used as vehicles for discussions. Child-oriented movies and books depicting the daily lives and feelings of people with physical limitations may be found through school or university libraries and media systems. These may be integrated with the teaching of reading or language skills so that discussion emerges naturally. Teachers should be encouraged to listen for the development of problems between and among students and be aware of their own behavior in relation to the handicapped child and other students (Hanna & Graff, 1977). The child with a disability wants to participate to his or her full ability, and generally wants to be treated like any other child. If the class misbehaves and brags about the fearsome punishment of the teacher, and the child with a disability is included among the group, the teacher does no service by exempting the child from appropriate punishment. Especially with younger children, whose past experiences make them particularly sensitive to differences, a focus by adults on the positive characteristics of the child with a disability will aid in easing the child's entry into the social life of the class and the school. Finally, taunting and ridicule should be discouraged as far as possible. While discussions and role-playing exercises may help by giving the able-bodied child an inside view of disability, breaking up teasing incidents may also be necessary. Too often a child with a physical limitation learns to agree with the bully that he or she is pitiful, rather than learning to maintain self-esteem in adversity. Even a single attack may have lasting emotional effects.

Adjustment of Others to the Child

In essence, the school psychologist and other outsiders must go through the same adjustment process as the child. Acceptance and natural ease in adjusting tasks or situations to the child's abilities while maintaining reasonable expectations for performance and behavior are very difficult as long as the child is judged comparatively. Professionals, too, may overprotect or isolate a child in response to their own unresolved feelings about disabilities. The tendencies to provide unneeded and unwanted help and to make special allowances for the child's behavior will be dysfunctional for the child in the long run. School psychologists may be able to assist teachers in resolving their feelings and in becoming aware of their assumptions about a child with physical or health problems, but they will be most effective if they have examined these things in themselves as well.

Adjustment as a Process

School psychologists and teachers need to be aware of the child's level of adjustment to the physical handicap in order to make adequate assessments of ability to handle social and academic tasks. For the psychologist this problem is crucial, since the child's motivation to succeed on aptitude tests may vary in different stages of adjustment. In turn, motivation can affect the validity of measurements used for educational planning. It will be important for all who work with the child to remember that adjustment is a *process* involving changes in mood, activity level, and commitment over time. It may also be influenced by the age of the child. For instance, a child who appeared to have made a satisfactory adjustment during latency may experience puberty as a crisis because of the importance of physique in establishing adult sexual identity and overlapping of "adult" and "child," "normal" and "disabled" determinants of behavior. Finally, if the child has a progressive disease, continuing decline may be associated with cognitive, emotional, and motivational fluctuations. Periodic reevaluations must take these factors into account.

Parent Counseling

At all times we must remember that the parent is the key to the child's psychological adjustment to disability (Wright, 1960). Parent counseling is not always part of the school psychologist's job, but if parental attitudes appear to be the source of school problems and if there are no other ancillary personnel available, then such counseling may be appropriate and necessary. The balance between an attitude of hope and acceptance of stark reality is important here, and requires sensitivity on the part of the school psychologist. The parents, as well as the teachers who work with the child, should be made aware of the differences among and between overprotection, realistic dependence, and independence; they should be especially encouraged to seek a balance between the last two.

EDUCATIONAL ISSUES

Integrating a child with physical limitations into the regular classroom immediately raises concern about such issues as making architectural modifications such as wider aisles to allow free passage of a wheelchair, selecting a room with ready access to a bathroom, or providing special chair-desk combinations to provide better support, perhaps with straps to hold the child on the chair. There are many other considerations as well. Psychological reports and recommendations must be clear and useful, particularly when the receiving teacher has had limited experience with physically- or health-limited children. School psychologists would be well advised to consider the situation from the teacher's perspective: What does the teacher need to know about the child, what teaching materials and methods should be used, to whom can the teacher turn for guidance or in a crisis, and, of particular interest, how can the teacher assist in the assessment process?

Architectural Modifications

Assuming that the child can get inside the building (as mandated by the Rehabilitation Act of 1973, Section 502), further modifications may be necessary within some classrooms: handrails to encourage independence and freedom to move around the room; higher desks to accommodate wheelchairs and crutches; a cot or mattress for rest periods (leg braces are *very* heavy and fatiguing). The list goes on: lowering blackboards that are too high to be reached by a child in a wheelchair to preferential seating to accommodate a reclining wheelchair or facilitate exiting during fire drills and real emergencies. The special education teacher-consultant can be invaluable in suggesting and making these physical modifications (Bigge, 1976).

Interdisciplinary Services

The teacher (and school psychologist) may be unaware of the myriad medical disciplines often involved with physically and multiply handicapped children. Most children are involved with the usual health service personnel of pediatrician, dentist, and sometimes a psychologist or psychiatrist. Mullins (1979) raised the point that physically handicapped children may be involved with any one of over 40 personnel, ranging from neurosurgeons, prosthetic dentists, and physical therapists to social workers and school psychologists. While the interdisciplinary team approach provides the opportunity for professionals to discuss their concerns and integrate their recommendations, the teacher may still lean heavily on the school psychologist for advice and interpretation. The more seriously involved a child's disabilities are, the more the teacher may need guidance in teaching methods and the more restrictions may be put on time spent with the student in class. A child who requires daily naps and daily physical therapy sessions may have little real time left for academic classroom activities.

In many cases, however, the child spends a good part of the day in the classroom. It is for this reason that the teacher's observations can provide valuable feedback to other support personnel; the teacher becomes a member of the team by encouraging and challenging the child to use new skills prescribed by the therapists. The child's passive or active participation in activities can be influenced by the teacher's attitudes. The teacher may assist by inspecting the child's therapeutic equipment, or better yet, by periodically asking about the status of braces or crutches and thereby encouraging the child to check the equipment. Through daily interactions with the child, the teacher will be able to detect atypical appearance or behavior and bring it to the attention of other professionals involved with the child. The teacher should not be made to feel solely responsible for observing and noting emotional or physical problems the child may be experiencing, but should be sensitized to potential psychological and physical issues.

Use of Task Analysis to Augment Assessment and Instruction

The assessment process can be augmented not only by the teacher's observations but also by the method of teaching. The use of task analysis or diagnostic-prescriptive teaching enables the teacher to identify what the child can and cannot do and then teach to the child's weaknesses by using the strengths (Bigge, 1976; Calhoun & Hawisher, 1979). Task analysis assumes that the reason a disabled person (or any other person) cannot accomplish a particular task is because of an inability to accomplish one or more subparts of the task (Bigge, 1976).

Information derived from task analyses can be used in formulating instructional objectives and goals. Defining target tasks and their subtasks is often an arbitrary process; however, it may help to review the following questions when analyzing a task:

1. What task or tasks should be learned next?
2. What parts of the target task are accomplished?
3. What parts of the target task are not accomplished?
4. What are all the probable steps necessary in order for a person to be able to accomplish the task of _____?
5. How should tasks be changed to accommodate persons with disabilities?
6. Under what conditions and to what degree are tasks accomplished? (Bigge, 1976, p. 7)

Diagnostic-prescriptive teaching makes use of the information derived from task analyses and other test results to ameliorate the effects of the child's weaknesses while capitalizing on strengths.

In general there is no single teaching method appropriate for these children. The physical or health limitations may or may not affect cognitive ability; the physically handicapped child may be gifted, learning disabled, or mentally impaired, or present behavior disorders. The focus of the teacher should be on the learning style, not the physical handicap per se.

Children who have physical limitations are heterogeneous in the nature of their educational needs. Modifying curriculum is rarely necessary, although some children may need to have one or more of the following areas emphasized in their individualized education program:

Habits of planning. Retracing one's route unnecessarily is too time and energy consuming for children and youth whose supply of those commodities is less than average.

Choosing the essentials. Most pupils can carry along an additional book just in case it is found to be required later. Not so for pupils who need one or both hands to help with movement and who may already be carrying a heavy brace.

Mobility training. All children have to learn how to travel with increasing independence. Special added instruction is required when only certain routes, buses, buildings, and streets are sufficiently barrier free to use and when weather changes pose extraordinary hazards.

Health habits. Personal health takes on special meaning when functionally limiting impairments already exist. For example. . .epileptic pupils who are liable to seizures or to brief blank periods must have instruction in the management of those incidents.

Physical education and recreation. Happily, physical educators. . . help pupils with physical and health impairments to acquire and maintain superior levels of general fitness through individualized programs termed *adaptive* physical education. Special attention spotlights body alignment, posture, and the adjustments needed to facilitate participation in recreational sports such as bowling, fishing, and golf.

Handwriting. Some pupils with hand or coordination difficulties will attain competence in writing if templates and line guides are employed and if simpler and larger letters are substituted for those conventionally used. Others may have to bypass handwriting altogether, except for learning a signature, and do all their writing on standard or modified typewriters.

Socialization and self development. This part of the curriculum refers to what students learn in school about cooperation, respect for individual rights (both personal and property), consideration for others, their own strengths and weaknesses, and the generally accepted values of the child and adult worlds in which they live. . .

Other curricular areas. Vocal music may be extremely difficult for pupils with slowed speech and distorted articulation due to cerebral palsy. Studio arts may require adaptations in technique and media for pupils without the use of hands and arms. Playing wind instruments may be too dangerous for pupils with weak arterial walls or asthma. Chemistry experiments may have to be adapted for youngsters still learning how to manipulate objects by means of prostheses. Wood or metalshop machinery may require added safety devices and special signs and fixtures. Calculators may have to be supplied in mathematics classes. Relevant adjustments may need to be made in all other curricular components, too. (Reynolds & Birch, 1982, pp. 315-316)

The school psychologist may become the one who orchestrates the child's programming during school time. In an effort to meet the child's physical needs, it is important to remember that these children are not easily whisked to and fro and that they may tire quickly. Attempts should be made to schedule physical therapy sessions, for example, at the end or beginning of the day. The child should be allowed maximum time in school for interaction with peers and the teacher.

The mainstreaming of children with physical limitations or health impairments may be a fluctuating process, with the children having good or bad times, lasting for minutes, days, or weeks. Adaptability on the part of the teacher is an essential component of a good teacher-student relationship. When communication between home and school is maintained, early recognition of new stressors or changes in physical and educational performance will be ensured. It is paramount that the child should never be discounted as a valuable contributor in programming and implementation.

THE ASSESSMENT PROCESS

The heterogeneity of this group of children precludes categorical statements about specific test instruments and procedures. The school psychologist must be flexible and creative in approach, bearing in mind the purpose for evaluation and conducting the evaluation in a non-biased manner. The assessment process is highly individualized. Cross and Goin (1977) have suggested that a diagnostic battery for children with physical limitations should include at least four types of data collection:

1. A structured or unstructured interview with parents, teacher, and, if appropriate, the child to obtain a detailed description of the child's current behavior (see Appendix D for a suggested format).
2. A history of the child's past disability and development, including a current report from the physician(s).
3. Observations including how and where the child was observed as well as the frequency and duration of the observation.
4. The use of standardized instruments.

The selection of test instruments should be based primarily on the reason for the evaluation. Extensive testing is not always in the best interest of the child. Careful and sensitive administration of one or two tests may provide much more qualitative and quantitative information than a lengthy barrage of instruments.

Once the purpose of the evaluation is clarified, the psychologist must determine the child's mode of communication, particularly if the child has no oral language. This may require observation as well as consultation with the child's teacher, parents, speech and language pathologist, or physical therapist. With severely involved children, the school psychologist must find at least one consistent response pattern, that is, a movement that is distinguishable from all other movements and that can be made by the child upon command. Once this movement has been identified, the child can be taught signals for communication. For example, a glance upward may indicate "yes," a glance to the side may mean "no," and a drop of the head may indicate "I don't know" (Allaire & Miller, 1983; Bigge, 1976; Silverman, 1980).

Depending on the child's mode of communication and the purpose for the evaluation, standardized tests may or may not require modifications. The time needed to complete the test may exceed the strength or endurance capability of the child, so that the psychologist may have a limited amount of real working time with the child. As discussed in Chapter 1, caution should be exercised in modifying standardized tests, for a change in test administration affects the meaning of scores. Tests that rely heavily on physical responses are clearly unsuitable for children with severe motor involvement, although one should never underestimate the child's capabilities; some children are as deft with their prostheses as others are with natural limbs. Before making any modifications, the psychologist must be certain that the proposed adjustments are necessary and warranted in order to assess a particular area of functioning or ability. When test results are reported, modifications must be explained. In addition, the classroom implications of the child's performance on standard and modified tasks should be considered in reports.

Criterion-referenced tests can be of great assistance to teachers in their daily programming for children. The reliability and validity of these tests are evaluated on the basis of the ability of the test to indicate growth or progress within an individual rather than between individuals. Content validity thus assumes great importance. Some norm-referenced tests can be used as criterion-referenced tests, but such a step should only be taken after careful examination of the instrument. Criterion-referenced instruments may be more beneficial for instructional programming because they usually contain more items and often cover many developmental areas. Their weaknesses lie in three areas:

1. Some are designed for use with a specific group of children and when used with other groups of children may not provide the type of information needed by the teacher.
2. The items are often very specific, measuring splinter skills but failing to yield a total picture of the child.
3. The items tend to measure the acquisition of skills only, not the child's ability to generalize the use of a skill. (Bigge, 1976)

In order to assess the development of living skills such as dressing, feeding, ambulation, and responsibility for personal hygiene, adaptive behavior scales can be particularly useful. Adaptive behavior scales that are commonly employed for any child suspected of having a mental impairment are often valuable instruments for use with other special needs children. The scales provide a chronological age-rating for acquisition of certain skills and much practical information for educational programming (Bigge, 1976).

No assessment of students with physical limitations or health impairments is complete without a current report from the physician(s). As mentioned earlier, these children may be involved with one or more medical disciplines as well as a variety of school personnel. Often, physicians are unable to attend school meetings and will send their reports to the school nurse. School staff must be assertive in requesting specific information from physicians about the child's physical and health capabilities and limitations, particularly when the child has a progressive disease. Parents can be valuable aids in hastening the release of reports from physicans and in conveying information about school performance to physicians.

The school psychologist would be well advised to become familiar with various support agencies in the community and ask to be put on their mailing lists (see Appendix F). Parents' opinions about the responsiveness of agencies to the needs of families and handicapped children are also valuable sources of information. Often a new problem area is identified by the interdisciplinary team. It is essential to have a working knowledge of community services as referrals for ancillary services.

MULTIPLE IMPAIRMENTS

Many of the physical impairments described in this chapter involve more than one disability. Other health complications are frequent, and sensory losses are associated with several of them, particularly mental retardation. In fact, multiple disabilities seem to be the rule rather than the exception, at least in disabilities not caused by trauma during childhood (such as amputations). Wolf and Anderson (1969) reported a number of studies indicating that 70 to 90% of handicapped children have two or more impairments.

The major disability types may be grouped as (a) motoric problems, including paralysis, ataxia, uncontrolled movements, debilitating weakness, and deformity; (b) sensory losses, especially visual and hearing impairments; (c) the various other health impairments; and (d) mental retardation, usually moderate, severe, or profound. Many school districts define ''multiply impaired'' as involving a cross-group combination of motor, sensory, and cognitive (retardation) problems. The combinations that seem to have received the most attention are those involving two or more groups, probably since these childen cannot be handled in programs designed for a single type of disability.

Incidence

Illustrative of the issues related to multiple impairments is the work of Wolf and Anderson (1969), who cited several studies showing a high rate of hearing impairment among retarded children—13 to 49%, depending on the hearing loss criteria used. Conversely, they cited studies indicating a 10 to 12% prevalence of retardation among children in special schools for the deaf, and about 40% among deaf children with other disabilities. The varying criteria for hearing loss and for retardation cast these results into some doubt, but there seems to be a significant group with such multiple disabilities. Often these children tend to have measured IQ's too high for placement in a special school or classes for mentally impaired students, yet do not flourish in regular classes for deaf students. Many teachers of mentally retarded children are not trained to teach deaf students, many teachers of deaf students are not qualified to teach children who are retarded. Most of these children appear to be enrolled in residential institutions for either deaf or retarded students, but Wolf and Anderson (1969) concluded that "without extensive changes in the present character of educational services, many of these children will not achieve social competence" (p. 26).

The combination of deafness and blindness is relatively rare, although it has been of concern to special educators for many years (Wolf, 1967). The National Study Committee on the Education of Deaf-Blind Children defines these children as those whose combination of handicaps prevents them from profiting satisfactorily from educational programs either for the hearing impaired or the visually impaired. Regional educational and rehabilitative programs make the selection of an appropriate educational placement more possible than has been true in the past (Dantona, 1976).

Studies regarding the prevalence of speech impairments among blind children are few and inconsistent, with estimates ranging from 6.7 to 49% requiring speech therapy. Studies of the blind-retarded group provide a rate of 7.9-42%. These children also are not adequately provided for in standard programs for blind retarded children, but more combined programs seem to exist for them than for deaf children (Wolf & Anderson, 1969).

A major question in all of these studies, and one with which the school psychologist may become directly concerned, is whether the retardation of children with sensory or physical impairments is organically based; is related to an impoverished or nonstimulating environment, especially during the early years; is a product of the primary impairment; or is simply a function of the assessment instruments. The latter question was discussed in the assessment section of this chapter, but it is wise to keep the lack of adequately validated and standardized assessment instruments in mind when viewing these incidence figures.

As for the children with mental retardation as a primary diagnosis, Wolf and Anderson estimated that "one fourth to one half of all mentally retarded children can also be considered multiply handicapped" (1969, p. 39). They summarized their research findings as follows:

1. There is a lack of a theoretical concept concerning multiple disabilities;
2. Confusion and lack of agreement on definitions, classifications, and terminology;
3. Inadequacy of a rationale by investigators in assigning priority to a disability;
4. Conflicting viewpoints concerning which facilities are most appropriate and the extent and availability of such facilities;
5. Inconsistencies in reported incidence and prevalence;

6. Lack of a precise methodology for teaching children with multiple disabilities;
7. The need for additional research on any or all of these findings. (pp. 39-40)

Role of the School Psychologist

Advances in medical science are saving many infants who in former years would have died. Many of these have one or more physical or mental impairments that contribute to later developmental problems having an impact on their education. These place increasing pressure on public schools to provide services for multiply handicapped children who formerly were placed in institutional settings or kept at home. For some severely handicapped pupils, the school psychologist may have limited involvement in the assessment and educational planning processes because of the severity of their impairments. However, the school psychologist should be familiar with the educational problems these children present and with alternate assessment strategies, such as those discussed in Chapter 3, which might be useful to the teacher and other members of the interdisciplinary team in arriving at decisions regarding educational placement and planning that will best meet the needs of the child.

Many school districts have special facilities for the education of multihandicapped students, and the school psychologist may or may not be involved in their assessment. Most children with orthopedic or other health impairments of varying degrees of severity are likely to be in the regular public schools, and the school psychologist may be involved in educational evaluation and planning for these students. As adolescence approaches, the school psychologist may need to facilitate referrals to rehabilitation agencies.

Definitions and eligibility requirements for special education programs and services for this group of pupils vary from state to state within the federal guidelines. The school psychologist must be knowledgeable about federal and state regulations pertaining to evaluation procedures. Assessment must take into account the child's mode of communication, and instruments should be selected to reflect the child's aptitude or achievement as accurately as possible. An evaluation of the child's suspected disability is required. With physically and otherwise health impaired children, a physician's report is often interpreted by the school nurse. The interdisciplinary team must include one or more specialists qualified to evaluate the suspected disability. School psychologists may be assigned to the team when it is necessary to evaluate intellectual and/or personality issues. No student should be determined eligible for special education services without considering the influence of environmental, cultural, or economic factors. If the disability can be attributed solely to any of these factors, then the student does not usually qualify for special education services.

SUMMARY

The heterogeneous characteristics and needs of children who have physical and health impairments require that the school psychologist work closely with other school personnel in the assessment process. The specific role played by the school psychologist as a member of the interdisciplinary team will vary from state to state and even within each state depending on the available resources and related services. In some districts the school psychologist will be responsible for not only educational and psychological assessment but also counseling with parents and pupils, consultation with teachers, and referral of children and/or parents to appropriate community and rehabilitation agencies. Thus the school psychologist must know the school and community resources.

Many of the children described in this chapter do not require special education programs and services. For these children the school psychologist may be requested to provide support services, counseling, and referral when appropriate and to function as an advocate interpreting the child's physical, social, and emotional needs to the regular classroom teachers. Children who have multiple impairments will require highly specialized programs and services that often must be supplemented with community resources in order that they may receive an appropriate education. The school psychologist's role with these children will include counseling and referral, when appropriate, in addition to the assessment and educational planning roles.

REFERENCES

Allaire, J. H., & Miller, J. M. (1983). Nonspeech communication. In M. E. Snell (Ed.), *Systematic instruction of the moderately and severely handicapped* (2nd ed.) (pp. 289-311). Columbus OH: Charles E. Merrill.

Bartel, N. E., & Guskin, S. L. (1971). A handicap as a social phenomenon. In W. M. Cruickshank (Ed.), *Psychology of exceptional children and youth* (3rd ed.) (pp. 75-114). Englewood Cliffs NJ: Prentice-Hall.

Bigge, J. L. (1976). *Teaching individuals with physical and multiple disabilities.* Columbus OH: Charles E. Merrill.

Blackman, J. A. (1983). Orthopedic problems. In J. A. Blackman (Ed.)., *Medical aspects of developmental disabilities in children birth to three* (pp. 179-186). Iowa City: University Hospital School, The University of Iowa.

Bleck, E. E., & Nagel, D. A. (Eds.). (1983) *Physically handicapped children—a medical atlas for teachers* (2nd ed.). New York: Grune & Stratton.

Calhoun, M. L., & Hawisher, M. F. (1979). *Teaching and learning strategies for physically handicapped students.* Baltimore: University Park Press.

Cegelka, P. T., & Prehm, H. J. (1982). *Mental retardation: From categories to people.* Columbus: Charles E. Merrill.

Cross, L., & Goin, K. (Eds.). (1977). *Identifying handicapped children: A guide to casefinding, screening, diagnosis, assessment, and evaluation.* New York: Walker and Company.

Dantona, R. (1976). Services for deaf-blind children. *Exceptional Children, 43,* 172-174.

Ellenberg, M. (1978). Diabetes Mellitus. In R. M. Goldenson (Ed.), *Disability and rehabilitation handbook* (pp. 353-362). New York: McGraw-Hill.

Goldenson, R. M. (1978a). Cerebral Palsy. In R. M. Goldenson (Ed.), *Disability and rehabilitation handbook* (pp. 331-343). New York: McGraw-Hill.

Goldenson, R. M. (Ed.). (1978b). *Disability and rehabilitation handbook.* New York: McGraw-Hill.

Gould Medical Dictionary. (3rd ed.). (1972). New York: McGraw-Hill.

Hanna, R. L., & Graff, D. L. (1977). *The physically handicapped child: Facilitating regular classroom adjustment.* Austin TX: Learning Concepts.

Healy, A. (1983). Cerebral palsy. In J. A. Blackman (Ed.), *Medical aspects of developmental disabilities in children birth to three* (pp. 31-37). Iowa City: The University of Iowa.

Howell, L. (1978a). Spina bifida. In R. M. Goldenson (Ed.), *Disability and rehabilitation handbook* (pp. 560-564). New York: McGraw-Hill.

Howell, L. (1978b). Epilepsy. In R. M. Goldenson (Ed.), *Disability and rehabilitation handbook* (pp. 381-388). New York: McGraw-Hill.

Kirk, S. A., & Gallagher, J. J. (1983). *Educating exceptional children* (4th ed.) (chap. 10). Boston: Houghton Mifflin.

Lewandowski, L. J., & Cruickshank, W. M. (1980). Psychological development of crippled children and youth. In W. M. Cruickshank (Ed.), *Psychology of exceptional children and youth.* (4th ed.) (pp. 345-380). Englewood Cliffs NJ: Prentice-Hall.

Mullins, J. B. (1979). *A teacher's guide to management of physically handicapped students.* Springfield IL: Charles C Thomas.

Ornitz, E. M., & Ritvo, E. R. (1976). Medical assessment. In E. R. Ritvo (Ed.), *Autism: Diagnosis, current research and management* (pp. 7-23). New York: Spectrum.

Reynolds, M. C. & Birch, J. W. (1982). *Teaching exceptional children in all America's schools.* (rev. ed.) (chap. 9, 13). Reston VA: The Council for Exceptional Children.

Ritvo, E. R. (1976). Autism: From adjective to noun. In E. R. Ritvo (Ed.), *Autism: Diagnosis, current research and management* (pp. 3-6). New York: Spectrum.

Robinson, N. M., & Robinson, H. B. (1976). *The mentally retarded child: A psychological approach.* New York: McGraw-Hill.

Schor, D. P. (1983a). Autism. In J. A. Blackman (Ed.), *Medical aspects of developmental disabilities in children birth to three* (pp. 11-13). Iowa City: University Hospital School, The University of Iowa.

Schor, D. P. (1983b). Cystic Fibrosis. In J. A. Blackman (Ed.), *Medical aspects of developmental disabilities in children birth to three* (pp. 77-80). Iowa City: University Hospital School, The University of Iowa.

Silverman, F. H. (1980). *Communication for the speechless.* Englewood Cliffs NJ: Prentice-Hall.

Wolf, J. M. (1967). *The blind child with concomitant disabilities.* New York: American Foundation for the Blind.

Wolf, J. M. & Anderson, R. M. (1969). *The multiply handicapped child.* Springfield IL: Charles C Thomas.

Wolraich, M. L. (1983). Seizure disorders. In J. A. Blackman (Ed.), *Medical aspects of developmental disabilities in children birth to three.* (pp. 215-221). Iowa City: University Hospital School, The University of Iowa.

Wright, B. A. (1960). *Physical disability—A psychological approach.* New York: Harper & Row.

ADDITIONAL RESOURCES

Campbell, H. (1981). *Measuring the abilities of severely handicapped students.* Springfield IL: Charles C Thomas.

Clements, S. D., & Hicks, T. J. (1974). Physically and neurologically impaired children. In M. V. Wisland (Ed.), *Psychoeducational diagnosis of exceptional children* (pp. 213-232). Springfield IL: Charles C Thomas.

DeLoach, C. & Greer, B. G. (1981). *Adjustment to severe physical disability: A metamorphosis.* New York: McGraw-Hill.

Eissler, R. S., Freud, A., Kris, M., & Solnit, A. J. (Eds.). (1977). *Physical illnesses and handicap in childhood: An anthology of The Psychoanalytic Study of the Child.* New Haven: Yale University Press.

Hamburg, B. A., Lipsett, L. F., Incoff, G. E., & Drash, A. L. (Eds.). (1980). *Behavioral and psychosocial issues in diabetes.* Washington DC: Department of Health and Human Services, NIH Publication No. 80-1993.

Newman, J. (1980). Psychological problems of children and youth with chronic medical disorders. In W. M. Cruickshank (Ed.), *Psychology of exceptional children and youth* (4th ed.) (pp. 381-434). Englewood Cliffs NJ: Prentice-Hall.

Rogers, S. J. (1982). Assessment considerations with the motor handicapped child. In G. Ulrey & S. J. Rogers (Eds.), *Psychological assessment of handicapped infants and young children* (pp. 85-107). New York: Thieme-Stratton.

Snell, M. E. (Ed.). (1983). *Systematic instruction of the moderately and severely handicapped* (2nd ed.). Columbus: Charles E. Merrill.

Vernon, M., Bair, R., & Lots, S. (1979, Summer). Psychological evaluation and testing of children who are deaf-blind. *School Psychology Digest, 8,* 281-296.

Wing, L. (1976). *Early childhood autism.* (2nd ed.). New York: Pergamon.

Yarnell, G. D., & Carlton, G. R. (1981). *Guidelines and manual of tests for educators interested in the assessment of handicapped children.* Austin TX: International Research Institute.

CHAPTER 9

Hearing Impairments

Jody Harrison

Children with auditory handicaps may have difficulty hearing in one or both ears or may virtually not hear at all. Professionals and laymen have used a variety of terms to refer to these children: hard of hearing, deaf, deaf-mute, deafened, partially deaf, partially hearing, hearing impaired. The latter term is preferred at the present time. Whatever the label, these children have a sensory impairment which limits their world of experience and requires a shift or reorganization of experience and psychological processes. Within the educational setting, it is imperative that the nature of the impact of the sensory impairment on learning and adjustment be ascertained for each child and that appropriate remedial procedures be facilitated.

School psychologists have the knowledge and training to make helpful contributions in this area. Therefore, it is crucial that they be informed about the important issues and considerations of working with a hearing impaired child. Equally important for school psychologists is knowledge about the physioanatomical nature of the impairment so that they can use the information in conferring with parents, teachers, and other specialists who have some responsibility for the education of the child.

This chapter discusses the hearing impaired child in terms of psychological, educational, and assessment issues. It begins with a broad overview of the process of hearing and definition and exposition of the population. Methods for measuring hearing loss are summarized. Implications are then discussed in each of the following areas: development, assessment, and educational needs.

THE PROCESS OF HEARING

A professional worker in the area of hearing impairments must have some knowledge of the sensory process itself. Many specialists work with the hearing impaired child. The otolaryngologist is concerned with the diseases causing deafness; the audiologist with the psychophysiology and psychoacoustics of hearing; and the educator and psychologist with the effects of the hearing loss on learning and development. However, no professional can be concerned with only one aspect of the problem without severely limiting both understanding of the child and effectiveness in helping and planning for that child. An interdisciplinary team relationship is necessary for an effective educational program.

Content for the remainder of this section is summarized from Dale (1962) and Yost & Nielson (1977).

Structure of the Ear

The ear is divided into three parts: the outer ear, the middle ear, and the inner ear. The outer ear "collects" sounds from the environment. It is composed of the visible part of the ear (pinna) and the canal leading to the eardrum. Its actual functions are protection of the middle and inner ear, amplification of sound, and localization of sound. It collects and transmits acoustic energy in the form of air vibration to the middle ear.

The middle ear begins with the tympanic membrane, or eardrum, and also consists of the ossicular chain, which is three small bones: the malleus, the incus, and stapes. The middle ear is referred to as the conductive mechanism since its function is to conduct the sound vibration to the inner ear through the passage of mechanical vibrations from the eardrum, which vibrates when the air vibrations contact it, through the ossicular chain, to the inner ear. The middle ear also contains the opening of the Eustachian tube, connecting the ear and the nasopharynx. Its purpose is to allow equalization of air pressure on both sides of the tympanic membrane. The stapes then delivers the mechanical sound vibrations to the inner ear.

The inner ear's function is to convert the mechanical energy into electrochemical energy for transmission of the sound via the nervous system. The inner ear is in the temporal bone, which provides maximum protection. It consists of a series of tubular structures referred to as the labyrinth. The latter includes the semicircular canals and vestibular mechanism, which are crucial for the sense of balance. The acoustic labyrinth includes the cochlea and the basilar membrane on which are sensory cells called the organ of Corti. The mechanical energy from the middle ear causes the basilar membrane to bulge, which activates the cilia on the organ of Corti. The movement of the cilia constitutes the conversion of mechanical energy into nerve impulses. These impulses reach the brain through the VIIIth nerve.

The Central Auditory Pathways

Each ear is connected by nerve pathways to both cerebral hemispheres. Both hemispheres are required for maximum effectiveness of audition, especially for some of the more complex sound discriminations such as foreground versus background and noise level versus speech. The nerve pathways lead to the temporal lobe or auditory cortex. Deficiencies in the nerve pathways up to and including the cochlea result in peripheral deafness; deficiencies from the VIIIth nerve to the cortex result in central deafness. Central deafness is of significance psychologically because learning and developmental issues must consider both neurological and sensory deficit. It is also possible that the individual with central deafness will have normal hearing for reflex functions (i.e., have no sensory deficit) but not hear speech, since the lesion precludes the stimulus from reaching the cortex.

In the process of hearing, it is necessary to distinguish startle or involuntary reactions to sound from listening or voluntary behavior. Listening is learned and is dependent on maturation. Thus, maturational aspects of auditory functioning must be taken into consideration in arriving at a differential diagnosis, especially in young children.

Fundamentals of Sound

Sound waves are the disturbance of air caused by vibrating objects. Sounds are perceived as having three psychological dimensions: pitch, loudness, and timbre. Each of these dimensions has a physical correlate: frequency, intensity, and complexity. *Frequency* is defined as the number of times per second that the sound wave completes a full cycle (cps). Humans can respond to a range of 20 to 20,000 cps. However, the range that is essential for hearing speech is from 250 to 4,000 cps. Higher frequency sounds are perceived as higher in pitch, lower frequencies as lower in pitch. *Intensity* refers to the magnitude or power of the sound, the amplitude of the sound waves. Intensity is measured in decibels (dB), which are comparable to "just noticeable differences" in sound intensity. Normal speech falls between 50 and 65 dB. *Complexity* refers to the mixture of frequencies, intensities, and rhythms contained within a single sound stimulus. Complexity allows us to distinguish one person's voice from another and to make other important discriminations.

DEFINITION OF THE POPULATION

There are many variables to be considered in describing the hearing impaired child. Because of the multidimensional nature of the problem and the implications of each dimension for treatment and education, it is necessary to consider all of the following variables for each individual child in the assessment process and in planning an education program: degree of loss, age at onset, causes, type of loss, and frequencies of remaining hearing.

Degree of Loss

Hearing impairments are typically measured with a pure tone audiometer and classified on the basis of the results into *deaf*, which is a loss greater than 70 dB in the better ear, or *hearing impaired*, which is a significant loss up to 70 dB. Such classification does not take into consideration other variables related to hearing, such as ability to discriminate various sounds. Terms such as *mild, moderate, severe,* and *profound* are now used more often (Sanders, 1980). A profound loss means that the child must be educated in sensory modalities other than hearing; a mild loss means the child can usually be educated in a regular program with some amplification and/or special help in speech and language; moderate and severe are intermediate stages between mild and profound.

Frisina (quoted in Kirk & Gallagher, 1983) defined a deaf person as "one whose hearing is disabled to an extent. . . that precludes the understanding of speech through the ear alone, without or with a hearing aid" (p. 232). Typically this includes a loss of 70 dB or greater. Persons who are deaf include those who are congenitally deaf, that is, born deaf (prelingual deafness) and those who are adventitiously deaf, that is born with normal hearing but whose hearing has become nonfunctional later through illness or accident (postlingual deafness).

A person classified as hard of hearing is "one whose hearing is disabled to an extent. . . that makes difficult, but does not preclude the understanding of speech through the ear alone, without or with a hearing aid." (Kirk & Gallagher, 1983, p. 232). Typically this includes a loss in the better ear from 35 to 69 dB.

Davis and Silverman (1978) have suggested the following classifications: mild (27–40 dB), moderate (41–55 dB), moderately severe (56–70 dB), severe (71–90 dB), and profound (91+ dB). It should be noted that how well the child is able to use the remaining hearing is more critical for the educational program than the actual dB loss.

Age at Onset

The differentiation of congenital deafness and adventitious deafness refers to the time of the onset of sensory deprivation. This distinction can be further differentiated in terms of when, developmentally, the adventitious deafness occurred. The educational and developmental implications of this distinction are obvious: the child who becomes deaf later in life has most probably acquired language, speech, and general communication facility, whereas the child who is deaf at birth or soon after might manifest severe language and communication difficulties and present a greater challenge in educational programming (Sanders, 1980).

Causes

The etiology of the hearing impairment has implications for subsequent medical treatment, psychological effects, and assessment issues. Certain etiologies, for example, rubella during the first trimester of pregnancy, may indicate possible multiple impairments that have educational and diagnostic significance but may not be immediately and outwardly apparent. Furthermore, relationships exist between the type of hearing loss and the cause. For example, chronic otitis media, an infection in the middle ear, may result in a conductive hearing loss. Therefore, knowledge of etiology allows inferences to be made concerning type of hearing loss. It is important to note that much of the etiological diagnosis is made by inference from the medical and family history.

Some hearing defects are predetermined by the genetic structure: abnormalities of the external auditory canal, deformed or absent structure of the middle ear, or arrested development of the neural mechanism of the inner ear. Others are due to a maternal infection or a toxic condition during pregnancy that may also influence the forming auditory structure. The rubella epidemic of 1964-1965, for example, caused deafness in an estimated 8,000 children (Kirk & Gallagher, 1983).

Hearing defects acquired at birth may result from traumatic delivery experiences, a prolonged lack of oxygen, or mother-child blood incompatibilities. Postnatal diseases and accidents account for a large percentage of hearing losses. These include meningitis; otitis media; and infected adenoids, tonsils, or sinuses. As medical treatment improves, the risks of the frequency and severity of hearing losses from childhood diseases decrease. However, medical advances in neonatology contribute to an increase in auditory impairments related to prematurity. Concussions, prolonged exposure to high-frequency sounds, cerebral hemorrhage, and intracranial tumors may all cause temporary or permanent loss of hearing also (Quigley & Kretschmer, 1982).

Types of Hearing Loss

Hearing impairments are mainly of two forms: conductive losses and sensorineural losses. A conductive hearing loss results from a deficiency of function in the middle and/or outer ear, the conductive mechanism, so that the intensity of the sound reaching the inner ear and auditory nerve is reduced. A conductive loss seldom causes a hearing impairment greater than 60 to 70 dB since there will still be bone conduction of vibrations to the inner ear. Therefore, children with this type of loss generally fall in the category of mild to moderate hearing loss (Kirk & Gallagher, 1983). A sensorineural or perceptive hearing loss is caused by defects of the inner ear or auditory nerve. It may be partial or complete and may affect frequencies differentially. Generally, there is a greater loss at higher frequencies. Since the effect is in the nerve or inner ear, bone conduction does not improve hearing (Kirk & Gallagher, 1983).

Conductive losses are frequently corrected by wearing a hearing aid that amplifies all sounds. Sensorineural losses, however, present a trickier problem, since it is the discrimination of sounds, not merely the intensity of sounds, that is affected. For example, consonants are a blend of frequencies. As higher frequencies escape detection, the sounds become less clear, analogous to a slow-playing record. Vowels, on the other hand, are low-frequency, and therefore discrimination among vowel sounds may be possible for the child who has sensorineural loss.

METHODS FOR MEASURING HEARING LOSS

Formal Methods

Formal tests of hearing are generally administered by the audiologist using an audiometer, a pure tone measure of hearing that usually ranges from a frequency of 125 up to 8,000, or one octave above and below the speech range, and from threshold audibility to 100 dB. An audiogram is plotted separately for each ear with plotting frequency shown as a function of the decibel threshold for detectability. A conductive hearing loss will generally approximate a flat loss in the audiogram, that is, equal loss across frequencies. Sensorineural losses generally show a descending audiogram, that is, greater loss at higher frequencies. Figures 9-1 and 9-2 show representative audiograms for each of these two types of hearing loss (Kirk & Gallagher, 1983, pp. 237-238). The frequencies between the dotted vertical lines indicate the range important for speech.

The audiometer can be used for both air conduction and bone conduction testing. In the former, the headset is placed over the ears; in the latter, the headset is placed over the mastoid process behind the ears. Bone conduction testing makes it possible to compare the responses of the middle and inner ear. When a loss is indicated by

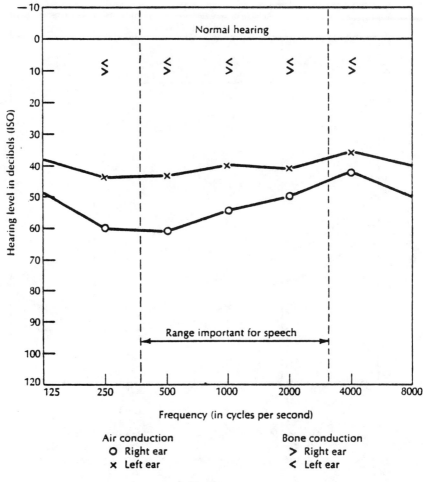

FIGURE 9-1.
Audiogram of child with a conductive hearing loss
(Kirk & Gallagher, 1983, p. 237).

air conduction but not by bone conduction, a middle and/or outer ear defect is assumed. When a loss is indicated by both bone conduction and air conduction equally, it is assumed the lesion is in the inner ear. When bone conduction reveals better hearing than air conduction but does not reach normal, both middle and inner ear factors are assumed.

Routine audiometric procedures are inappropriate for use with infants or young children. Although they will not be discussed here, audiology clinics can use such techniques as electrodermal procedures, EEG audiometry, and operant conditioning audiometry (Butterfield, 1982; Rapin & Ruben, 1982).

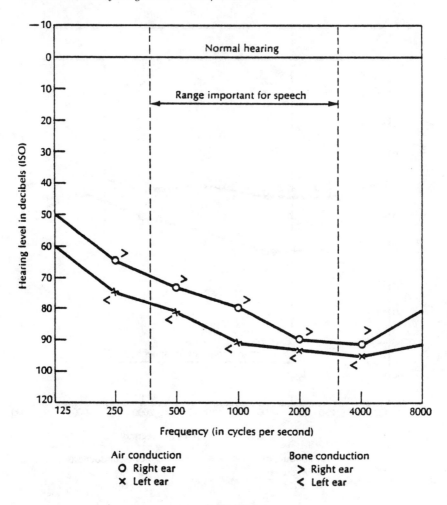

FIGURE 9-2.
Audiogram of child with sensorineural hearing loss
(Kirk & Gallagher, 1983, p. 238).

In addition to pure tone testing, it is advisable to gather information on a speech test of hearing. Such tests typically use consonant-vowel-consonant syllables and paired vowel discrimination. The results from these tests have practical implications in the classroom and in special auditory training (Egan, 1948; Fry, 1939; Hudgins, Hawkind, Karlin, & Stevens, 1947). These tests are usually administered by a speech, hearing, and language pathologist (see Chapter 11).

Informal Methods

Often hearing loss is detected by informal means. For clinical purposes, the school psychologist may wish to accumulate a variety of informal measures. This information can then be used in forming recommendations for the classroom teacher concerning the range of situations in which residual hearing is or is not useful for the child. Informal techniques are limited only by the needs and imagination of the psychologist. Suggested techniques include the following: conversation at 20 feet, whisper tests, watch tick tests, response to music, responses to voices out of line of vision, response to environmental sounds. In addition, observations of behavior and careful note of speech patterns, distortions, and omissions and of language patterns can provide clues and other information (Reynolds & Birch, 1982). For example, possible behaviors include turning the head to catch sounds, more than normal use of the hands to communicate, difficulty in balance, lack of attention, difficulty following directions, irrelevant answers, requests for repetition of instructions or questions, complaints of head noises or earaches, and restlessness. Possible speech and language observations include defective speech, loud or soft voice, lack of intonation and resonance, dropped consonants, and dropped prepositions or connecting words.

IMPLICATIONS FOR DEVELOPMENT

Mental Development

The principal question considered here is whether or not deafness influences mental development. The relationship is a complex one (Furth, 1966, 1973; Quigley & Kretschmer, 1982; Ruben & Rapin, 1982). In some instances, the factor that causes the deafness may also have caused brain damage and/or mental impairment. However, since the basic instruments for measuring intellectual capacity are language-based or language-mediated, the relationship becomes less clear in many instances in which language development is obviously related to the hearing loss alone. However, it also seems obvious that there must be some significant auditory experience involved in the growth of intellectual processes even without the language issue. Therefore, the hearing impaired child may be functionally mentally impaired. Considerations of intelligence testing will be discussed under assessment at a later point in this chapter and will, therefore, not be given full treatment here. However, the studies to date seem to indicate that a hearing loss has a selective effect on intellectual abilities, but a generalized effect is not suggested (Sanders, 1980). For example, tasks of a verbal-symbolic nature may be affected while nonverbal tasks of cognition may not be affected.

Emotional Development

In the psychology of deafness, the problem is not limited to the effects of communication and language difficulties. Infants with hearing losses do not hear the "cooing" of their mother, their own babbling, or the laughter and crying of others. They do not hear intonations and implied meanings in normal conversation that transmit biases and taboos that characterize society. Furthermore, they do not have access to the usual identification process that is related to language acquisition and audition. Sounds that enhance interpersonal relationships and feedback regarding the self are restricted (Sanders, 1980).

What is the effect of these limitations in experience on emotional development? The deaf child shares many of the experiences of an institutionalized infant: isolation, lack of stimulation (or impoverished stimulation), and lack of integration between parent and child. Isolation is perhaps the most important factor. The deaf child is deprived of the monitoring function of hearing. A fundamental criterion for maintaining emotional stability is being able to compare one's thinking and feeling with others. The deaf child is faced with the difficulty of monitoring his or her own feelings, attitudes, and ideas in a socially restricted context. The individual is naturally more isolated by peers, with the possible effect of becoming more detached, preferring to be alone. Social relationships with hearing children are difficult to sustain. The extreme response is a drift toward autistic-like behavior. Isolation is perpetuated by seemingly trivial and meaningless things such as the difficulty of keeping the hearing impaired child informed of daily occurrences. Furthermore, paranoid reactions may develop, since the hearing impaired child has limited checks on the content and intent of behaviors of others. It is little wonder, therefore, that hearing impaired children face greater problems than their normal peers in social and emotional development (Myklebust, 1964; Quigley & Kretschmer, 1982; Ruben & Rapin, 1982; Sanders, 1980).

Motor Development

The relationship between hearing loss and motor functioning involves the obvious association of defects in the inner ear and motor disequilibrium. This association is caused by a concomitant impairment of the semicircular canals. For example, in cases of severe loss, there may be a change in visual-motor organization and behavior, since the child experiences an altered perceptual organization. There also may be an effect upon reaction time, since one very important channel for processing stimuli is restricted. This has some implications for testing. Since the concept of speed is altered for the hearing impaired child, timed tests may not be appropriate. Profoundly deaf children may be observed to shuffle their feet as they walk, ostensibly because they have not learned, through sound feedback, to pick up their feet. The child who has hearing loss early in life may also experience laterality problems, possibly due to central nervous system involvement (see Ruben & Rapin, 1982; Sanders, 1980).

Social Maturity

Social maturity refers to the ability to care for one's self and assist others (Quigley & Kretschmer, 1982). Scales measuring social maturity usually include items of self-help, self-direction, locomotion, communication, and social relations. Quigley and Kretschmer (1982) have suggested that the lower level of social maturity in deaf children may be related to variables of age, quality of parent-child communication, and educational setting. Furth (1973) has concluded, however, that by adulthood, those differences tend to disappear for most deaf persons.

Sanders (1980) has suggested that dependency defines a handicap. For the child with a hearing impairment the lack of the usual avenues of communication causes the child to become more dependent on parents and teachers than the child with hearing. The challenge for educators and school psychologists becomes the extent to which the child can be taught the skills necessary to alleviate dependency. It can be assumed that the question of social maturity is bound up in the issues of altered perceptual processes, altered memory, and altered ego development. If, in addition to language development, these three areas can be given psychological and educational support, it is likely that there will be a concomitant increase in social maturity.

Language Development

The hearing impaired child is limited in both the receptive and expressive areas of speech and language. First, the child has limited channels for relating words to experiences, and second, the child has limited speech skills for relating experiences to others. Because of the limitations in input and output and the mere fact of less frequent exposure to and experience of speech and language, the hearing impaired child does not acquire meanings, symbols, and concepts as quickly or in the same ways as a hearing child. It is difficult for the hearing impaired child to acquire the meaning to be associated with a word. Furthermore, there is a relationship between the spoken word and the written word; that is, language acquisition is a prerequisite to reading and reading comprehension. This fact often places the hearing impaired child at a distinct academic disadvantage. Language may need to be acquired through visual or tactile-kinesthetic channels. The methods for using these channels are speechreading, manual communication, and a combination of the two. However, all of these methods are inferior to hearing; each has advantages and disadvantages (see Quigley & Kretschmer, 1982; Sanders, 1980).

IMPLICATIONS FOR ASSESSMENT

Communication Skills

Routine psychological batteries may not be appropriate for hearing impaired children because of the possible communication difficulties. Three ramifications of the communication problem are salient in subsequent assessment procedures and findings. First, if the child depends primarily on speechreading (lipreading) to comprehend others' speech, comprehension will be imprecise at best and fatigue will set in quickly. Second, the child's own speech may show distortions in pronunciation, pitch, or volume and thus be unintelligible to the untrained ear of the school psychologist. Third, the level of language development may itself affect assessment findings. The deaf child usually begins school with less understanding of English syntax than the average hearing first grader.

It is important for the school psychologist to have prior information regarding the child's communication abilities and disabilities. Is the child primarily oral or manual? Does the child speechread? Is speech intelligible? What is the comprehension level? These questions may be referred to the audiologist, speech and language pathologist, classroom teacher, or other professional who has had contact with the child. In addition, the psychologist should collect anecdotal material from interviewing the child and from classroom observations. Sentence completions and other educational tests can be used to assess the child's ability to read and write. The intelligibility and pleasantness of the child's speech should be noted. The extent to which the child is able to understand conversation on a one-to-one basis, the relative reliance on visual cues versus residual hearing, and the ability to communicate in groups should all be observed and noted. In addition, if the child communicates manually, fingerspelling and/or signing should be addressed to determine the child's fluency. The audiologist and speech and language pathologist are the most appropriate authorities in the area of communication; however, the school psychologist can and should function as a lay observer to provide additional information about the child's functioning.

Collection of Additional Information

The findings of the audiologist and speech and language pathologist are crucial to a meaningful evaluation of a hearing impaired child. In addition, reports of physical examinations and medical history provide useful information about etiology and possible related impairments and conditions. A complete social case history is necessary in light of the fact that psychological assessment may not be accurate. Therefore, background information supplements obtained knowledge about abilities, performance, and achievements. A parent interview is of value in gaining insight into the child's acceptance of the handicap and the parents' attitudes toward the child. Classroom observations are essential. These procedures are described in Chapters 2 and 3.

Rapport

Rapport should be established in a manner natural to the school psychologist. In general, in communicating with hearing impaired children, the psychologist should maintain and use eye contact; always sit facing the child, with face toward the light and the child's view of it clear; work on a level with the child; articulate carefully; speak in a normal tone and at a normal speed; use short simple sentences; and do not expect the child to understand everything that is said.

When to Use Regular Psychological Procedures

The determining factor for selection of evaluation instruments is the extent of the communication impairment. Children with a hearing loss of less than 15 dB may have little or no impairment of communication skills and should, therefore, be given the same set of standard psychological instruments and interviews as those used with the hearing child if these are needed.

In general, those with a loss of 75 dB or more may have a communication impairment serious enough to warrant special procedures devised for children who have hearing losses. Children in the middle group, 20 to 70 dB loss, need to be carefully assessed for communication skills. If there is a severe communication problem, special procedures should be used. If, however, communication skills appear to be good, conventional instruments may be used, perhaps with some modifications. If there is some question, parts of both types of evaluation can be administered. Large discrepancies between scores on verbal compared to nonverbal tasks suggest that a significant communication impairment may exist and that the child should be evaluated on the basis of specially devised procedures. If the hearing loss occurred after age 3½, or when scores on the special psychological tests for the profoundly deaf are exceptionally high, the regular evaluation for the hearing child should also be given for comparative purposes.

Considerations in Intelligence Testing

Most assessment procedures include some measures of intellectual functioning. It should be emphasized that such tests should not be the sole focus of the assessment but rather should be only one part. The following points are relevant for use of such instruments.

1. Verbal tests of intelligence may measure the language deficiency due to hearing loss, rather than intelligence, but they can be used by school psychologists to determine what the child is able to pick up through the auditory sense (Sullivan & Vernon, 1979). In general, for a valid measure of intelligence, a nonverbal/performance type of instrument should be used. However, care must be taken in the selection of such instruments to avoid nonverbal tests that have verbal directions. The psychologist must also exercise care in determining the appropriateness of verbal tests with children who have less severe hearing losses. These children may give the impression of understanding the verbal tasks when in fact they do not. It is often advisable in this case to begin with a performance measure and then, if indicated, administer a verbal measure using gestures to supplement the verbal instructions (Rogers & Soper, 1982). If the former indicates higher ability, it is probably a more valid measure of intelligence.

2. Intelligence testing of preschool and early-school-age hearing impaired children should be held suspect. Nonverbal tests that employ nonlanguage tasks and informal assessment procedures are suggested at these ages (Rogers & Soper, 1982).

3. It is more likely that a low IQ is an underestimation of ability than that a high one is an overestimation of ability. This probability should be included in the consideration of final test scores and in the preparation of reports and recommendations (Quigley & Kretschmer, 1982).

4. Tests that are administered by a school psychologist who is not experienced with hearing impaired children are highly susceptible to error. The hearing impaired child may have an atypical attention set that becomes reflected in lower scores and that may go unnoticed or be wrongly interpreted by the inexperienced school psychologist (Vernon, 1974).

5. The performance part of many conventional intelligence tests is only half or less of the total test. Therefore, it is advisable to give more than one performance scale so as to improve validity (Rogers & Soper, 1982).

6. Intelligence tests that emphasize time are not usually appropriate for hearing impaired children, since many of these children have

an altered perception or understanding of speech and a lowered rate of absorbing instruction (Rogers & Soper, 1982).

7. Group testing should be used only as a gross screening device, especially with hearing impaired children (Vernon, 1974).

Evaluations of some selected intelligence tests for use with hearing impaired children are included in Table 9-1.

TABLE 9-1

Evaluation of Intelligence Tests Used With Hearing Impaired Children

Test	Appropriate Age Range Covered by the Test	Evaluation of the Test
Wechsler Performance Scale for Children from Wechsler Intelligence Scale for Children—Revised	9-16 years	The Wechsler Performance Scale for Children is at present the best test for deaf children ages 9-16. It yields a relatively valid IQ score, and offers opportunities for qualitative interpretations of factors such as brain injury or emotional disturbances. It has good interest appeal and is relatively easy to administer and reasonable in cost.
Wechsler Adult Intelligence Scale—Revised	16-70 years	The rating of the Wechsler Performance Scale for Adults is the same as the rating on the Wechsler Performance Scale for children.
Wechsler Preschool and Primary Scale of Intelligence Performance subtests	3 yrs, 11 months-6 yrs, 8 months	This scale is not as good for use with deaf and hard of hearing children as the other Wechsler Scales. Picture Completion and Mazes are difficult to explain nonverbally. Other performance subtests are excellent. Standardization seems a little high.
Leiter International Performance Scale	4-12 years (also suitable for older mentally retarded deaf subjects)	This test has good interest appeal. It can be used to evaluate relatively disturbed deaf children who could not otherwise be tested. This test is expensive and lacking somewhat in validation. In general, however, it is an excellent test for young deaf children. Timing is a minor factor in this test. One disadvantage is in the interpretation of the IQ scores because the mean of the test is 95 and the standard deviation is 20. This means that the absolute normal score on this test is 95 instead of 100 as on other intelligence tests. For example, scores of 60, therefore, do not indicate mental deficiency but correspond more to about a 70 on a test such as the Wechsler or Binet. Great care must be taken in interpreting Leiter IQ scores for these reasons.

TABLE 9-1 (Continued)

Evaluation of Intelligence Tests Used With Hearing Impaired Children

Test	Appropriate Age Range Covered by the Test	Evaluation of the Test
Raven's Progressive Matrices	9 yrs-adulthood	Raven's Progressive Matrices is good as a second test to substantiate another more comprehensive intelligence test. The advantage of the Matrices is that it is extremely easy to administer and score, taking relatively little of the examiner's time and is very inexpensive. It yields invalid test scores of impulsive deaf children, who tend to respond randomly rather than with accuracy and care. For this reason, the examiner should observe the child carefully to assure that he is really trying.
Chicago Non-Verbal Examination	7-12 years	This test rates fair if given as an individual test; very poor, if given as a group test. The scoring is tedious and reliability is rather low.
Arthur Point Scale of Performance Tests: Revised	4.5-15.5 years	This is a test that is poor to fair due to the fact that timing is heavily emphasized, norms are not adequate, and directions are somewhat unsatisfactory. This test is especially unsatisfactory for emotionally disturbed children who are also deaf. With this type subject this test will sometimes yield a score indicating extreme retardation when the difficulty is actually one of maladjustment. It is also poor for young deaf children who are of below average intelligence because they often respond randomly instead of rationally.
Merrill-Palmer Scale	2-4 years	The Merrill-Palmer is a fair test for young deaf children, but it must be adapted in order to be used and would require a skilled examiner with a thorough knowledge of deaf children.
Goodenough Draw-A-Man	8.5-11 years	Directions are very difficult to give to young children in a standardized manner. Scoring is less objective than would be desired, so this test is relatively unreliable. It does, however, have some projective value in terms of personality assessment.
Vineland Adaptive Behavior Scale	1-25 years	This is a questionable test for deaf and hard of hearing children generally, but can be used for extremely difficult-to-test emotionally disturbed youngsters. It is given by asking the parents questions on the development of their child. The norms of this test have to be adapted for the hard of hearing because many of the questions involve items such as onset of speech, length of sentences, vocabulary, etc. This test is inexpensive and can be given to otherwise untestable children.

Note. Adapted from Vernon, M. (1974). Deaf and hard of hearing. In M. V. Wisland (Ed.), *Psychoeducational Diagnosis of Exceptional Children* (pp. 198-201). Springfield IL: Charles C Thomas. Reprinted by permission.

Screening for Brain Injury

Because of the high incidence of brain injury among hearing impaired children, it is often appropriate to use screening procedures for brain damage or central nervous system involvement. If the etiology of the hearing impairment indicates the possibility of brain damage or if there are specific learning difficulties that are not attributed to the hearing loss, the child should be referred for a complete neurological assessment. The suggested tests and items from tests useful as screening devices for brain injury that are included in Table 9-1 are discussed in greater detail in Vernon (1974) and Sullivan and Vernon (1979).

Modification in Administration

Whether administering a conventional test or one specifically devised for use with hearing impaired children, there are certain basic considerations in administration that the school psychologist should know. These include:

1. Hearing impaired children seek visual cues as feedback on their performance and whether they have done well or not. Therefore, the school psychologist should be aware of his or her gestures and facial expressions. Even a smile might encourage the continuation of wrong responses if it occurs at an inappropriate time. Testing hearing impaired children requires a sensitivity to even slight movements and possible cues of behavior and expression.

2. All children need appropriate lighting and seating during testing. However, these features are particularly important for hearing impaired children. They should sit directly across from the examiner with a well lighted work area. The examiner should not have his or her face or hands in shadow nor in the glare of sunlight nor with back to the light.

3. For children who are not proficient in speechreading or who do not have adequate residual hearing for oral instructions, alternate methods of giving instructions must be considered. Pantomime instructions may be used to supplement oral instructions. A simple demonstration of the demands of the task generally give the child a clearer understanding of expectations but may indicate the answer to a scorable item or be inappropriate at certain complexity levels where the test does not provide a sample item. To get around these difficulties the school psychologist can administer some of his or her own sample items by demonstration instead of beginning with the test items themselves. For the child who can read and shows adequate reading comprehension, the instructions may be provided in a written form. Instructions may be given in sign language or

fingerspelled if the child can communicate manually and if the examiner is fairly fluent in manual communication. School psychologists assigned to assess hearing impaired children and others with limited verbal language, such as trainable mentally retarded pupils, are advised to acquire sufficient skills in manual communication to enable them to work more effectively with these groups.

4. Certain items may have to be changed in some way to be appropriate to the experience of hearing impaired children. For example, an item that asks children what they should do if they hear a fire alarm should be deleted or altered to fit their world of experience. With the increased availability of flashing lights in conjunction with fire alarms, the school psychologist may wish to re-word the statement first to accommodate this variation.

Since the school psychologist will frequently use the Wechsler Performance Scales for assessing hearing impaired children, specific considerations for the administration of each of the subtests on the WISC-R are discussed here (Glasser & Zimmerman, 1967; Sattler, 1974).

1. *Picture completion.* The examiner can show pencil drawings of a face, each with a different part missing. The missing part on the first drawing can be drawn in for the child; on subsequent drawings, the child can draw it in for him or herself. When it is certain that the child understands the demands of the task, the school psychologist can proceed with the test materials, giving the child a dry paintbrush to indicate the missing part. Alternately, the school psychologist can show three trial items of paired pictures, one with a part missing, the other with the detail filled in, clearly indicating the missing part in each pair. The goal is to determine whether the child understands the instructions before beginning the task.

2. *Picture arrangement.* The child can be presented with a series of numbers, a series of letters, and finally a series of sample pictures to place in order. Each trial should be accompanied by a demonstration. The school psychologist may also wish to use cardboard strips on which are drawn the outlines of boxes the size of the cards to be used. Each box should have a number inside it in sequence (1 through 3, 4, or 5). The sample item can then be demonstrated by placing the pictures in order within the proper boxes on the strip. The child should also be taught to indicate to the examiner when he or she has completed each item.

3. *Object assembly.* This subtest generally presents no problems since the child easily understands the puzzlelike nature of the task. If difficulties do arise, the school psychologist may show a picture of the completed puzzle.

4. *Block design.* The school psychologist must clearly communicate the sameness of the blocks. Therefore, all the blocks should be set out in a single line with one color on top. The child can be asked to name the color. Each side should then be shown in turn, turning all blocks in the line simultaneously. Demonstrations are part of the standard administration for this subtest and should be adhered to, although it is advisable to allow the child to complete the first design even if the allotted time has expired. Furthermore, during demonstrations, the examiner should use both hands.

5. *Coding.* Coding can be accurately pantomimed since it is also pantomimed for the hearing child. The important consideration here is to communicate the notion of speed, during the sample items and by extra cues. If necessary, the examiner can point to the next item quickly after the child has completed the previous one.

Differential Assessment

Many behavioral symptoms of a hearing impairment parallel the behavioral manifestations of other impairments such as mental or emotional impairments. Therefore, it is important to make careful differential assessments of children who display such symptoms. These symptoms include: ignoring, confusing, or not complying with directions; daydreaming; academic difficulties; speech defects; lack of speech; and lassitude. The definitive assessment tool is usually the audiological examination. This technical field has advanced so that there are techniques of measuring hearing that do not require the sophistication or verbalization of response required by some standard instruments (Rapin & Ruben, 1982). Therefore, it is imperative that a child be referred for a complete audiological examination if hearing impairment is even suspected as a cause of behavior, academic, or speech difficulties. If a hearing loss is found, the behavior difficulties must then be evaluated in relationship to the hearing impairment, generally as secondary to the primary disability of hearing loss. This, of course, has implications for placement and treatment.

It is possible that the emotional or mental impairments may be severe enough and substantial enough, given the medical and family history, to warrant classification as primary. Again, it is important that the medical and family history adequately support such a classification. However, the hearing loss must still be recognized and treated, and therefore the school psychologist must try to assess the range of functioning given the degree and type of hearing loss.

Other Assessment Areas

Assessment should not be restricted to measures of intellectual ability. A variety of information is essential in order to plan an appropriate educational program for hearing impaired children. Zieziula (1982) has prepared a comprehensive listing of 62 instruments that may be used for assessment with hearing impaired persons in the areas of achievement, communication, intelligence, personality, visual perception, vocational aptitude and interest, and work evaluation measures. He has described each instrument including such information as age levels, validity, reliability, appropriateness for the hearing impaired, and relevant references. The reader is also referred to Rogers and Soper (1982), Sullivan and Vernon (1979), Vernon (1974), and Yarnell and Carlton (1981) for evaluations of measures useful in assessing hearing impaired children.

IMPLICATIONS FOR EDUCATION

The educational provisions and techniques for hearing impaired children or children with some degree of functional hearing and communication skills, are significantly different from those used with childen who have a profound loss (Quigley & Kretschmer, 1982). The former have the ability to acquire speech and language through hearing and essentially require support and aids to help them learn through the methods used with hearing children. The latter, however, require more specialized techniques and training since they cannot develop speech and language through the sense of hearing. Therefore, quite frequently the latter children will require placement in special classes whereas the former may be placed in regular classrooms. Some considerations for hearing impaired children are discussed below.

Hearing Aids

Use of a hearing aid requires training and supervision by a professional. The child needs to learn how to use the aid. The hearing aid amplifies sounds in the environment, thereby facilitating the child's ability to hear speech and use residual hearing. However, the aid cannot restore normal hearing. Although aids are technically more sophisticated now and can perform some differential amplifications of frequencies, a hearing aid will still not "flatten out" the hearing loss in specific frequencies evenly across all frequencies, nor does it block out extraneous environmental noises. The child who can benefit from a hearing aid should be encouraged to wear it. However, teachers and psychologists should not expect miracles from the hearing aid and should be aware of its limitations (Kirk & Gallagher, 1983).

Auditory Training

The child should be taught to use residual hearing to listen to sound clues, and to discriminate between different sounds. Such training should be started at an early age, preferably during the preschool years, and should emphasize parent involvement (Quigley & Kretschmer, 1982).

Speechreading (Lipreading)

Speechreading involves directing the child's attention to the visual cues of facial expressions and lip movements to fill in the sounds that are not heard and the words that are indistinct. Many words look alike and cannot be discriminated visually unless picked up in context. Other words are fairly easy to differentiate. Vowels are more difficult to identify visually, but since they belong to the lower frequency ranges, they are easier to discriminate auditorily with residual hearing. In general, three methods of teaching speechreading are used: the phonetic approach, the whole method, and the syllable approach (Kirk & Gallagher, 1983).

Speech Correction

The aim of speech correction is to find out what errors in articulation, loudness, or pitch the child is making and initiate corrective measures. The child has limited ability to monitor his or her own speech and therefore requires the support and help of a specially trained speech teacher or other professional. Most effective results are obtained when speech training is integrated with work in the classroom and with parent involvement in the home (see Chapter 11).

Methods of Instruction

Personnel concerned with the education of the profoundly hearing impaired have held sharply differing views on the methods of instruction in communication and language. One method, the oral approach, develops communication strictly through speech and speechreading and the use of residual hearing. The second method emphasizes the development of communication through manual methods. The third, the total communication approach, combines the use of fingerspelling and signing with speech and speechreading and auditory training. All three approaches are in use today and the conflict between the approaches remains at a high emotional level. The reader is referred to Furth (1973), Quigley and Kretschmer (1982), and Sanders (1980) for more detailed discussion of the issues surrounding those methods.

Although the school psychologist may be limited by the available district programs for placement of a child, he or she should be informed of the advantages of each approach for individual children with different needs and abilities and be able to make clear recommendations for placement based on the specific needs of the child. Assignment to a particular program because it is the only one available is not in keeping with the intent of P.L. 94-142. This problem was discussed in Chapter 1.

Speech Development

The child who has not yet acquired speech and language needs specialized help in these areas. Since the child is apt to have a profound loss, the acquisition of speech will have to proceed through channels other than hearing. This training is highly technical and requires a trained professional in speech and language. Channels and methods used include: vibration, the sense of touch, visual aids, kinesthetic or proprioceptive cues, auditory stimulation and residual hearing through hearing aid use, and electronically displayed "visible" speech (see Chapter 11).

SUMMARY

Assessment of children with hearing impairments presents a strong challenge to the school psychologist. This is one of the low incidence categorical areas, and there may be few opportunities to acquire sufficient experience to work comfortably and confidently with these children. Hence, the school psychologist must rely on the application of knowledge about hearing impairments and their impact on development in order to modify and adapt the typical assessment procedures for hearing impaired children who may be encountered in the school district. Standardized tests must frequently be modified in administration, scoring, and interpretation so that the hearing impaired child is not placed at a disadvantage because of the disability. In any case, such instruments should be supplemented with other procedures, especially classroom observation, in order to obtain as complete a picture as possible of the child's present level of functioning relative to potential as determined by a variety of formal and informal assessment measures.

REFERENCES

Butterfield, E. C. (1982). Behavioral assessment of infants' hearing. In M. Lewis & L. T. Taft (Eds.), *Developmental disabilities: Theory, assessment and intervention* (pp. 101-113). New York: S. P. Medical & Scientific Books.

Dale, D. M. C. (1962). *Applied audiology for children.* Springfield IL: Charles C Thomas.

Davis, H., & Silverman, R. (Eds.). (1978). *Hearing and deafness.* New York: Holt, Rinehart & Winston.

Egan, J. P. (1948). Articulation testing methods. *Archives of Laryngology, 58,* 955-959.

Fry, D. B., & Kerridge, P. M. J. (1939). Tests for the hearing of speech by deaf people. *The Lancet, 1,* 106.

Furth, H. G. (1973). *Deafness and learning.* Belmont CA: Wadsworth.

Furth, H. G. (1966). *Thinking without language: Psychological implications of deafness.* New York: The Free Press.

Glasser, A. J., & Zimmerman, I. L. (1967). *Clinical interpretation of the Wechsler Intelligence Scale for Children.* New York: Grune & Stratton.

Hudgins, C. V., Hawkind, J. E., Karlin, S. E., & Stevens, S. S. (1947). The development of recorded auditory tests for measuring hearing loss for speech. *Archives of Laryngology, 57,* 57-89.

Kirk, S. A., & Gallagher, J. J. (1983). *Educating exceptional children.* Boston: Houghton Mifflin.

Myklebust, H. R. (1964). *The psychology of deafness.* New York: Grune & Stratton.

Quigley, S. P., & Kretschmer, R. E. (1982). *The education of deaf children.* Baltimore: University Park Press.

Rapin, I., & Ruben, R. J. (1982). Appraisal of auditory function in children. In M. Lewis & L. T. Taft (Eds.). *Developmental disabilities: Theory, assessment, and intervention* (pp. 79-100). New York: S. P. Medical & Scientific Books.

Reynolds, M. C., & Birch, J. W. (1982). *Teaching exceptional children in all America's schools* (pp. 356-396). Reston VA: The Council for Exceptional Children.

Rogers, S. J., & Soper, E. (1982). Assessment considerations with hearing impaired preschoolers. In G. Ulrey & S. J. Rogers (Eds.), *Psychological assessment of handicapped infants and young children* (pp. 115-122). New York: Thieme & Stratton.

Ruben, R. J., & Rapin, I. (1982). Theoretical issues in the development of audition. In M. Lewis & L. T. Taft (Eds.), *Developmental disabilities: Theory, assessment, and intervention.* (pp. 63-78). New York: S. P. Medical & Scientific Books.

Sanders, D. A. (1980). Psychological implications of hearing impairments. In W. M. Cruickshank (Ed.), *Psychology of exceptional children and youth.* (4th ed.) (pp. 218-254). Englewood Cliffs NJ: Prentice-Hall.

Sattler, J. M. (1974). *Assessment of children's intelligence.* Philadelphia: W. B. Saunders.

Sullivan, P. M., & Vernon, M. (1979). Psychological assessment of hearing impaired children. In K. Gerken (Ed.), *School Psychology Digest, 8,* 271-290.

Vernon, M. (1974). Deaf and hard of hearing. In M. V. Wisland (Ed.), *Psychoeducational diagnosis of exceptional children* (pp. 190-212). Springfield IL: Charles C Thomas.

Yarnell, G. D., & Carlton, G. R. (1981). *Guidelines and manual of tests for educators interested in the assessment of handicapped children.* Austin TX: International Research Institute.

Yost, W. A., & Nielson, D. W. (1977). *Fundamentals of hearing.* New York: Holt, Rinehart & Winston.

Zieziula, F. R. (1982). *Assessment of hearing impaired people.* Washington DC: Gallaudet College Press.

ADDITIONAL RESOURCES

Birch, J. W. (1975). *Hearing impaired pupils in the mainstream.* Reston VA: The Council for Exceptional Children.

Bishop, M. E. (1979). *Mainstreaming: Practical ideas for educating hearing-impaired students.* Washington DC: Alexander Graham Bell Association for the Deaf.

Brookhouser, P. E. (1983). *Sensory impaired project: A report to the Nebraska Department of Education.* Lincoln: Nebraska Department of Education.

Fine, P. J. (Ed.). (1974). *Deafness in infancy and early childhood.* New York: Medcom Press.

Froehlinger, V. J. (Ed.). (1981). *Today's hearing impaired child: Into the mainstream of education.* Washington DC: Alexander Graham Bell Association for the Deaf.

Gustason, G., Pfetzing, D., & Zawalkow, E. (1980) *Signing exact English* (3rd ed.). Los Alamitos CA: Modern Signs Press.

Hicks, W. (n.d.). *Add-a-fact-deafness, associated and unassociated disorders.* Washington DC: Gallaudet College.

Jacobs, L. M. (1974). *A deaf child speaks out.* Washington, DC: Gallaudet College Press.

Levine, E. S. (1974). *Lisa and her soundless world.* New York: Human Sciences Press.

Mindel, E. D., & Vernon, M. (1971). *They grow in silence.* Silver Spring MD: National Association of the Deaf.

Northern, J. L., & Downs, M. P. (1974). *Hearing in children.* Baltimore: Williams & Wilkins.

O'Rourke, J. J., Humphries, T., & Padden, C. (1980). *A basic course in American sign language.* Silver Spring MD: T. J. Publishers.

Schlesinger, H. S., & Meadow, K. P. (1972). *Sound and sign: Childhood deafness and mental health.* Berkeley CA: University of California Press.

Silverman, F. H. (1980). *Communication for the speechless.* Englewood Cliffs NJ: Prentice-Hall.

CHAPTER 10

Visual Impairments

Geraldine T. Scholl

Visual impairments are a common human problem. Almost every one who lives a long life will develop some type of restriction or impairment in visual functioning. Most of these impairments can be corrected or at least alleviated through surgery, such as for the removal of cataracts; or through corrective lenses, which will improve defective near or distance vision. Severe visual limitations are found in a relatively small proportion of the population. In the United States persons classified as legally blind number about 500,000 and more than half are over the age of 65.

In the school-age population, pupils with severe visual impairments account for about 1% of the handicapped children who need special education programs and services (Kirchner, 1983). About one school-age pupil in 10,000 will have a moderate to severe visual impairment that requires some type of educational remediation or modification so that the pupil can participate in the regular school program. About 1 in 500 will have a mild visual impairment that usually can be remediated through corrective lenses. The challenge for both parents and educators is to find these pupils with mild impairments. It is difficult for young children to assess their own visual efficiency. Hence, unless some very observant adult notes signs of visual problems, such children may be labeled as slow and even retarded. They fall behind consistently in their school work, and few teachers or parents suspect that the source of the problem is a visual impairment.

All school personnel should be aware of the following signs of visual problems: (NSPB, 1978).

BEHAVIOR

Rubs eyes excessively.

Shuts or covers one eye, tilts head or thrusts head forward.

Has difficulty in reading or in other work requiring close use of the eyes.

Blinks more than usual or is irritable when doing close work.

Is unable to see distant things clearly.

Squints eyelids together or frowns.

APPEARANCE

Crossed eyes.

Red-rimmed, encrusted, or swollen eyelids.

Inflamed or watery eyes.

Recurring styes.

COMPLAINTS

Eyes itch, burn or feel scratchy.

Cannot see well.

Dizziness, headaches, or nausea following close work.

Blurred or double vision

Pupils who consistently show any of these signs should be referred to the school nurse for further screening and possible examination by a medical specialist.

The purpose of this chapter is to describe the types and characteristics of visual impairments found in the school-age population, to summarize the major impact of such impairments on growth and development, and to review implications for the assessment process that are important for school psychologists.

TERMINOLOGY

This section defines some of the labels that are used by school districts for describing children with visual impairments.

Blind: Relatively few persons, both adults and children, are *blind* in the strict definition of the term, meaning "unable to see" or "without the use of sight." Most persons do retain some vision. The term *blind* is most often used to label those persons who are eligible for some form of public assistance including those who claim an extra exemption on their income tax. Legal blindness is less than 20/200 best corrected vision in the better eye or a field of vision restricted to a diameter no greater than 20 degrees.

The legal definition of blindness has limited use for educators because most pupils whose vision corrects to 20/200 in the better eye are able to make effective use of visual materials in the classroom. Although some states still retain the definition of legal blindness to certify pupils as eligible for special education programs and services, it is becoming increasingly obsolete for educators.

The term *blind* is appropriately applied to pupils who must use senses other than vision in their educational process.

Partially sighted or partially seeing: These terms are used less frequently by schools partly because they have little educational meaning. When the terms are used, they usually refer to persons whose best corrected vision in the better eye falls between 20/70 and 20/200.

Low vision: This term is applied to those pupils who can see objects held close to their eyes and who may or may not require the use of tactual materials in their education.

Limited Vision: This term is used for those pupils who have some limitations in their visual functioning but who will usually be educated through their visual sense.

Mild, moderate, and severe visual impairments: The term *mild* is applied to pupils whose visual impairment is usually correctable with glasses. Such pupils require no modification in their educational programs other than sitting close the chalkboard. *Moderate* is applied to pupils who require modifications such as special books in large type, magnifiers, or similar materials, but whose educational program is conducted primarily through the sense of sight. *Severe* is applied to pupils whose vision is absent or so defective that the educational program must be conducted through senses other than vision.

Visually impaired/visually handicapped: These are terms applied to persons who have any degree of limitation on visual functioning. Impairment indicates the physiological, medical, or anatomical loss or abnormality. *Handicap* refers to the limitations imposed on a person by society or by the person himself or herself as a result of the impairment. The term *visually handicapped* will be used in this chapter to describe all ranges of impaired vision.

School psychologists should know the terms used by school/agency/state department of education to label pupils with visual impairments. They should, however, realize that the label may have little meaning for visual functioning; and that they should observe the degree to which the pupil uses vision for school-related activities and not conclude on the basis of an eye report or a label, that visual materials cannot be used.

CHARACTERISTICS OF VISUAL IMPAIRMENTS RELEVANT FOR ASSESSMENT

There are several characteristics of visual impairments that will have an impact on understanding the pupil and are of concern to the psychologist preparing for the assessment. Information about these may be available in the eye report. If not, parents and teachers may be able to supply missing facts, or the school psychologist should consult with the examining physician.

The topics included in this section are organized around the information provided in the typical report from an examining ophthamologist or optometrist. For additional information about any characteristic, the reader is referred to Chalkey (1974), Harley and Lawrence (1977), Jose (1983), Kirk (1981), or Vaughan & Asbury (1977). The latter presents a more technical treatment of the subject.

Pupils who have already been identified as having a visual impairment should have an eye examination report in their file. A report from a medical specialist, an *ophthalmologist* or *oculist*, will include the medical diagnosis and other medical information related to the eye condition. The medical specialist will also assess the degree of vision in each eye, and this information will be noted in addition to the type of correction through lenses if they are necessary. Prognosis and recommendations for treatment are also included.

Some pupils may have an examination by an *optometrist*, a nonmedical specialist in vision. If there is a medical problem or need for medical remediation for the problem, the optometrist usually refers the pupil to an ophthalmologist. Optometrists are particularly interested in the use of low vision aids and corrective lenses. The eye report will often include information about type of lenses prescribed.

Both the opthalmologist and the optometrist usually refer their patients to an *optician* who will make the glasses to fit the prescription for the individual. This specialist will also repair glasses. Opticians do not do refractions or give eye examinations. Reports from ophthalmologists and sometimes from optometrists should include information about the eye condition.

Onset

School psychologists will want to know the age of onset and the type of onset of the visual impairment. If the pupil was born with the condition, it is considered as a *congenital* impairment. In this case, it may be the result of heredity or may be attributed to some prenatal cause, such as rubella during pregnancy. If the condition occurs after birth, it is listed as *acquired* or adventitious. Most visual impairments in the school-age population are congenital. If it is an acquired condition, it most likely will be the result of an accident or some disease.

The onset may be *gradual*, that is, decreasing vision over a long period of time, or *traumatic*, that is, occurring instantly. Some congenital conditions cause a gradual loss of vision that may extend to adulthood. This is important information to the school psychologist because such students may require emotional support as they face the realities of their deteriorating vision.

Knowing age of onset and type of onset can furnish important clues to the school psychologist. For example, a child who lost his or her vision prior to the age of 5 is usually considered as congenitally blind because very little visual imagery is retained. In general, physical coordination and spatial orientation tend to be less smooth in the congenitally visually handicapped. An older pupil losing vision may evidence more emotional problems than the congenitally handicapped, especially if the onset occurs during adolescence. Similarly, emotional reactions may accompany both gradual loss and traumatic loss. Discussions of the dynamics of visual loss relative to emotional adjustment may be found in Cholden (1958) and Cowen, Underberg, Verrillo, & Benham (1961).

Degree of Vision

Several aspects of the degree of vision should be included in the eye report. If they are not, the school psychologist should request the information from the examining specialist. *Near vision* will be reported in terms of the smallest size of print that can be read at a distance, usually, of 14 inches from the eye. (The distance will be indicated in the report.) *Distance vision* is reported as a fraction in feet. For example, 20/20 means that the individual sees at 20 feet what the person with normal vision sees at 20 feet; 20/200 means that person sees at 20 feet what the person with normal vision sees at 200 feet. Distance vision may sometimes be reported in the metric system: 6/6, 6/60.

Children who have good near vision but poor distance vision are nearsighted or *myopic*; they are able to see the print in their books but may not be able to see the chalkboard or a baseball on the playground. Children with good distance vision and poor near vision are farsighted or *hyperopic*; they do well in activities that require them to see distant objects, such as a baseball or basketball or the chalkboard, but are unable to see clearly the print in their books.

The eye examination should also assess any limitations in the *field of vision*. A person with normal vision in both eyes is able to see along a 180-degree plane, up/down and side-to-side. Restrictions in any part of that field will cause such problems as slowness in reading (because not so much can be taken in during a single eye movement) or stumbling over objects left on the floor.

The fourth aspect of importance is how well the muscles in the eyes work together so that a single image is seen by both eyes. Young children in particular should be tested for *fusion*, because if both eyes are not working together, there is a possibility of blindness developing in the eye that is not being used.

Causes of Visual Impairments

Two common eye problems in school-age pupils have been mentioned: *myopia*, or nearsightedness, and *hyperopia*, or farsightedness. *Strabismus*, or crossed eyes, and *nystagmus*, or involuntary eye movements, are eye muscle problems. Strabismus should be corrected during the preschool period to avoid the possibility of loss of vision in one eye due to lack of use. Nystagmus can sometimes be alleviated by medical intervention and in fact has been helped by behavior modification techniques. It will cause the child to have difficulty focusing on an object for any extended period of time (Jose, 1983).

The eye is a very complex part of the body, and thus many possibilities exist for malfunction. The most common eye conditions in the school-age population are retrolental fibroplasia, congenital cataracts, optic nerve atrophy, and albinism (Hatfield, 1975).

Retrolental fibroplasia is an eye condition resulting from excess oxygen administered to premature and low-birth-weight infants. Although the cause of the condition is known, large amounts of oxygen must often be administered to keep the neonate alive. During recent years, as advances in science have enabled the medical profession to save neonates with increasingly shorter gestation periods, more of them are showing evidence of other handicapping conditions in addition to the visual impairment (Silverman, 1980).

Congenital cataracts, an opacity of the lens in the eye, may result from a variety of causes including heredity and rubella (German measles). Surgery and corrective lenses will frequently improve the condition and enable the child to use his or her vision effectively for school tasks.

Optic atrophy is a degeneration of the optic nerve, usually caused by a lesion. Under the present state of medical knowledge, it results in a gradual, irreversible loss of vision.

Albinism is a congenital lack of pigment that may involve a part or all of the body. Albino children whose eyes are affected will have severe photophobia (sensitivity to light). They are frequently fitted with tinted lenses to reduce this light sensitivity. Care should be taken they are not exposed to the sun for long periods of time because they also tend to burn easily.

School psychologists wishing more information about a particular child's eye condition should consult directly with the examining specialist. The school nurse is another valuable resource for information about medical and potential educational implications of specific eye conditions.

IMPACT ON GROWTH AND DEVELOPMENT

Any sensory loss will have consequences for growth and development, some of which may be related to the extent of the loss but which more often may be due to the presence of other disabilities or to the amount of stimulation provided in the environment. If a child with a vision problem is found to be deficient in a developmental skill, school psychologists should not immediately conclude that it is due to the sensory loss; other factors may be more important. This section reviews briefly the potential impact of the visual impairment on physical, mental/intellectual, social, and emotional growth and development and draws some implications for the assessment process. For a more detailed discussion, see Scholl (1973).

Physical Development

Impact

The impact of the visual impairment on physical development is indirect, rather than direct; that is, the impairment itself does not cause retardation but rather the lack of opportunities for adequate physical experience does. Restricted mobility causes the child to be sedentary; large muscles are not exercised, and this may result in deficiencies in gross motor skills. The dangers of riding a tricycle or bicycle when one cannot see what lies ahead deprive some youngsters of this valuable muscle exercise. The lack of ability to see small objects clearly or not at all deprives the toddler, in particular, of a valuable experience in picking up small objects such as bits of paper from the floor, which would help to improve fine muscle coordination. Thus, both fine and gross muscle development may be retarded compared with that of the normal child. Since much of the retardation is attributed to lack of experience, the school program must often remediate these problems by providing an enriched environment and by helping parents to also provide more opportunities for physical activities.

Implications

Noting such deficiencies in a child with no other impairments, the school psychologist should consider recommending that the school program include large and small muscle activities since they will enhance physical growth. Extra work or a special program in physical education may be appropriate. If the child is not receiving orientation and mobility instruction, this specialized instruction should also be recommended. Such instruction is a needed part of every visually handicapped child's school program. A recommendation to the regular teacher about encouraging the child to move about in the classroom or sending the child on errands within the building will encourage movement and contribute to improving physical development.

Mental/Intellectual Development

Impact

Vision is a valuable source of information for mental and cognitive development. Without vision the child is deprived of many cognitive experiences, and many concepts are beyond his abilities to grasp, for example, colors, the concept of three dimensions, or size and shape when the gestalt of the object cannot be perceived by touch. While the sense of hearing is also essential in the learning process, it gives no information about the object world to the child who has no vision. Vision is also a unifying force in cognition. The concept of a large object may be inadequate because exploration by touch of individual parts does not necessarily result in a concept of the whole. Thus, defective or limited vision will have some impact on cognitive development.

Much early learning depends on imitation. Activities such as skipping, which children learn naturally through imitation, must often be taught to visually handicapped children. If the environment has not provided a wealth of experiences, visually handicapped children may become labeled as "retarded" when in reality they should be considered "disadvantaged" because their environment has not provided them with sufficient meaningful sensory stimulation or experiences.

The visual impairment does not usually hinder verbal communication; in fact, many visually handicapped children and adults are avid conversationalists partly because talking provides them with contact with their environment. This characteristic sometimes leads to verbalism, the use of words without real comprehension of their meaning (Harley, 1963).

Implications

Because the major contact of the child with another person lies in verbal communication, school psychologists should talk and explain what they are doing while doing it. In establishing rapport, they should also probe for meanings of words used by the child to determine whether there is true understanding. There is no need to hesitate to use such words as "look" and "see."

If the child appears to have vision or the eye examination record indicates some vision, try it out informally on tasks such as identifying objects in the room and picking out details in pictures or photographs. This helps determine whether or not there is sufficient vision to complete satisfactorily the performance items included in the assessment instruments.

Social Development

Impact

The absence of vision will sometimes give a person the appearance of being a social isolate. Many of our social contacts are initiated through nonverbal communication. Without vision such contacts are lacking, and the person remains silent and seemingly aloof. In fact, unless there is some sound from the group, the blind person would have no knowledge of the presence of others.

Implications

The social integration of visually handicapped children should be encouraged through the development of association with peers both in and out of school. Delays in social development are probably due to lack of experience. Thus, true integration of all handicapped children should be a major objective both within the school setting and in extracurricular activities. Participation in group activities such as clubs should be encouraged to reduce the effects of social isolation.

Emotional Development

Impact

Emotional adjustment for visually handicapped children involves an acceptance of themselves as persons of worth; acceptance of their impairment; and finally, acceptance of the limitations imposed by the impairment. The development of self-concept may be delayed because children with defective vision have limited opportunities to view themselves as people in relationship with others. As toddlers, these children lack the experiences of mirror play and visual opportunities of comparing themselves with others. Their minority status as handicapped persons is usually not reinforced by contacts with others of similar minority status, and thus they lack opportunities for being with others like themselves.

Acceptance of limitations is determined for children largely by attitudes of those around them, primarily their parents. If the parents help children view their impairment as a challenge to be met rather than as an all-pervasive handicap, then the children, too, will be more accepting. However, acceptance must also be tempered with realism. The child should not be encouraged to do things that cannot be done. For example, it is a mistake to encourage a blind child in an ambition to become an airline pilot, at least in the present stage of our technological development.

Adolescence presents unique problems for all persons; for those with disabilities, these may become intensified. In general, the problems of adolescence must usually be resolved before visually handicapped adolescents can deal with their struggles to see themselves as persons of worth who have an impairment (Cholden, 1958).

Implications

The school psychologist is usually the professional who has the greatest understanding of the dynamics of growth and development, mental hygiene, and therapeutic techniques. Thus, the psychologist may be most helpful in working with parents and teachers to assist the child with a visual impairment to develop a realistic appraisal of self and abilities. This may be accomplished in a number of ways. Elementary teachers can be encouraged to use substitute experiences for the mirror play available to nonhandicapped children in order to assist visually impaired children in making a realistic appraisal of the physical self. Cultural taboos concerning touching need to be set aside as parents and teachers help visually handicapped children explore their own bodies and those of their peers and adults. Descriptions of appearance compared with the norm of peers and adults need to be provided so that visually handicapped children can compare themselves with others. Supportive help through group counseling is often advisable. Contact with others like one's self is necessary to develop an adequate self-concept. Particularly during adolescence, counseling sessions with groups of other visually handicapped peers and contacts with visually handicapped adults may help the adjustment process.

THE ASSESSMENT PROCESS

Knowing some of the characteristics and needs of the visually handicapped child will help the school psychologist structure a more meaningful assessment from the initial meeting to the interpretation of the report.

Establishing Rapport

Touch or sound, and to a limited degree smell, are the major sensory avenues that tell the blind child who is around. Thus, talking to the child to let him or her know where in the room you are located will help the child become oriented to the room. The initial greeting should include touching to establish contact. In most cases, it is not necessary to lead the child to a chair; instead verbal directions should be given. This exercise will provide an opportunity to observe physical movement, orientation to space, ability to follow directions, and a general indication of how well the child is able to manage in space. Directions and instructions should be clear and as specific as possible. For example, tell the child that a chair or table is at the left about two steps and that the back of the chair faces the child. Normal language should be used. There is no need to eliminate words for visual concepts such as "see," "look," names of colors, and so forth from normal conversation.

Determining the Extent of the Impairment

Classroom observations can help in the assessment of the visual functioning or efficiency of the child. In addition, the initial observation of the child entering the school psychologist's office—together with previous observations in the classrooms, playground, lunch room, and halls—should help in the assessment of how well the child uses vision and thus whether or not visual materials in test instruments may be tried.

The school psychologist should also find out whether the child uses a low vision aid or wears glasses and, if so, make certain the child brings them to the office. Asking the child to describe what he or she sees in the room, such as any pictures or objects or the placement of furniture, and probing for details about any objects mentioned will provide further cues on how much the child can see. If there is doubt about whether the child can see sufficiently for some of the assessment tasks, they should be tried anyway. Such trials will provide a better idea of visual functioning even if the results are not used in the report.

Selecting Appropriate Measures

In general, visually handicapped pupils will not have difficulty with verbal tests. In giving verbal tests such as vocabulary tests, it is sometimes necessary to probe more deeply to ascertain whether or not the child really does understand the concept. Sometimes visually handicapped children can give acceptable verbal responses without true understanding or meaning. Manipulative or performance tests may require more careful selection, depending on the assessment of visual efficiency and hand coordination. More time may need to be allowed to get acquainted with materials. The child should be encouraged to explore materials thoroughly by use of vision if possible and tactually if the child cannot see them. The school psychologist should place the child's hands on the materials while explaining where they are located. Plenty of time should be allowed for both visual and tactual exploration.

There will always be questions about using specially adapted tests. In general, school psychologists should develop their own philosophy on this issue. If assessment is viewed as attempting to arrive at a comparison of the child's abilities with the so-called normal, then it is essential to adhere strictly to commonly used tests and their published norms. If assessment is viewed as a process of attempting to find out all one possibly can about a child, then a variety of tests should be tried, both those commonly used and some "special" ones. In this latter instance, portions of tests rather than complete batteries may be more appropriate.

In general, group tests are not recommended for visually handicapped children because of the varied and greatly reduced speed of reading both in braille and in print. Most group tests are timed, and thus the slower reading rate penalizes these children in their performance.

There are several resources for lists of instruments that have been used in assessing children with visual impairments. Scholl and Schnur (1976) have provided a comprehensive review of measures used with visually impaired persons, including those used with preschool age children, for assessing intellectual, personality, vocational, and educational functioning. The book includes measures developed for a specific research project, instruments commonly used by psychologists in their clinical practice, and instruments developed specifically for the visually handicapped population. Yarnall and Carlton (1981) have reviewed 29 tools useful for assessing children who have sensory, physical, and severe mental handicaps. In their article on assessing visually handicapped individuals from a school psychology point of view, Genshaft, Dare, and O'Malley (1980) provided a list of instruments for assessing residual vision; cognitive abilities; academic achievement; physical, behavioral, and social development; language skills; and vocational skills and interests. Vander Kolk (1981) included in his chapter on assessing children and youth a summary of instruments used with visually handicapped and multihandicapped children.

School psychologists may wish to consult one or more of these resources about currently used instruments but should keep in mind that there are minimal statistical data about validity and reliability for most of the instruments listed. In most cases, professional judgment must be exercised in the selection, administration, and interpretation of any assessment measure used with visually handicapped pupils. The following sections provide some guidelines for this process.

Needed Modifications

Some experienced psychologists modify administration, scoring, and use of norms when working with handicapped pupils. Whether school psychologists wish to follow this practice will usually depend upon their philosophy of testing and their answer to the question "Why assess?" (see Chapter 1).

In administration, modifications can be made in the time limits and in the instructions. If modifications are made in time limits, mentally noting where the child would be stopped if timed and then letting him or her continue until finished will result in some measure of abilities that will permit a comparison with norms but will also be a measure of how far the child can go. Instructions may be modified depending on the abilities and understanding of the child. It should be recalled that many visually handicapped children are lacking in experiential background and may not understand words, concepts, or other allusions that are ordinarily expected of children with vision (Bauman, 1973).

Scoring

Flexibility in scoring is sometimes necessary, especially with young children. Responses based on their experiences may not be found in the acceptable category of the test manual. In Chapter 1, the response of the blind child to the question about what we do with our eyes was related to both the need for flexibility in scoring and the need to probe further. As it stands, this child gave the most appropriate response based on a different experience, and the item should be given credit. However, the school psychologist may also wish to probe further and ask what people usually do with their eyes to determine whether or not the acceptable response can be elicited.

Use of Norms

Another question arises about the use of special or regular norms. Again, the purpose of the assessment must be considered. If a strict comparison with so-called normal children is desired, then the regular norms should be used; however, if the purpose of the assessment is to compare the child with others with similar handicapping conditions, then special norms may be more appropriate.

SUMMARY

Although school psychologists may feel some initial reluctance about assessing a child with a visual impairment, the experience can be challenging and rewarding. This chapter summarized characteristics of visual impairments and their impact on physical, mental, emotional and social growth and development. This background information was then applied to the assessment process. Commonly used instruments can frequently be used in whole or in part in assessing visually handicapped pupils and in arriving at decisions about educational placement and developing individualized education programs.

REFERENCES

Bauman, M. K. (1973). Psychological and educational assessment. In B. Lowenfeld (Ed.), *The visually handicapped child in school* (pp. 93-115). New York: John Day.

Chalkey, T. (1974). *Your eyes.* Springfield IL: Charles C Thomas.

Cholden, L. S. (1958). *A psychiatrist works with blindness.* New York: American Foundation for the Blind.

Cowen, E. L., Underberg, R. P., Verrillo, R. T., & Benham, F. G. (1961). *Adjustment to visual disability in adolescence.* New York: American Foundation for the Blind.

Genshaft, J. L., Dare, N. L., & O'Malley, P. L. (1980, November). Assesing the visually impaired child: A school psychology view. *Journal of Visual Impairment and Blindness, 74,* 344-350.

Harley, R. K. (1963). *Verbalism among blind children.* New York: American Foundation for the Blind.

Harley, R. K., & Lawrence, G. A. (1977). *Visual impairment in the schools.* Springfield IL: Charles C Thomas.

Hatfield, E. M. (1975). Why are they blind? *Sightsaving Review, 45,* 3-22.

Jose, R. T. (Ed.). (1983) *Understanding low vision.* New York: American Foundation for the Blind.

Kirchner, C. (1983, May). Special education for visually handicapped children: A critique of data on numbers served and costs. *Journal of Visual Impairment and Blindness, 77*(5), 219-223.

Kirk, E. C. (1981). *Vision pathology in education.* Springfield IL: Charles C Thomas.

National Society for the Prevention of Blindness. (1978). *Signs of possible eye trouble in children.* Pub. G-102. New York: NSPB.

National Society to Prevent Blindness. (1981). *Vision problems in the U.S.* New York: NSPB.

Scholl, G. T. (1973). Understanding and meeting developmental needs. In B. Lowenfeld (Ed.), *The visually handicapped child in school* (pp. 61-92). New York: John Day.

Scholl, G. T., & Schnur, R. (1976). *Measures of psychological, vocational and educational functioning in the blind and visually handicapped.* New York: American Foundation for the Blind.

Silverman, W. A. (1980). *Retrolental fibroplasia: A modern parable.* New York: Grune & Stratton.

Vander Kolk, C. J. (1981). *Assessment and planning with the visually impaired.* Baltimore: University Park Press.

Vaughan, D., & Asbury, T. (1977). *General ophthalmology.* Los Altos CA: Lange Medical Publications.

Yarnall, G. D., & Carlton, G. R. (1981). *Guidelines and manual of tests for educators interested in the assessment of handicapped children.* Austin TX: International Research Institute.

ADDITIONAL RESOURCES

Barraga, N. (1983). *Visual handicaps and learning* (rev. ed.). Austin TX: Exceptional Resources.

Bauman, M. K. (1974). Blind and partially sighted. In M. V. Wisland (Ed.), *Psycho-educational diagnosis of exceptional children* (pp. 159-189). Springfield IL: Charles C Thomas.

Bauman, M. K., & Kropf, C. A. (1979). Psychological tests used with blind and visually handicapped persons. *School Psychology Digest, 8*(3), 257-270.

Hansen, R., Young, J., & Ulrey, G. (1982). Assessment considerations with the visually handicapped child. In G. Ulrey & S. J. Rogers (Eds.), *Psychological assessment of infants and young children,* (pp. 108-114). New York: Thieme-Stratton.

Lowenfeld, B. (1973). *The visually handicapped child in school.* New York: John Day.

Lowenfeld, B. (1980). Psychological problems of children with severely impaired vision. In W. M. Cruickshank (Ed.), *Psychology of exceptional children and youth,* (4th ed.) (pp. 255-342). Englewood Cliffs NJ: Prentice-Hall.

Morse, J. L. (1975). Answering the questions of the psychologist assessing the visually handicapped child. *The New Outlook, 69*(8), 350-353.

Smits, B. W. G. M., & Mommers, M. J. C. (1976). Differences between blind and sighted children on WISC verbal subtests. *The New Outlook, 70,* 240-246.

Swallow, R. M. (1977). *Assessment for visually handicapped children and youth.* New York: American Foundation for the Blind.

Swallow, R. M., Mangold, S., & Mangold, P. (1978). *Informal assessment of developmental skills for visually handicapped students.* New York: American Foundation for the Blind.

Tillman, M. H., & Osborne, R. T. (1969). The performance of blind and sighted children on the Weschler Intelligence Scale for Children: Interaction effects. *Education of the Visually Handicapped, 1,* 1-4.

CHAPTER 11

Communication Disorders

Geraldine T. Scholl
Sister Yvonne Mary Loucks

Children with communication disorders are found among the school population classified as "normal" as well as those classified as "exceptional." The school psychologist however, is not ordinarily the primary assessment specialist, since most referrals for communication problems are made directly to the speech and language pathologist in the school district. Referrals to the school psychologist for educational and psychological assessment may be made by this specialist if there are additional questions about intellectual, academic, or social/emotional functioning. Speech and language problems are found among exceptional children, however, and school psychologists should have some background about these conditions since they may be secondary problems for the children they are assessing. In such cases, the school psychologist would work cooperatively with the speech and language pathologist in assessment, selection of an appropriate placement, and development of an individualized education program.

Communication problems are roughly divided into those related to speech itself and those related to language. In the past, the primary remedial function of the specialist focused on speech and correction of speech defects, and the specialist was called a speech correctionist or speech therapist. Because of the close interaction of the auditory system with speech development, the role was later expanded to include work with children who had mild to moderate hearing disorders, and the title of the specialist became "speech and hearing therapist."

More recently, the role was expanded to include language disorders, and the title became "speech and language pathologist" (Kirk & Gallagher, 1983).

Speech problems are found in approximately 5% of the school-age population, with a greater proportion among children in the kindergarten and early elementary grades (Kirk & Gallagher, 1983). The prevalence of language problems is more difficult to determine because of the occurrence of such problems among other groups, primarily hearing impaired, severely mentally impaired, and learning disabled children. Language disorders are also a frequent problem among preschool children (Ulrey, 1982). The school psychologist assessing any of these groups may wish to consult with the speech and language pathologist about appropriate instruments to use for language assessment or request that specialist to do such an assessment.

This chapter includes a summary of the major language and speech problems together with assessment implications for the school psychologist.

LANGUAGE

General Considerations

Language binds and creates relationships among persons, events, and situations. Bloom and Lahey (1978) described language as a "code whereby ideas about the world are represented through a convenient system of arbitrary signals for communication" (p. 4). Language presupposes and depends on some conventional experience of the world systematically mapped out in ways that permit and provide speakers with the tools to exchange ideas about their perceptions of that world. The number of possible transactions in the system of language is infinite when both speakers know the system of rules for their language.

In language disordered children, many aspects of communication can be deviant. They may not be aware of or have the rule system necessary for the communication of ideas; they may have the correct form of language, but may not apply the conventional meaning to those forms; their use of form and/or meaning may be inappropriate; or they may perseverate, mimic, demonstrate inappropriate affect, and be unaware of conversational turntaking and conversational subtleties such as entrance and termination behaviors.

Language disordered children may be behavior problems in the classroom, partly because they have not learned the communicative code used by the majority of persons in society. They may not be able to read facial expressions of approval and disapproval, and therefore lack necessary formative feedback; or they may not be able to read subtleties in language. For example, the statement "It's cold in here" can have several meanings, based on the context. It could be a remark; it could be an affirmative acknowledgment; it could be an indirect request to close the window. A language disordered child might hear and interpret the statement only in its literal sense. The response of the conversational partner in a situation where an individual misinterpets an indirect request, such as the above example, is most often irritation. Peers, family, and teachers become irritated with the child for appearing obstinate, illusive, or nonattentive. The problem lies in the fact that the child may not know the communicative code necessary for normal exchange between persons.

Language problems cover a broad category of communication disorders, including language delay, language deficiency, childhood aphasia, mental retardation, and learning disabilities. The latter two conditions are discussed in Chapters 5 and 6, respectively. Language problems are also prevalent in children with hearing disorders; they are discussed in Chapter 9.

Language Delay

During the first 2 years of normal development, verbal behavior progresses from the crying vocalization of the infant to babbling, to imitation of the child's own voice production or that of others in the environment, to single words, to two-word sentences. Beginning around age 2 to 3, children begin to acquire the grammatical system of those around them (Ulrey, 1982; Wilkinson & Saywitz, 1982). Any retardation in this progression is usually termed a *language delay*. Two major causes of delayed language development are mental retardation and hearing impairment. Before initiating a remedial program for a language delay, the speech and language pathologist will first rule out these two conditions.

If the delay cannot be attributed to either of these two major causes and there are no overlays of severe emotional disturbance, autism, or aphasia, then the speech and language pathologist may suspect that the child has no use for speech and language because every need is met without verbal behavior, or that there is some emotional problem in the relationship between child and family (Eisenson, 1980). School psychologists may be called upon to assist in working with the family and child in order to create an environment that encourages and rewards the use of speech and language.

Language Deficiency

Some children have difficulty in using the linguistic characteristics or features of language. Such difficulties are manifested as phonologic disorders (deviations in the sound patterns of the language); morphologic disorders (difficulty in clustering sounds into units, which lead to difficulties in learning sound/symbol relationships); syntactic disorders (deviations in the derivation of meaning from the system of grammar of the language); and semantic disorders (difficulties in acquiring the meaning of utterances) (Wilkinson & Saywitz, 1982).

Remediation of these disorders requires the skill of a language specialist; school psychologists would probably be involved in those situations where emotional problems are also present.

Aphasia

Childhood aphasia is a severe language disorder in which the child either has not acquired speech and language or has acquired and then lost them at a later time. Usually brain injury or trauma is involved (Emerick & Hatten, 1979). Treatment requires the skills of a speech and language pathologist. Involvement of school psychologists in the process will be particularly important to assess and remediate any emotional problems that may accompany the condition. Aphasia and delayed speech are difficult to differentiate. As noted above, the speech and language pathologist first rules out all other conditions—mental retardation, hearing impairment, emotional disturbance, autism, and environmental influences—before arriving at a diagnosis of aphasia. Remediation for children with aphasia will usually require a multidisciplinary team approach that includes not only the speech and language specialist and school psychologist but also the learning disabilities teacher and the school social worker. The treatment plan must also include the child's family.

SPEECH

Speech is defined by the American Speech-Language-Hearing Association as the vocal-motor channel of language performance. It is the means by which language is communicated and thus is basic to good oral communication. Speech is considered defective when it calls attention to itself, interferes with communication, or affects the speaker or listener negatively (Van Riper, 1978). Remedial programs for children with speech defects have been conducted by the public schools since 1908 (Reynolds & Birch, 1982). Service delivery is typically an itinerant teacher model wherein the speech and language pathologist conducts sessions once or twice weekly for children, either individually or in small groups. The children spend the remainder of the school day in a regular class. The speech and language pathologist works with the regular teacher to facilitate the transfer of remediation to the classroom situation.

The speech pathologist usually conducts routine screening examinations for all children in the kindergarten and early elementary grades. Early remediation is essential in order to prevent not only related problems with other aspects of communication such as reading, but also emotional problems that may result from prolonged speech disorders. Many speech pathologists work with regular kindergarten and early elementary grade teachers on speech improvement programs designed to help all children in the classroom to become more sensitive to their speech.

Speech defects are divided into three major categories: articulation, which accounts for about 70-80% of speech problems; fluency disorders; and voice disorders.

Articulation Disorders

Articulation disorders range in severity from a simple lisp to a severe apraxia and/or dysarthria, which can cause a person to be completely unintelligible. Apraxia is caused by a cortical disorder that renders voluntary movement of the articulators very difficult or impossible. Dysarthria is a paralysis or paresis of the musculature of the oral cavity that leads to slurred and unintelligible speech. These conditions usually require more intensive treatment than can be accomplished by the typical public school speech and language pathologist. Less severe articulation disorders include substitutions (e.g., wabbit for rabbit); omissions (e.g., ump for jump); distortions (e.g., schtop for stop); or additions (e.g., sumber for summer). Since the ability to make certain sounds (e.g., /s/ as in biscuit) may be delayed until as late as the third grade, speech and language pathologists may postpone any formal therapy sessions for some children until there is evidence that the maturation process will not remediate the problem (Emerick & Hatten, 1979; Reynolds & Birch, 1982).

Children with cleft palates present a special challenge because their highly nasalized speech definitely calls attention to itself. Therapy for these cases requires a team approach (Emerick & Hatten, 1979). From the plastic surgeon they require a thorough oral peripheral examination, which may involve the use of electromyography, a test used to determine phonations through measurement of electrical activity accompanying muscle contraction (Hutchinson, Hanson, & Mecham, 1979). From the orthodontist they often require specialized care to ensure the best possible alignment of the teeth so that speech production may be facilitated. The speech and language pathologist must work closely with these specialists in the rehabilitation of the child. The objective of therapy is to work the child into a gradually more socially acceptable form of speech production. It is essential that this rehabilitation begin as early as possible to avoid social stigma and possibly rejection by peers.

School psychologists should be alert to articulation problems that may cause them to misinterpret a child's oral responses because of sound substitutions or other abnormalities. A longer period of talking with the child prior to initiating the assessment may be necessary in order for the ear to become accustomed to the deviant speech. This may be especially true in the case of children with cleft palates, who sometimes can be understood only by their parents.

Fluency Disorders

The most common fluency problem among children is stuttering. This is a many-faceted problem and, like other communication problems, involves listeners as well as the speaker. Van Riper (1978) pointed out that "stuttering occurs when the forward flow of speech is interrupted abnormally by repetitions and prolongations of a sound or syllable, or articulatory posture, or by avoidance or struggle reactions" (p. 249).

Dysfluences are normal in all speakers at one time or another, particularly in tense situations or during times of fatigue (Emerick & Hatten, 1979). However, they are never as severe as that experienced by the stutterer. The important psychological aspects of stuttering are not readily apparent through visual observation. Measurements such as electromyography and air flow and pressure measurements are often used to determine the severity of the dysfluency (Hutchinson et al., 1979).

Often when stuttering first occurs in early childhood, the child does not notice it and shows no anxious behaviors. Unfortunately, the parents frequently become anxious and, if they are not assured by a professional person at this point, their anxiety may transfer to the child, who will begin to develop signs of avoidance and struggle. When this occurs, the child may demonstrate marked frustration with his or her own communication abilities and use a great deal of energy avoiding speaking situations in which he or she feels increasingly inferior and incapable.

Additional problems are often created for the young stutterer by the listener. Listening to and watching someone stutter severely on an utterance can be an unpleasant and unnerving experience. Many persons practice the same avoidance behaviors toward the stutterer that the stutterer does. Williams (1978) stated that in the initial evaluation the speech and language pathologist should answer the following questions:

a) What specific behavior patterns require change in their frequency of occurrence, intensity, duration, or in the conditions under which they occur?
b) What are the conditions under which the behavior was acquired? What factors are currently maintaining it?
c) What are the best practical means which can produce the desired changes in this individual? (p. 285)

Responses to these questions can lead the speech and language pathologist into initiating collaborative work with the school psychologist, the school social worker, and other support pesonnel. Stuttering is a communication disorder that usually requires interdisciplinary professional assistance.

For the stuttering child and his or her family, the school psychologist can be supportive and helpful in interpreting the child's emotional and social needs. Since there is some research evidence that parents of children with speech impairments tend to show more maladjusted behavior than control groups of parents of nonimpaired children (Eisenson, 1980), school psychologists in collaboration with school social workers and the speech and language pathologist can often play a vital role in helping parents work through their emotional problems whether they are related to the speech defect or not.

In the assessment situation it may be necessary for the school psychologist to set aside time restrictions because of the child's lengthy speech hesitations. Making the child feel as comfortable and relaxed as possible may also reduce the stuttering. Play therapy techniques outlined in Chapter 7 may be useful for these pupils as well. In extreme cases, the school psychologist might try having the pupil sing or chant the responses since stutterers rarely stutter while singing.

Voice Disorders

Although voice disorders are probably more prevalent in the adult population, it is not uncommon for vocally active children, and adolescents in particular, to have problems with the quality, pitch, and loudness of the voice (Emerick & Hatten, 1979). Some of these problems may be due to vocal nodules and/or polyps that require the attention of a medical specialist. Assessment of voice disorders requires skilled techniques. Emerick and Hatten (1979) have stated that voice production is influenced by the respiratory, resonatory, phonotory, endocrine, and neural systems, any one of which may cause a voice disorder. The muscles that function to produce a normal voice are not readily visible for observation. Therefore, in diagnosing voice disorders it is necessary to rely on such instrument techniques as electromyography to measure adequate functioning; indirect laryngoscopy, which enables the clinician to examine the adequacy of the the child's vocal folds; or the use of a sonograph, a voice print machine. (Emerick and Hatton, 1979).

Aside from the unpleasantness of voice problems, if vocal pathologies are not corrected, more serious problems may develop that can require invasive forms of treatment such as medication and surgery. Although the impaired voice is not as socially penalizing on the whole as some other communication problems, it can lead to serious debilitating conditions if not treated. It is important that referrals be made as soon as possible to avoid further complications.

For diagnosis and remediation of voice disorder problems, the school psychologist must rely on direction and guidance from the speech and language pathologist as a member of the interdisciplinary team.

ASSESSMENT

The speech and language pathologist is the most appropriate specialist to assess the child and differentially diagnose the language or speech problem. Standardized tests are available for the assessment of appropriate use, form, and content of speech and language (Darley, F., & Spriesterbach, D.C., 1978; Ferry, 1982; Swanson & Watson, 1982). Diagnosis includes observation in various communicative settings as well as use of standardized instruments.

The school psychologist should refer children who are being assessed for other reasons to the speech and language pathologist for a more complete diagnosis when speech or language problems are evident. Similarly, the school psychologist may receive referrals for diagnosis and therapy from the speech and language pathologist, especially for emotional problems that may accompany severe speech defects such as stuttering and cleft palate and severe language problems such as aphasia.

SUMMARY

The same speech and language problems found among nonhandicapped children will also be found among handicapped children. Remedial education programs for some categories should also include the services of a speech and language pathologist, particularly for hard-of-hearing, mentally retarded or learning disabled children. In assessing these groups the school psychologist should note any deficiencies in speech and language and assure that remediation is included in the individualized education program.

The school psychologist can be a valuable member of the multidisciplinary team by working in conjunction with the speech and language pathologist in the assessment process and in dealing with emotional problems that may accompany the communication disorder. School psychologists should refer children who evidence speech or language disorders to the speech and language pathologist for more intensive diagnosis.

REFERENCES

Bloom, L., & Lahey, M. (1978). *Language development and language disorders.* New York: John Wiley.

Darley, F. & Spriesterbach, D.C. (Eds.). 1978. *Diagnostic methods in speech pathology* (2nd ed.). New York: Harper & Row.

Eisenson, J. (1980). Speech defects: Nature, causes, and psychological concomitants. In W. M. Cruickshank (Ed.), *Psychology of exceptional children and youth* (4th ed.) (pp. 173-218). Englewood Cliffs NJ: Prentice-Hall.

Emerick, L., & Hatten, J. (1979). *Diagnosis and evaluation in speech pathology* (2nd ed.). Englewood Cliffs NJ: Prentice-Hall.

Ferry, P. C. (1982). Clinical appraisal of language functions in the preschool child. In M. Lewis & L. T. Taft (Eds.), *Developmental disabilities: Theory, assessment and intervention.* New York: Spectrum.

Hutchinson, B., Hanson, J., & Mecham, M. (1979). *Diagnostic handbook of speech pathology.* Baltimore: Williams & Wilkins.

Kirk, S. A., & Gallagher, J. J. (1983). *Educating exceptional children.* Boston: Houghton-Mifflin.

Reynolds, M. C., & Birch, J. W. (1982). *Teaching exceptional children in all America's schools.* Reston VA: The Council for Exceptional Children.

Swanson, H.L. & Watson, B. L. (1982). *Educational and psychological assessment of exceptional children.* St. Louis: C. V. Mosby.

Ulrey, G. (1982). Assessment considerations with language impaired children. In G. Ulrey & Rogers S. J. (Eds.), *Psychological assessment of handicapped infants and young children* (pp. 123-134). New York: Thieme-Stratton.

Van Riper, C. (1978). *Speech correction: Principles and methods* (6th ed.). Englewood Cliffs NJ: Prentice-Hall.

Wilkinson, L. C., & Saywitz, K. (1982). Theoretical bases of language and communication development in preschool children. In M. Lewis & L. T. Taft (Eds.), *Developmental disabilities: Theory, assessment and intervention* (pp. 301-319). New York: Spectrum.

Williams, D. E. (1978). The problem of stuttering. In F. Darley & D. C. Spriesterbach (Eds.), *Diagnostic methods in speech pathology* (2nd ed.) (pp. 284-321). New York: Harper & Row.

ADDITIONAL RESOURCES

Freeman, G. G. (1977). *Speech and language services and the classroom teacher.* Minneapolis: University of Minnesota, National Support Systems Project.

Hixon, T., Shriberg, L., & Saxman, J. (Eds.). (1980). *Introduction to communication disorders.* Englewood Cliffs NJ: Prentice-Hall.

Yoder, D. E. (1974). Evaluation and assessment of children's language and speech behavior. In M. V. Wisland (Ed.), *Psychoeducational diagnosis of exceptional children* (pp. 320-380). Springfield IL: Charles C Thomas.

APPENDIX A

Sample Referral Form

Name: Address:

Birthdate: Phone:

Grade: Parent's Name(s):

Referring Teacher:

Referral Date:

Please answer these questions as completely as you can. This information will be used to plan assessment and intervention procedures.

Why are you referring this child?

Describe the child's learning and/or behavioral problem(s) in some detail: (include onset, duration, frequency. Examples or anecdotes would be helpful).

How have you attempted to deal with this problem and what were the results?

If you have discussed the problem with the child, describe the child's reaction and perception of the problem.

In general, how would you describe this child's behavior and relationships with peers? With teachers? In structured situations? In unstructured situations?

Describe the child's motivation and attitudes toward academic work, own behavior, and self.

What are the child's strengths? Weaknessess?

What is the child's reading level? Math level? Spelling level? General performance level?

What is your subjective impression of the child's home environment? Describe any interactions you have had with the parents that support this impression.

Does the child have any health, medical, or physical handicaps that you feel are relevant?

Has the child received (or is he or she receiving) any special education or other supportive services?

What is your impression of the nature of the child's problem? What do you feel the child's needs are? How do you think the child might best be helped?

How can the school psychologist be of most help to you?

Are there any additional comments or information you would like me to know?

APPENDIX B

Common Behaviors and Attitudes During Assessment

1. Extreme shyness, inhibitions

   Suggests: threatened by situation, authority
   severe withdrawal
   school phobia

2. Apprehension, anxiety

   Suggests: inability to deal with new situations

3. Defensiveness

   Suggests: fear of failure or ridicule
   fear of emotional involvement, closeness with others
   feeling threatened

4. Overfriendliness

   Suggests: immaturity
   need to defend against possible harm

5. Brashness

   Suggests: inability to restrain behavior
   tendency to act out
   rejection by peers or teachers

6. Need to impress

   Suggests: insecurity
   denial against failure
   inability to tolerate frustration

7. Hyperactivity

   Suggests: brain damage
                 immaturity
                 overt anxiety

8. Impulsiveness:

   Suggests: immaturity (8 years and up)
                 regression
                 defense against anxiety arousing feelings

9. Dependency

   Suggests: immaturity
                 retardation
                 anxiety
                 avoidance of responsibility
                 passivity

10. Over-questioning

    Suggests: brain damage
                  anxiety
                  emotional conflicts
                  poor self-esteem

11. Extreme overdeliberateness, meticulousness

    Suggests: fear of failure
                  obsessiveness, compulsiveness
                  perfectionism

12. Giving up

    Suggests: passive-aggressiveness
                  neurological problems
                  poor self-esteem

13. Negative reaction to success

    Suggests: driving conscience or parent

14. Negative reaction to failure

    Suggests: fragile self-concept
                  low frustration tolerance

15. Intellectuality

    Suggests: need to control threatening situations
                  fear of feelings or thoughts
                  repression

16. Use of personal experiences in answering test questions

   Suggests: immaturity, self-centeredness
   poor judgment
   emotional conflicts

17. Tendency to free associate

   Suggests: emotional conflicts and concerns
   inability to focus attention

18. Variability of mood

   Suggests: emotional conflicts
   brain damage

Observations That May Be Helpful in Writing Reports

1. Ability to incorporate and process new stimuli in order to deal with the situation.
   a. The child's response to assessment itself should be noted. Of the wide range of responses possible, high levels of anxiety, withdrawal, physical intrusiveness, or destructive manipulation of objects may indicate emotional disturbance.
   b. The child's prevailing mood is important. Fearfulness, sadness, anger, anxiety, apathy, docility, sulking, and/or rapid changes in mood should be noted.

2. Perception—ability to understand the physical environment.
   a. Does the child discriminate between the examiner's role and the role of parent or teacher or see them as having the same role?
   b. How does the child perceive the physical environment? This includes what sensory processes the child uses to gather information about surroundings and whether perceptions are accurate or distorted. Neurological deficits may be a factor if perceptual difficulties are present.
   c. Does the child use objects in the environment appropriately? Bizarre or idiosyncratic uses are to be noted (e.g., treating people as objects, eating crayons, distorted concepts of space and time).

3. Self-concept—the child's attitudes toward self.
   a. Much can be revealed in the child's dress, hygiene, posture, and mannerisms. Obesity, being excessively underweight, lack of attention to grooming or dress, excessive neatness or cleanliness, and/or stiffness of posture should be noted.

b. Signs of self-abusive behaviors should be noted. If these are not directly observed or reported by others, signs of such behavior should be kept in mind. Lip biting, picking at the body, and hair pulling all leave physical signs on the child.

c. Reactions to successes and failures are important sources of information about the child's self-image.

d. Hesitancy to attempt novel or difficult tasks may indicate lack of self-confidence as does a need for much praise, encouragement, or reassurance.

4. Ability to control impulses.
   a. Excessive motor activity, impulsive behavior, tantrums, and/or lack of goal-directed behavior or verbalizations should be noted.

   b. Bowel and/or bladder control that are inappropriate for the child's age should be noted (enuresis or encopresis).

   c. If excessive activity or hyperactivity is present, certain questions should be asked to determine whether or not it may be organically based: Does it occur consistently or *episodically*? Is it random behavior or *purposive*? Does it seem to be *triggered by anxiety*? Is it accompanied by impulsive and uninhibited behavior? Are there also attentional deficits? Is it correlated with *low frustration tolerance*? (The italicized options indicate a likely emotional basis, and the others a possible organic basis.)

5. Cognitive abilities—intellectual functioning and quality and content of thought processes.
   a. What is the level of abstract thinking, and is it age appropriate?

   b. Is the child's general fund of information and vocabulary appropriate to age, grade, level of intellectual functioning, and cultural background?

   c. What is the child's level of educational achievement? Is this level discrepant from the child's ability level? Is there a discrepancy between educational achievement and classroom performance (tests and homework)?

   d. Can the child follow through his or her thoughts in a logical manner, or are associations loose and unrelated? Are the child's thoughts goal-directed?

   e. What themes exist in the child's fantasies? Can the child distinguish fantasies from reality?

   f. What level of social awareness does the child have? Is the child able to understand the situation and make good judgments as to how to act?

6. Ability to communicate—both nonverbal and verbal skills.
   a. Presence of age-appropriate speech and language should be noted. Problems with articulation, dysrhythmias, pitch, or volume should be noted since they can indicate neurological dysfunction, maturational lags, or interpersonal problems.
   b. Speed, amount, and spontaneity of speech should be noted.
   c. Does the child use speech to communicate with others or for self-stimulation? Echolalia, word distortions, humming, rhyming, and irrelevant talk may indicate speech used for self-stimulation.
   d. The content of the child's verbalizations is important. Themes, preoccupations, concerns, interests, and experiences should be recorded as well as the child's syntax, use of pronouns, and completeness of thought expressed. Thought fragmentation, running together of ideas, including excessive details, misuse of pronouns, and odd syntax patterns may all be indicators of emotional problems.

7. Interpersonal and social relationships—the child's interest in these as well as skills.
   a. The child's response to the examiner's requests are an important source of information. Overcompliance, ignoring, and refusal (oppositionalism) are responses to be noted.
   b. What demands does the child make on the examiner? Are they attempts to gain control of the situation?
   c. The child's level of exploratory and curiosity-motivated behavior is important. Is the child interested in the new environment or aloof and indifferent? If the child is aloof and indifferent, it is necessary to look for indications of whether this is a result of anxiety, lack of interest in social interactions, withdrawal, or depression.
   d. The child's manner of relating to the examiner should be noted. Is the child friendly or withdrawn, responding only when the examiner initiates interaction? Behavior on the extreme end of the continuum, such as negative—cooperative or passive—aggressive, should be noted. Expressions of hostility should be noted. Can the child enter into teasing or game playing?
   e. Is the child interested in what the examiner has to say or contribute, or is the child egocentric in his or her interactions?
   f. What is the quality of the child's peer relationships? Are the child's interactions with peers age-appropriate?

g. How does the child resolve conflicts with others? Does the child rely on an adult for resolution or deal with it independently?

h. What is the nature of the child's relationship with family members? With teachers?

i. Does the child have the ability to empathize with others? What are the child's role-taking skills?

8. Value development.
a. What are the child's values? To what degree have they been internalized?

b. What is the child's understanding of rules? What are the child's attitudes toward obeying them and reasons for doing so?

c. Is the child's behavior consistent with his or her values and rules? If not, is the child aware of this discrepancy?

d. Where does the child attribute responsibility for wrongdoings? If the child sees himself or herself responsible, is there evidence of excessive guilt feelings or no guilt?

e. Can the child be flexible and adaptive in use of ethical principles, or are they used rigidly?

APPENDIX D

Suggested Format for Interview with Parents

General

Family members: Names, age, grade, occupation
Describe the problem.
How is the problem manifested at home?

Family History

Marriage: How long; any separations; previous marriages; if divorced, custody agreement and visiting patterns; general tone of marriage

Mother, Father

Place of birth and where grew up
Family make-up
Childhood illnesses, deaths, divorces
Education
Work experience
Aspirations: early and present, satisfaction with progress
Current relationship with extended family
Current health, physical and emotional
Alcohol or drug abuse
Family moves and living arrangements
Family separations when child was separated from parents
Familial diseases
Family activities
Sibling(s) age(s), adjustment, and relationship with child
Discipline techniques and consistency

Developmental History

Pregnancy:

Planned or unplanned; parent's attitude when learned of pregnancy
Age of parents and marital status
Mother's health during (vomiting, weight gain, blood pressure
  problems, swelling, kidney problems, etc.)
Complications, such as threatened or voluntary abortions
Parent's emotional state during

Birth:

Labor and delivery
Complications
Birth weight
Postpartum course
Postnatal difficulties (anoxia, jaundice, etc.)
Any evidence of infection or damage

Development:

Infancy: Feeding, respiration, sleep, colic, general mood, respon-
        siveness, sensory deficit, temperament
Milestones: Sitting, standing, talking (first word and sentences),
        walking, toilet training

Medical History

Serious illnesses, accidents, head injuries, operations, hospitalizations, convulsions/seizures, allergies, current medications, and
health status

School History

Preschool:

Separation difficulties, temper tantrums
Peer relations
General adjustment

Elementary School, Junior and Senior High:

Academic performance
Social: peer relationships, teacher relationships
Refusals to attend
Problems or disciplinary actions

Parents' Perceptions

Father's/Mother's view of their relationship with the child
Child's current personality
  general view of
  frustration tolerance, anxiety, fears
  what arouses aggression/anger
  general mood, feelings, attitudes
Child's behavior
  interests, friends
  drug, alcohol, tobacco usage
  police contacts
  suicide or homicide attempts, cruelty to animals
Child's experiences
  physical assaults (beatings, animal attacks)
  sexual trauma, interests, attitudes and concerns about sex
Father's/mother's view of the cause of the problem
Father's/mother's expectations and desired solution

APPENDIX E

Suggested Format for Interview with Child

General conversation: Where the child lives, interests, hobbies, sports, music, vacations.

Why the child is here: The child's understanding of what will happen and the purpose of the process.

Friends: Activities, view of friends, ages of friends, what the child feels parents think of friends' problems.

School: Likes or dislikes
Subjects of interest
General attitude toward grades: If poor, why the child thinks they are
How the child feels about peers in class and how he or she gets along with them
Attitudes toward teachers
Problems with teachers

Family: How the child gets along with mother, father, each sibling
Worst thing about relationship with each parent
Best thing about relationship with each parent
Which sibling the child gets along with best, worst; why
Worries about each parent
Worries about family
Whether the child thinks parents' discipline is fair
Where the child thinks he or she fits into the family
If child is adopted and knows this fact, feelings, fantasies regarding natural parents

Affect: How the child feels most of the time
When trying to fall asleep, what thought or fantasies the child often has
When in a really boring class at school, what the child thinks about and what feelings are associated
Whether the child sometimes imagines being someplace else or someone else; if so where, who, why, what better
Daydreams, what about
Fears, what makes the child angry, sad, happy

The following sections should be used as appropriate to age and referral problems.

Drug usage: Age of first use, which drug tried first
Other drugs in order of experimentation (check specifically: marijuana, hash, THC, PCP, downers, Quaaludes, Valium, acid/mescaline, speed, cocaine, heroin, other). For each drug used, age at first use, number of times used, last time taken and how much, effects (How does the child feel; what does the child like about it.)

Alcohol usage: Age began, how often, kinds and quantity, how often drunk, when was last time

Tobacco usage: Age began, quantity

Sexuality: Dating
Girlfriends/boyfriends
Experiences such as first intercourse and at what age, frequency, contraceptives used
Feelings regarding sexual involvement
Concerns, attitudes

Organization for Data Collection in the Ecological Approach

I. Initial description of the environment

   A. The environment is engaged for data collection on perception of the problem.

   B. Information is gathered from the particular setting(s) in which the problem is most noticeable.

   C. Information is gathered from the settings in which the problem is not noticeable.

II. Expectations

   A. Information is gathered about the expectations of the environments in which the child is experiencing problems.

   B. Information is gathered about the expectations of the environment in which the child is not having problems.

III. Behavioral descriptions

   A. Data are collected on the interactions and skills of the people involved in the problematic situations.
      1. Present data
      2. Historical data
      3. Interactional analysis
      4. Functional analysis

B. Data are collected on the interactions and skills of the people involved in successful situations.
   1. Present data
   2. Historical data
   3. Interactional analysis
   4. Functional analysis

C. Assessment is made of the skills needed by the child to function successfully in different environments.

IV. Data are summarized.

V. Reasonable expectations are set for the child and for teachers for situations in which the problem is most noticeable.

Adapted from Laten, S., and Katz, G. (1975). *A theoretical model for assessment of adolescents: The ecological/behavioral approach.* Madison WI: Madison Public Schools.

APPENDIX G

National Organization Sources for Further Information

The following list of national organizations is not meant to be exhaustive. For more complete listing the reader is referred to R. M. Goldenson, *Disability and Rehabilitation Handbook* (New York: McGraw-Hill, 1978). Many national organizations have regional, state, or local chapters, offices, or branches. The reader should check local telephone directories of social service agencies and organizations for such groups.

GENERAL

The Council for Exceptional Children (CEC)
1920 Association Drive
Reston VA 22091

The following divisions of CEC are especially relevant:

Council of Administrators of Special Education (CASE)
Council for Educational Diagnostic Services (CEDS)
Division on Career Development (DCD)
Division for Early Childhood (DEC)
Teacher Education Division (TED)

Division of School Psychology
American Psychological Association
1200 17th Street, NW
Washington DC 20036

National Association of School Psychologists
1511 K Street, NW, Suite 927
Washington DC 20005

National Association of State Directors of
   Special Education (NASDE)
1201 16th Street, NW
Washington DC 20036

GIFTED

American Association for Gifted Children
15 Gramercy Park South
New York NY 10003

The Association for the Gifted (TAG)
A Division of The Council for Exceptional Children
1920 Association Drive
Reston VA 22091

MENTAL RETARDATION

American Association on Mental Deficiency
5201 Connecticut Avenue, NW
Washington DC 20015

Division on Mental Retardation (CEC-MR)
A Division of The Council for Exceptional Children
1920 Association Drive
Reston VA 22091

National Association for Retarded Citizens
2709 Avenue E East
Arlington TX 76011

LEARNING DISABILITIES

Association for Children with Learning Disabilities
4156 Library Road
Pittsburgh PA 15234

Division for Learning Disabilities (DLD)
A Division of The Council for Exceptional Children
1920 Association Drive
Reston VA 22091

EMOTIONALLY DISTURBED

American Orthopsychiatric Association
1790 Broadway
New York NY 10019

Council for Children with Behavioral Disorders (CCBD)
A Division of The Council for Exceptional Children
1920 Association Drive
Reston VA 20091

PHYSICALLY HANDICAPPED

American Diabetes Association
1 West 48th Street
New York NY 10020

Division for Physically Handicapped (DPH)
A Division of The Council for Exceptional Children
1920 Association Drive
Reston VA 22091

Epilepsy Foundation of America
1828 L Street, NW
Washington DC 20036

National Easter Seal Society for Crippled Children and Adults
2023 West Ogden Avenue
Chicago IL 60612

National Society for Autistic Children
306 31st Street
Huntington WV 25702

United Cerebral Palsy Association
66 East 34th Street
New York NY 10016

HEARING IMPAIRED

Alexander Graham Bell Association for the Deaf
3417 Volta Place, NW
Washington DC 20017

Division for Children with Communication Disorders (DCCD)
A Division of The Council for Exceptional Children
1920 Association Drive
Reston VA 22091

National Association of the Deaf
813 Thayer Avenue
Silver Spring MD 20910

National Information Center on Deafness
Gallaudet College
Kendall Green
Washington DC 20002

VISUALLY IMPAIRED

American Foundation for the Blind
15 West 16th Street
New York NY 10011

Division for the Visually Handicapped (DVH)
A Division of The Council for Exceptional Children
1920 Association Drive
Reston VA 22091

National Society to Prevent Blindness
79 Madison Avenue
New York NY 10016

COMMUNICATION DISORDERS

American Speech and Hearing Association
9030 Old Georgetown Road
Washington DC 20014

Division for Children with Communication Disorders (DCCD)
A Division of The Council for Exceptional Children
1920 Association Drive
Reston VA 22091

APPENDIX H

Resources for Assessment Instruments

This listing includes publishers of the assessment instruments mentioned in the text. The reader is referred to the following resources for additional information about these instruments as well as others that are available:

Buros, O. K. (Ed.). (1978). *The eighth mental measurements yearbook* (Vols. I & II). Highland Park NJ: The Gryphon Press.

Includes a description of 1,184 tests, with statistical data on standardization, validity, and reliability. Test reviews and references are included for specific tests.

Johnson, O. G. (Ed.). (1976). *Tests and measurements in child development: Handbook II* (2 vols.). San Francisco: Jossey-Bass.

A listing of published and unpublished measures including behavior rating scales, measures of attitudes, and instruments appropriate for assessing various aspects in the child's environment. Descriptions of reliability and validity are included when available. Instruments are appropriate for ages 0 to 18.

Mitchell, J. V., Jr. (Ed.). (1983). *Test in print III*. Lincoln NB: The University of Nebraska Press.

A description, with references, of 2,672 commercially published tests in print and currently available. Reviews are not included. The book serves as a master index to the content of the *Mental Measurements Yearbook* series.

Sweetland, R. C., & Keyser, D. J. (1983). *Tests*. Kansas City MO: Test Corporation of America.

A comprehensive listing of over 3,000 tests in the English language divided into three main sections: psychology, education, and business. Information on each test includes its purpose, a description of the test, and availability. No reliability or validity data are provided.

Part A: Listing of Assessment Instruments

Assessment instruments, with the publisher, are listed in alphabetical order. Publishers and addresses are listed in alphabetical order in Part B.

AAMD Adaptive Behavior Scale (Publishers Test Service)

AAMD Adaptive Behavior Scale: School Edition (Publishers Test Service)

Arthur Point Scale of Performance Tests: Revised (Psychological Corporation)

Bayley Scale of Infant Development (Psychological Corporation)

Behavior Problem Checklist (unpublished) (D. Peterson)

Bender Visual Motor Gestalt Test (American Orthopsychiatric Association)

Cain-Levine Social Competency Scale (Consulting Psychologists Press)

Cattell Infant Intelligence Scale (Psychological Corporation)

Chicago Non-Verbal Examination (Psychological Corporation)

Child Behavior Rating Scale (Western Psychological Services)

Children's Apperception Test (Psychological Corporation)

Columbia Mental Maturity Scale (Harcourt, Brace & World)

Creativity Assessment Packet (Publishers Test Service)

Devereux Adolescent Behavior Rating Scale (Devereux Foundation)

Devereux Child Behavior Rating Scale (Devereux Foundation)

Devereux Elementary School Behavior Rating Scale (Devereux Foundation)

Draw-a-Person Test (Western Psychological Services)

Durrell Analysis of Reading Difficulty (Harcourt, Brace & World)

Family Drawings (Grune & Stratton)

Gates-McKellop Reading Diagnostic Tests (Teachers College Press)

Gesell Developmental Schedules (Psychological Corporation)

Goodenough Draw-A-Man Test (Harcourt, Brace & World)

Hahnemann High School Behavior Rating Scale (Hahnemann Mental Health/Mental Retardation Center)

Henderson Environmental Learning Process Scale (Office of Child Research)

Home Observation for Measurement of the Environment (Robert H. Bradley)

Illinois Test of Psycholinguistic Abilities (Publishers Test Service)

Kaufman Assessment Battery for Children (American Guidance Service)

Key Math Diagnostic Test (American Guidance Service)

Leiter International Performance Scale (Stoelting Company)

Louisville Behavior Check List (Child Psychiatry Research Center)

McCarthy Scales of Children's Abilities (Psychological Corporation)

Make a Picture Story (Psychological Corporation)

Merrill-Palmer Scale (Stoelting Company)

Nebraska Test of Learning (Psychological Corporation)

Peabody Picture Vocabulary Test (American Guidance Service)

Peabody Individual Achievements Test (American Guidance Service)

Pictorial Test of Intelligence (Houghton Mifflin)

Pupil Behavior Rating Scale (Publishers Test Service)

Raven's Progressive Matrices (Psychological Corporation)

Rohde Sentence Completion (Western Psychological Services)

Rorschach Psychodiagnostic Plates (Psychological Corporation)

Rotter Sentence Completion (Psychological Corporation)

Slosson Intelligence Test (Publishers Test Service)

Social Climate Scales (Consulting Psychologists Press)

Stanford-Binet Intelligence Scale (Houghton Mifflin Company)

Stanford Diagnostic Arithmetic Test (Harcourt, Brace & World)

Stern Personality and Associates Environmental Indexes (Evaluation Research)

System of Multicultural Pluralistic Assessment (Psychological Corporation)

Thematic Apperception Test (Psychological Corporation)

Torrance Tests of Creative Thinking (Personnel Press)

Vineland Adaptive Behavior Scale (American Guidance Service)

Walker Problem Behavior Identification Checklist (Western Psychological Services)

Wechsler Adult Intelligence Scale-Revised (Psychological Corporation)

Wechsler Intelligence Scale for Children-Revised (Psychological Corporation)

Weschsler Preschool and Primary Scale of Intelligence (Psychological Corporation)

Wide Range Achievement Test (Publishers Test Service)

Woodcock Reading Tests (American Guidance Service)

Part B: Address of Publisher

American Guidance Service, Inc.
Publisher's Building
Circle Pines MN 55014-1796

American Orthopsychiatric Association, Inc.
1775 Broadway
New York NY 10019

Bobbs-Merrill Educational Publishing Company
4300 West 62nd Street
Indianapolis IN 46206

R. H. Bradley
University of Arkansas at Little Rock
33rd & University
Little Rock AR 72204

Child Psychiatry Research Center
608 South Jackson Street
Louisville KY 40202

Consulting Psychologists Press, Inc.
577 College Avenue
Palo Alto CA 94306

Devereux Foundation Press
19 South Waterloo Road
Devon PA 19333

Evaluation Research Associates
P.O. Box 6503 Teall Station
Syracuse NY 13217

Grune & Stratton, Inc.
757 Third Avenue
New York NY 10017

Hahnemann Community Mental Health/
  Mental Retardation Center
314 North Broad Street
Philadelphia, PA 19102

Harcourt, Brace & World, Inc.
757 Third Avenue
New York NY 10017

Houghton Mifflin Company
Test Editorial Offices
P.O. Box 1970
Iowa City IA 52240

Charles E. Merrill Publishing Company
Test Division
1300 Alum Creek Drive/Box 508
Columbus OH 43216

Office of Child Research
Arizona Center for Educational Research and Development
College of Education
University of Arizona
Tucson AZ 85721

Personnel Press
191 Spring Street
Lexington MA 02173

D. Peterson
39 North 5th Avenue
Highland Park NJ 08904

Publishers Test Service
2500 Garden Road
Monterey CA 93940-5380

Psychological Assessment Resource, Inc.
P.O. Box 98
Odessa FL 33556

Psychological Corporation
7500 Old Oak Boulevard
Cleveland OH 44130

Stoelting Company
424 N. Moman Avenue
Chicago IL 60624

Teachers College Press
Teachers College
525 West 121st Street
New York NY 10027

Western Psychological Services
12035 Wilshire Boulevard
Los Angeles CA 90025